T0085778

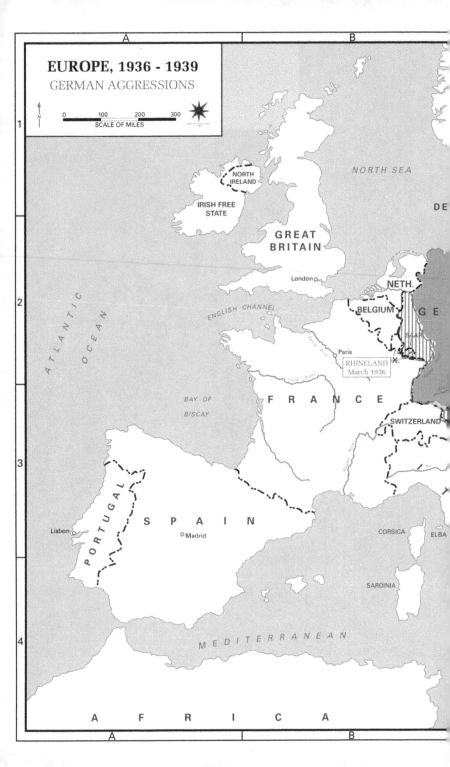

A grateful thanks to Friedel Hosenfeld for his generous help in providing family photographs, correspondence, and other documents central to the life story of his grandfather Wilm Hosenfeld.

I ONLY SEE THE PERSON IN FRONT OF ME

THE LIFE OF GERMAN OFFICER WILM HOSENFELD

By **HERMANN VINKE**

STAR BRIGHT BOOKS
Cambridge Massachusetts

Published in the United States by Star Bright Books.
The name Star Bright Books and the Star Bright Books logo are registered trademarks of Star Bright Books, Inc. Please visit: www.starbrightbooks.com.
To order, please email: orders@starbrightbooks.com, or call: (617) 354-1300.

Hermann Vinke: *"Ich sehe immer den Menschen vor mir": Das Leben des deutschen Offiziers Wilm Hosenfeld, Eine Biographie* © Arche Literatur Verlag AG. Published by agreement with Arche Literatur Verlag AG. First edition published in German in 2015.

Translated to English by H. B. Babiar.

Paperback ISBN: 978-1-59572-853-1
Star Bright Books / MA / 00206230
Printed in Canada / Marquis / 9 8 7 6 5 4 3 2

Printed on paper from sustainable forests.

Library of Congress Cataloging-in-Publication Data

Names: Vinke, Hermann, author. | Babiar, H. B. (Translator), translator.
Title: I only see the person in front of me : the life of German officer Wilm
  Hosenfeld / By Hermann Vinke ; Translated by H. B. Babiar.
Other titles: Ich sehe immer den Menschen vor mir. English
Description: Cambridge, MA : Star Bright Books, [2019] | Includes
  bibliographical references and index.
Identifiers: LCCN 2018044288 | ISBN 9781595728531 (paperback)
Subjects: LCSH: Hosenfeld, Wilm. | Soldiers--Germany--Biography. | World War,
  1939-1945--Germany--Biography. | World War,
  1939-1945--Jews--Rescue--Poland--Warsaw. | Righteous Gentiles in the
  Holocaust--Biography.
Classification: LCC DD247.H66 V5613 2019 | DDC 940.53/18092 [B] --dc23
LC record available at https://lccn.loc.gov/2018044288

— Table of Contents —

I Only See the Person in Front of Me

If there were just one person who deserved to be called a "human being," then that would already be enough to believe in humans, to believe in humanity.

—Julius Spier, Jewish immigrant to the Netherlands, 1941, speaking to Etty Hillesum, a fellow Jew, who was murdered two years later at Auschwitz.

In November 1944, as World War II neared its close, an exceptional encounter occurred in Warsaw, Poland, in a building where the Wehrmacht was in the process of establishing its command headquarters. It was in this building that German army captain Wilm Hosenfeld discovered the Polish pianist Władysław Szpilman, who had been hiding in the attic and was close to starvation. Hosenfeld, a teacher in civilian life, did not hand the Jewish musician over to Nazi authorities. Instead, he provided Szpilman with food over a period of several weeks, thereby saving his life.

No other large European city was ravaged by the German occupiers in World War II to the extent of Warsaw. Almost all that remained of the once sophisticated and culturally flourishing city was a smoldering heap of rubble. Behind an inferno of mass killings and destruction, Adolf Hitler had ordered the Polish capital razed to the ground. By the autumn of 1944 the German occupiers, comprising tens of thousands of soldiers and security agents, had liquidated most of Poland's ruling class and intelligentsia during their merciless demolition campaign—while committing genocide against the Jews.

Nonetheless, there were exceptions among the Germans—people like Wilm Hosenfeld, whose story has remained largely unknown to the general public. It was only after a short scene in the 2002 award-winning film about the life of Władysław Szpilman, *The Pianist*, that Hosenfeld's courageous rescue was, for the first time, brought to the attention of a global audience. Although the film made Szpilman world-famous, Hosenfeld was not even mentioned by name.

Wilm Hosenfeld saved not only Władysław Szpilman from certain death, but also countless other Polish citizens, including additional Jews. Against the murderous background of Warsaw, the officer appears to us today as a shining figure during a time of darkness. It is likely that over 60 people managed to survive the war with Hosenfeld's help. He was a savior and, to some extent, also a victim—he died in Soviet captivity without ever seeing his family again.

***

This biography, *I Only See the Person in Front of Me: The Life of German Officer Wilm Hosenfeld*, brings to light the extraordinary story of this man's life—a story of admirable courage, contradictions, cruel coincidences, and finally, profound tragedy. It will show how it is possible, even under the most barbaric conditions, to preserve and act in accordance with one's beliefs and moral conscience. Hosenfeld did that. He gained recognition for his courageous acts at a much later point in time; the Holocaust memorial Yad Vashem honored him in 2008 as a "Righteous Among the Nations." His "rescue resistance" serves as a shining example for today and the future.

Born in central Germany's Rhön Mountains, Hosenfeld spent his World War II years exclusively in Poland, where he initially helped build and organize a camp for Polish prisoners of war before leading a sports and vocational school for Wehrmacht troops. These six years were a turning point in his life, in which he evolved from an enthusiastic follower of Hitler to one of the most fervent and clear-minded critics of the Nazi regime. From the start, Wilm Hosenfeld showed himself to be helpful, generous, and decisive toward the Polish people, disregarding official regulations and personal risk to save people from the terror of his own compatriots.

There is probably no other German officer who documented the crimes of the Nazis during World War II as comprehensively as Hosenfeld did. He kept a journal and wrote over 800 letters to his family at home in Thalau, Germany, where, prior to the war, he had taught at the village school. Hosenfeld thus became a chronicler of the murderous day-to-day life in occupied Warsaw, including the uprising in the Jewish ghetto in 1943 and the Warsaw Uprising in 1944. The majority of his letters were to his wife, Annemarie Hosenfeld (née Krummacher), a pacifist who grew up in a family of artists in Worpswede, Germany, near Bremen, and was left to raise their five children on her own during the war.

To a significant extent, this book is based on the correspondence between Wilm Hosenfeld and his wife and the writings in his unique Warsaw journals. His letters, notes, and journal entries were collectively published in the 2004 book *Wilm Hosenfeld, "Ich versuche jeden zu retten": Das Leben eines deutschen Offiziers in Briefen und Tagebüchern* (*Wilm Hosenfeld, "I Try to Save Everyone": The Life of a German Officer in Letters and Diaries*). The comprehensive documentation of almost 1,200 pages (the appendix alone comprises over 200 pages), written by historian Thomas Vogel and published by the Military History Research Institute in Potsdam, Germany, served as the first academically based work affording a look at the life of Wilm Hosenfeld.

For this book, I was able to interview the rescued pianist's widow, Halina Szpilman, and also had access to material supplied by their son Andrzej Szpilman. The archive of complete correspondence and documents from the Hosenfeld family was likewise made available. Numerous conversations and interviews with the Hosenfeld children, among others, round out the research material. For the first time, excerpts of Annemarie Hosenfeld's letters are published here. She was also an excellent writer. While her husband was being held captive, she would tell her children: "When Father comes home, he will become a writer."

PART I:
DISCOVERING NEW PATHS

Early Years

Wilm (born Wilhelm) Hosenfeld wrote an essay in Warsaw, Poland, on December 17, 1943, that appears to have been intended for his children. It is called "When Father Was a Young Boy." Writing, for Hosenfeld, was a way to reflect on his roots and his life. Hosenfeld's life catapulted him from a tranquil farming village in the former Prussian province of Hesse-Nassau into the heart of a criminal war of extermination.

Wilm Hosenfeld was born on May 2, 1895, in Mackenzell, Germany, near the town of Hünfeld, on the edge of the Rhön Mountains. He was the seventh of nine children and grew up in a conservative Catholic home. The ancestors of his father, Adalbert Hosenfeld, were farmers and artisans. His mother, Friederike Hosenfeld (née Krich), was the daughter of an exceptionally gifted teacher. Adalbert was a teacher who worked his way up to Mackenzell schoolmaster. The parents ran a small livestock business on the side, something that was common in those days since a teacher's salary was seldom enough to sustain a family.

The Hosenfelds raised their children in strict adherence to Catholic teachings. Corporal punishment was quite common at the time. The children feared their father, who disciplined them and was the unquestioned figure of authority, both at home and at school. Adalbert Hosenfeld treated his own children no differently than his students.

As a boy, Wilm Hosenfeld liked to play pranks. He avoided home whenever he could. He would rather help a peasant boy his age chop wood in the forest or assist with the beet harvest in the fields. When he saw his father walking through the village, Hosenfeld and his friends would hide behind a barn door or the wall of a house. He never received preferential treatment at school. Hosenfeld was questioned, scolded, and beaten like the other students. He feared the teacher as much as they did.

When the family went on an excursion to visit relatives, though, Adalbert was sweet to his children and presented himself as a kind person. In reviewing his childhood, Wilm Hosenfeld tried to do his father justice. Maybe it was Adalbert's austerity or his peasant upbringing that led him to be so strict with his children, rather than show them his emotions.

After World War I, when Wilm Hosenfeld asked for the hand of Annemarie Krummacher in marriage, he composed a letter dated December 30, 1919, to his future father-in-law in Worpswede, Germany. He wrote:

> *He* [Adalbert] *fears that Annemarie is not the right wife for a rural teacher, from what he knows of her. He knows me too little. My world is foreign to him. He is unlikely to understand it. He has to very slowly find his way across to us, without ever crossing fully. He will always see his boy in me, who does things differently and thus, more or less, does things wrong.*

As a teacher, Hosenfeld rejected his father's educational techniques, especially beatings with a cane. Even so, his parents taught him to respect them and the Catholic church with its Ten Commandments. This shaped Hosenfeld, and he never abandoned these principles.

He remained loyal to his Christian beliefs, even in the most difficult of times. They provided him with support and a sense of orientation. In this light, his attitude toward the Poles during World War II was pre-ordained. Hosenfeld did not regard the Poles as slaves of the German conquerors; instead, he saw them as equal human beings. Given their Catholic faith, most Poles thought and acted like him.

The immediate influence of Hosenfeld's childhood home lessened once he left primary school at age 11. He transferred to Hünfeld, where he enrolled at the Latin grammar school. Unlike in Mackenzell, he no longer accepted everything the teachers expected of him during their lessons. His sense of justice rose up when one of his teachers slapped him in the face. In protest, he did not attend class for a short time.

Wilm Hosenfeld knew relatively early he wanted to follow in his father's footsteps, but without Adalbert's teaching methods. Hosenfeld wanted to prove it was possible to raise and educate children without using physical punishment. In the years to come, modern education theories would be of great interest to Hosenfeld.

From 1910 to 1913, Hosenfeld attended a preparatory teaching school in Fritzlar, where he readied himself for studies to become a teacher. A year before the outbreak of World War I, he enrolled at the Catholic teachers' seminary in Fulda. Hosenfeld now had his own room and began to orient himself.

***

One of the many groups that attracted young people prior to the turn of the 20th century was the Wandervogel movement. Wandervogel can be loosely translated to "wandering bird." Youths rediscovered nature and the environment. They gathered around campfires at night, sang songs, and enjoyed each other's company in an informal way. They longed to leave behind the noisy factories, the

Traditional emblem of the Wandervogel youth movement.

cramped living conditions of the city, and the conventional lifestyle of imperial Germany.

Wandervogel youth viewed themselves as part of a movement beyond politics and social conventions. The movement was characterized by songs in praise of being German; poetic, intellectual flights of fancy; and a self-assertiveness in everyday life. But to the adult world, this push for independence represented unrest and rebellion. The older generation felt its existing order—with Prussian virtues like obedience and a sense of duty—was in jeopardy.

The movement, which comprised various trends, actually had little to do with subversion and revolution. Instead, it was a way to rise up against the older generation, which wanted to dictate everything to the young and push them into an entrenched structure. Wilm Hosenfeld—lean, athletic, outgoing, and adventurous—immediately felt a close connection with the Wandervogel movement. A lot of things attracted him: the outdoors, the open and informal interaction among young adults, and the enthusiasm for freedom and self-determination. Hosenfeld joined because of his desire to free himself of stiff restraints and discover new paths for his own life. He had inherited his mother's sensibilities and her keen sense of nuance. He took pleasure in interacting with other people and had an amazing ability to take in surrounding events and accurately describe them.

It was under the influence of the Wandervogel movement that Hosenfeld changed his name to Wilm, which was shorter and catchier than Wilhelm. He most likely embraced a clause in the "Meißner formula," which stated, "The *Freideutsche Jugend* [free German youth] wants to shape its own life through self-determination, self-responsibility, and inner truthfulness."

In a sense, these ideals, accompanied by his Catholic faith, became a second anchor in Wilm Hosenfeld's life. He kept Wandervogel beliefs close, even after the movement lost its relevance. Later, after World War I—most likely in 1921 or 1922—Hosenfeld dedicated a lengthy essay titled "The German Youth Movement" to his personal awakening.

He listed all the achievements of the Wandervogel movement, perhaps in the hope that its ghost might be revived in light of the brutal war.

Hosenfeld wrote that Wandervogel youth created a new kind of community and developed their own hiking technique. Moreover, the movement reinvigorated folk songs and dances. *It was the first to push for the welfare of the youth in an idealistic sense, established the first youth hostels, encouraged physical training, and staged exercise competitions,* Hosenfeld observed. *It allowed for a simple, natural, and comradely character for the relationship between the genders.* The movement drew a line when it came to the adult world. *The youth does not want to be a hollow vessel that the older generation would be allowed to unquestionably fill with their ideals and outlook on life,* Hosenfeld wrote. *It now sees itself as strong and judicious enough to create its own youth culture.* Hosenfeld also contrasted the big city—with its bustling restlessness, its soullessness, and its enslavement of people—with the inner strength of the youthful spirit, the hiking, distant trips, and the solitude in nature.

Wilm Hosenfeld (*standing, right*) with a group of fellow Wandervogel youth in 1912 or 1913.

Wandervogel youth saw themselves as a countermovement to the industrialization and commercialization that precipitated an unimagined economic blossoming in Europe, particularly in England and Germany. At the same time, the movement was of an anti-bourgeois spirit. There had been peace for four decades following the Franco-German War of 1870 and 1871. During those years, Germany became the leading industrial nation in Europe. Advances in the areas of technology, science, and medicine were astonishing. Long distances shrank because of the development of passenger trains. Art and culture tested the limits of what was deemed acceptable before crossing them. Women fought for rights that had been denied them for centuries. Anything and everything seemed possible and within reach.

The flame of this new age also burned bright in heroic Wandervogel slogans. Inherent in the message was a willingness to sacrifice, to advocate for a sufficiently large and noble goal. The love for the fatherland was such an ideal. The pillars of society—schools, churches, the military, and the rulers all the way up to the kaiser—had planted patriotic devotion deep within the souls of young people. This virtue could be called upon at will, which was just enough to paint the danger to the fatherland in bright colors.

World War I

The Wandervogel movement was only one episode in the life of Wilm Hosenfeld, despite the lasting impact it had on him. The outbreak of World War I on August 1, 1914, put an end to all activities that intended to pave the way for a new attitude toward life. Young men like 19-year-old Hosenfeld, who recently had been rhapsodizing about freedom and self-determination, now voluntarily rushed to the military barracks.

Things moved fast for the teacher-to-be Hosenfeld, who had only completed half of his studies in Fulda. His schooling came to a premature end. In a 1917 essay titled "Recollections from the Field," Wilm Hosenfeld described the great excitement that defined the summer of 1914. *War was now the solution*, he wrote. *Hey, who would not have followed?*

Germany called an entire generation to arms for World War I. Hosenfeld could not be held back. His parents already expected that he and his brother Martin would volunteer to serve. On August 21, 1914, Hosenfeld first wore the gray army uniform of the 167th regiment in the Prussian infantry in Kassel. He completed basic training without difficulty. While others complained of the drudgery, humiliation, and harassment, Hosenfeld offered no resistance as he learned how to use his weapons. He wrote: *Our instructors found great pleasure with these recruits, and I did not feel the rigors of military discipline because we were always ready and willing to obey.*

From the start, Hosenfeld's path to an officer's rank was wide open due to his advanced level of schooling. The ascent within the military hierarchy ladder meant a lot to him. Hosenfeld's first deployment, at

Wilm Hosenfeld, age 19, in his World War I uniform.

the beginning of November 1914, was to the Flanders province in Belgium. This was the site of one of the fiercest battles of the war. The German army was expected to break the wall of French, British, and Belgian troops around the city of Ypres and then advance to the coast of the English Channel. This way, the Germans could keep their backs clear and focus on their goal: the capture of Paris.

What Hosenfeld saw during the train ride to the war front dampened his enthusiasm. Upon seeing German soldiers, Belgian women stuck out their tongues and, as Hosenfeld described, made a *throat-cutting motion* with their hands. However, the exhilaration of being allowed to take part in the war resurfaced during the march to the front. Hosenfeld wrote: *For the first time, I now experienced with an absolute power and intensity, the love and loyalty that connected me to the fatherland. The combination of thankfulness and pride provided me with strength, great courage, and a firm will.*

The soldier's strength, courage, and will to persevere were put to the test with the first assault in Flanders. During a nocturnal advance into no-man's-land, across slippery beet fields and through muddy ditches, Hosenfeld intermittently lost contact with the soldier before him. He wandered, disoriented, across the terrain and found himself between barbed wire and telephone lines and saw unfamiliar figures approaching him. Hosenfeld thought about *the humiliation of captivity* and *the futility of his existence as a soldier.* The bullets whistling past frightened him. At daybreak, he saw soldiers moving back and forth between splattering fountains of dirt until they suddenly fell to the ground. Were these his own comrades or the French? Soon after, Hosenfeld came across the first dead soldier. The sight unsettled him. *His eyes look straight at the gray sky, eternity looks at me,* he wrote.

Both sides, the Allies and the Germans, suffered heavy casualties in Flanders. The intense fighting and occasional use of chemical weapons eventually led to trench warfare. After the failed assault on Langemarck in early November 1914, Hosenfeld and his unit remained in the nearby village of Poelkapelle. From there, he and several comrades would relieve guards at the frontline. This was the case on the evening before December 24, 1914. Hosenfeld later described in a 1928 article for the German newspaper *Fuldaer Zeitung* how he spent *four Christmases during war.*

From November 1914 until April 1915 Wilm Hosenfeld participated in trench warfare in West Flanders. After the grueling wait was interrupted by artillery fire and individual battles, German detachments planned to force a breakthrough advance with a new offensive in the spring of 1915.

On April 24, 1915, near a farm, Hosenfeld was injured by shrapnel in his right leg, chest, and shoulder. Aides took him to the first-aid post. In the military hospital in Aachen, Germany (where he celebrated his 20th birthday), Hosenfeld underwent treatment for several weeks. The bullet wounds healed relatively fast.

At the end of June, Hosenfeld received new marching orders. This time, he was to head east to the second front. Germany and its ally Austria-Hungary had been active there since the start of the war.

Hosenfeld was initially stationed in Lithuania and Courland in modern-day Latvia. The aim was to drive Russian troops out of

An explosion rips through a battlefield in Flanders during World War I.

individual Baltic cities. In August, the Germans occupied Kaunas, Lithuania. Around three months later, the Germans' pursuit of the Russians stalled at the Daugava River to the south of Riga. Hosenfeld spent the ensuing weeks in rather subdued trench warfare. *Our life is pretty comfortable,* he wrote. *We are mostly young guys. Peace just does not want to come.*

Before arriving near Sibiu in Transylvania, Romania, in September 1916, after a seven-day train journey, Hosenfeld took a step up in the military hierarchy. He was promoted to sergeant, which authorized him to command a squadron of around a dozen soldiers. He received the coveted Iron Cross, Second Class, in April 1916 for his "bravery against the enemy on the battlefield of the Eastern Front."

***

The war continued in Romania. Almost restrained at first, it soon became unrelentingly harsh again. Hosenfeld fought alongside Austrians and Hungarians for the first time. He was highly impressed with their magnificent uniforms. At first, the forward advance in the Transylvanian Alps resembled a hiking tour—the actual fighting started at the end of September 1916. As the Romanians retreated, Hosenfeld's unit pursued them to the vicinity of Kronstadt, near Saint Petersburg, Russia.

The rearguard battles were ferocious. The sight of the battlefield, with torn people and horses rearing up in mortal agony, almost made Hosenfeld lose his mind. *We did the animals a favor and shot a bullet in their eye,* he wrote. *But I cannot do that with the people. . . .*

Roaming around the area, Hosenfeld came across a man he initially thought to be dead. It was a Romanian soldier who had been shot in the thigh. The man begged for help. Hosenfeld fetched water and gave him matches and cigarettes, a piece of bread, and a jacket. As he walked away, he heard the injured man begin to cry aloud. Hosenfeld wrote, *I will never forget the beautiful face of this man with its dark eyes that spoke more clearly than the most eloquent mouth.* His suggestion to the company commander, to take a few men and retrieve the injured man, was rejected. But the next day Hosenfeld was relieved to learn an injured Romanian with a gunshot wound in the thigh had been rescued.

The fate of Romanian military forces was decided during the last three months of 1916. They had to vacate Kronstadt and pulled back over the passes of the Transylvanian Alps with the Germans in pursuit. In the process, Hosenfeld met Transylvanian Saxons, who had lived in Romania for centuries, but had preserved their native German language and culture. *I would never have imagined coming here, where Germans live with an unfamiliar and elegant national pride that is greater than it is at home,* he wrote.

At the end of November 1916, German troops advanced deep into southern Romania, pushing forward to the Wallachia region. Hosenfeld's part in the advance ended in Ploiești, a town at the foot of the Carpathian Mountains about 40 miles north of Bucharest. The Germans then captured Bucharest with almost no resistance.

Wilm Hosenfeld spent his third wartime Christmas in an acacia forest in Romanian Moldavia. Grenades had shredded trees, and shell holes and trenches ravaged the ground. The enemy was situated less than a mile away. On Christmas Day Hosenfeld attended a Catholic field mass. He wrote in his journal, *No church in the world could have awoken the amount of devotion that this starry sky, dark ground, silent forest, and blazing fire did.* He felt a wonderful peace in his heart, he wrote, *in this setting, with combat, death, and horror all around us.*

As January 1917 drew to a close, the cold became unbearable. *A stiff, icy wind blew out of the northeast and continued for days and nights,* Hosenfeld wrote in his journal. *This was a storm, a hurricane, that cut through the uniforms and froze limbs.* Many suffered frostbite. After the Germans captured the city of Focşani, another round of trench warfare began. Dysentery and cholera were rampant. Hosenfeld, who had been promoted to second staff sergeant, spent four weeks in a military hospital due to illness, until early May. No specific details of his hospital stay are known.

As soon as he recovered, his superiors authorized him for a three-week home leave. By way of coincidence, his brother Martin was in Mackenzell at the same time. *On Ascension Day, the family was back together again for the first time in years, to the great delight of everyone in the household,* Hosenfeld wrote. *The time for farewells drew near again and on June 1* [1917] *I left.*

Hosenfeld's route back to Focşani took him through Wrocław, Kronstadt, and Ploieşti. When he rejoined his company in a village on the southern edge of the Carpathians, the summer weather was warm and there was a break in the fighting. This gave Hosenfeld a chance to observe the country and its people. He felt sorry for the Romanians. Hosenfeld approached the people and tried to communicate with them. He observed desperation and grief, but not hate. He admired the hardworking farmers and their skilled craftsmanship.

Hosenfeld was again injured in early August as the Germans advanced on Russian units in the Bukovina region of northeast

Romania. Hosenfeld made every effort to avoid the hail of bullets, but to no avail. He was shot in the left leg and became separated from his platoon. He fell to the ground and crawled on all fours into a cornfield, where two comrades found him.

In the second half of August a military hospital train took him to Gera, Germany. He had had enough of the war. *I am as happy as a child to be home and cannot believe my luck*, he wrote. His father was also relieved. *Keep yourself in the hospital for as long as you can*, Adalbert wrote. *I'm glad that the "home shot" has allowed you to escape the great danger*. Wilm Hosenfeld's biggest worry, though, was having to live with a stiff leg. To never be able to hike again—this was a dreadful thought. Toward the end of September, he transferred to a rehabilitation unit in Jena, Germany.

The follow-up care in Jena left Hosenfeld with much free time. He used this time to write down his recollections of the war. It was his intention to record events without glorifying them or presenting himself as a hero. Nor was he interested in making a critical analysis of the war or questioning the purpose of mutually murdering and slaughtering one another. Wilm Hosenfeld remained both a patriot and an enthusiastic Wandervogel follower. While still in the hospital in Jena, he found some like-minded contacts and took part in a regional leadership day of the Thuringia state association. There, he met Otger Gräff, a powerfully eloquent leader of the movement, who made no secret of his nationalistic and anti-Semitic beliefs. After the event, Hosenfeld wrote in his journal: *He wants to integrate us older Wandervogel into a Germanic, pure-blooded bond with the Young German Confederation, which he founded.*

Since Hosenfeld was classified as "unfit for active service," there was no chance of him returning to the front. He was at the garrison hospital in Weimar, Germany, at the turn of the year from 1917 to 1918. The surgeon there was able to repair the nerve pathways of his injured leg so well he was able to walk normally again.

Hosenfeld would long remember spending his last wartime Christmas with other wounded comrades. On Christmas Eve, the pastor said the German sword had not lost any of its edge. The year 1917 had been another glorious chapter on the garland of German victories, the pastor proclaimed, but Hosenfeld saw it differently. *We don't like this Christmas sermon*, Hosenfeld wrote. *We are all so tired. Nobody can deceive us. Not like that!*

On Christmas Day, Hosenfeld met a Catholic chaplain and became aware a new phase of his life was imminent. *And I noticed, what an inactive, lackluster, and wild life I had lived*, he wrote. *That is now over. For me, the war is over. The sound of the bells this morning, which I had not heard for three years, are calling out the peace to me, the peace of a conventional life.* In May 1918, Hosenfeld's superiors ordered his release from active military duty. The war was over for him; his comrades had to wait for the armistice on November 11, 1918.

Wilm Hosenfeld (*front left*) with a group of Prussian officers and nurses in September 1917.

A New Beginning

Wilm Hosenfeld was now finally able to look ahead and plan for the future. He had met Annemarie Krummacher, who was to be more than just a fleeting encounter. Hosenfeld first met her on August 8, 1918, during a Wandervogel meeting at a former colonial school in Witzenhausen, Germany. Annemarie later told their son Detlev in an ironic tone that Wilm had a simple and innocent way about him at the beginning of their relationship. He was adventurous and always ready for a joke, no doubt to please the girls in the group. One evening, he spoke very seriously with her about the war in Romania, telling her about the fighting and his injuries there. This conversation, more than anything else, impressed her. Annemarie liked the aspiring teacher with dark hair and athletic build more than the other young men in the Wandervogel group. However, she did not agree with Wilm Hosenfeld's populist-nationalistic views.

Annemarie Krummacher was born on April 6, 1898, in the Wilmersdorf section of Berlin. She grew up in Worpswede, Germany, an artist village near Bremen. Together with her younger sister, Gertrud, she had experienced the liberal element of the Wandervogel movement.

Annemarie's father was the painter and author Karl Krummacher, who was born into a Protestant pastor's family. He belonged to a circle of Worpswede painters whose works had brought the artist colony acclaim throughout Germany. Other prominent Worpswede artists at the time were Otto Modersohn, Fritz Overbeck, Fritz Mackensen, Heinrich Vogeler, and Hans am Ende.

The painter Carl Vinnen had convinced Krummacher to move to Worpswede from Berlin, where he was barely able to live off of his work as an art and theater critic. Heinrich Vogeler provided a place for Karl Krummacher to live. He focused extensively on painting, and his impressionistic artwork sold well. Close and friendly relations existed between most of the artists; they helped one another and celebrated together.

While in Worpswede, Karl Krummacher and his wife, Anna (née Brodkorb), moved their family three times until eventually settling on a large farm. For Annemarie, as she later described it, this was paradise. She wrote:

> In addition to the house we lived in, the extensive property, where we could do as we pleased, consisted of a courtyard, a garden and grasslands, and a grove. . . . Sometimes I would push my doll carriage through the dark ground of the narrow paths in the garden, past the fragrant jasmine bushes to the golden chain tree, whose heavy clusters of golden-yellow flowers reached to the ground.

Many guests came and went at her parent's home in those days. Annemarie described them as . . . *young, high-spirited artistic people. They played music, painted and discussed, and appreciated the hospitality of my parents.* Sometimes the house's large hall served as an artist studio when the painters of Worpswede gathered there to draw; sometimes it was used to play tennis when it was raining or too cold outside.

After his first wife died, Otto Modersohn married the painter Paula Becker. The new couple traveled to Paris shortly thereafter. Elsbeth, Otto's daughter, stayed with the Krummacher family. Shortly after the couple returned from Paris, Paula Modersohn-Becker—only a few weeks before her death—encouraged Annemarie and Elsbeth to accompany her on a visit with an old woman. The woman, because of her disfigured face, was branded among the children as being evil and ugly. The girls were reluctant, but Paula convinced them to come along. Annemarie reflected on the visit in her journal:

In the wretched dwelling, biting peat smoke assaulted us. Filled with
secret fear and childish curiosity, we eavesdropped on the conversation
of the women by the open hearth fire. Paula Modersohn[-Becker]
was speaking with the old woman in a Worpswede Low German
accent. I was amazed to observe how the poor woman lost all shyness
and opened up to the listener about her troubles. . . . I can never forget
this beautiful and soulful face of the great woman and artist, so full
of kindness. This is how I saw her for the last time.

Annemarie came into contact with many extraordinary people in
Worpswede. She met Clara Rilke-Westhoff and Heinrich Vogeler, as
well as people in the Barkenhoff, the socialist commune that Vogeler
founded. Many people who wanted to try new art forms and cohabi-
tation were attracted to the Barkenhoff. Following the death of Paula,
Otto Modersohn moved to the nearby village of Fischerhude. There,
he married Louise Breling. The Krummacher children visited Otto
and kept up contact.

Annemarie's parents, Karl and Anna Krummacher, ensured
their children received a solid education. Annemarie possessed a nice
soprano voice and took singing lessons. She attended a private school
in Sondershausen, where among other things, she learned English
and French. She then studied social education in Bremen. Annemarie
wanted to stand on her own two feet as a professional woman. She was
interested in art and literature. Her sister, Gertrud, was also musical
and played piano, and, because she could draw very well, acquired
graphic expertise and learned arts and crafts skills.

Karl and Anna also allowed their children sufficient freedom in
order to develop their own personal growth. Whenever the opportunity
arose, Annemarie and Gertrud went on excursions and trips throughout
Germany, either on their own or as part of a Wandervogel group.

***

From their first encounter, Annemarie Krummacher and Wilm
Hosenfeld were attracted to each other. Their opposing views about

the Wandervogel movement was of little importance. Indeed, they came from different worlds. Annemarie belonged to the cosmopolitan, progressive wing of the new youth movement. Having been influenced by the pacifist and author Bertha von Suttner, she also rejected the war on principle. Wilm, on the other hand, was committed to the populist-nationalistic aspect of the Wandervogel, while distancing himself from the anti-Semitic leanings of the movement.

Nevertheless, Wilm and Annemarie discovered they had many things in common, such as their mutual interests in art, literature, music, and of course, the outdoors. In a 2005 lecture, their daughter Uta Hosenfeld, a psychologist, presented the view that Annemarie's pacifism had fascinated Wilm. She said, "My mother belonged to these 'free Germans,' this left-leaning spectrum of the Wandervogel, and the two of them were able to give each other new impulses time and time again through intellectual exchanges. And I believe that my mother was the alter ego of my father."

Wilm Hosenfeld already had been acquainted with other women, but was still searching for the one with whom he would spend his life. As he admitted to a friend, none of the others had brought him total happiness. In his personal relationships, Hosenfeld did not exactly follow the precepts of the church. He wrote in his journal:

> *Concerning our Catholic church, I am still absolutely convinced of its value, but for some things I allow myself my own opinion and follow the principle: believe in God, but not in the dogma. . . . I don't consider it necessary to follow the rules of the church at all times if I can substitute something better in place of its position, and my inner law proves me right.*

From their first meeting, Wilm Hosenfeld was confident he had found the right woman. She also soon dropped her reserve. Six months after having met, they were engaged. The couple hesitated to inform their parents about their plans because they understood the obstacles a marriage would present. Hosenfeld's parents did not consider

Wilm and Annemarie in 1919.

Annemarie, the daughter of a higher-class family, a suitable wife for a future village schoolteacher. More than that, though, they opposed the marriage of their son to a Protestant.

The couple waited until fall 1919 to announce their intentions. Wilm Hosenfeld wanted a church wedding, but certain hurdles needed to be cleared. The Catholic church expected a bride to raise children in the Catholic faith. It was not easy for her, but in the end, Annemarie finally converted to Catholicism. At that time, it would have been difficult for Wilm Hosenfeld to teach Catholic classes if his wife were a Protestant.

Annemarie's parents also had reservations about the marriage. Was their daughter's future husband even in a position to support a family? In the years directly after World War I, there was great economic hardship in Germany and the salary of a young teacher was barely sufficient for one person.

Finally, on May 23, 1920, Annemarie Krummacher and Wilm Hosenfeld exchanged vows at the St. Johannis Catholic Church in

Bremen. Apart from the bride's concession, the couple had pushed aside all concerns and objections to their marriage to have their way. They had a great passion for one another and were a happy, young couple—despite the predictable financial difficulties.

Soon, family ties grew even tighter. Annemarie's sister, Gertrud, married Martin Hosenfeld, Wilm's older brother. They eventually also married at St. Johannis. Gertrud and Martin were the godparents to Helmut Hosenfeld, Annemarie and Wilm's oldest son, when he was baptized in 1921.

Wilm Hosenfeld was impressed by the welcoming atmosphere and tolerance he encountered among his Worpswede in-laws. During a discussion with Annemarie's uncle, the scientist Otto Krummacher, he observed certain differences to his own political views. *He is a freemason and social democrat, both of which require a supranational outlook, which I, with my nationalistically based worldview, can partially respect,* Hosenfeld wrote. *Of course, he also rejects any ties to the church.* He also noted that during their discussion, Otto had not made the slightest attempt to influence him. Hosenfeld wrote, *That's the reason why speaking with him is so pleasant. If you encounter differences, then one respects the other's viewpoint, and it stays that way.*

Wilm Hosenfeld and Annemarie Krummacher were engaged in 1919.

— 4 —

A Dedicated Teacher

Despite the influence of his Catholic childhood and his oft-mentioned populist-nationalistic worldview, Wilm Hosenfeld remained a seeker, hungry for knowledge, new ideas, and new insights. As early as 1912 or 1913, he subscribed to the *Weltrundschau* (*World Review*), published by Reclams, an illustrated journal that reported on the latest technical advancements and scientific research activities. Examining the long list of books, magazines, and newspapers that Hosenfeld read in the 1920s, one first notices titles related to the Wandervogel movement, to nature and regional studies, to German classics, and to World War I. Scattered among these are also periodicals from the All-German Union, a group of warmongers, as well as investigations on issues of race and the Jews.

Hosenfeld's priority, though, was progressive education. He may have followed in the footsteps of his father, but he wanted to be a different type of teacher. Hosenfeld outlined his guiding principle in his journal: I *will do all I can and not focus on the drill, but on the cultivation of the personality of the child. The child will undoubtedly profit more if I awaken abilities within him* [or her] *and develop these, than follow the written rules and teach him* [or her] *a mechanical skill that will later just fall away much like old plaster.*

In May 1918, Hosenfeld started as a student teacher in Rudolphshan. His energetic drive was expressed in his starting his own Wandervogel group. Teachers from the far and near surrounding areas met on weekends and during holidays in an old house in Rudolphshan that Hosenfeld rented as a place to discuss educational reform. Hosenfeld called it The Nest. Among the participants was Adolf Reichwein, who went on to become a distinguished advocate for modern education and who influenced Hosenfeld in talks and writings.

The Wandervogel meetings appeared somewhat alien to the village residents. Some of them, including the parish priest, wildly speculated without ever considering the group's focus was on the welfare of children. The priest also did not approve that the house became a meeting place for boys and girls. This was not proper in his view.

After only a few months, Hosenfeld was forced to sever ties with his Wandervogel project. He and his family moved to Rossbach, a village southeast of Gelnhausen. It was there that his oldest son, Helmut, was born, and where he completed his student teaching—both in February 1921. After passing his teaching exam, Hosenfeld officially became a civil servant.

Wilm and Annemarie Hosenfeld with their first child, Helmut, in 1921.

***

Wilm Hosenfeld received his first full-time position in the village school in Kassel, near Rossbach, in the summer of 1921. The young family was now financially secure for the first time, even if Hosenfeld's salary did not allow for much outside of the necessities of life.

Hosenfeld's ideas for reform were also not warmly received in Kassel. The school consisted of several classes. Most of his colleagues saw it as self-evident to continue traditional teaching methods. Hosenfeld wrote about this in his journal:

> *The teacher, the ruler, the monarch, the despot, the students* [are] *mere subjects without input on the lesson plan. Of course, the children are nothing more than subjects, and the spirit of being a subject is ingrained in them. Obedient without question or thought, untruthfulness, craving for admiration, deceitfulness, affectation, undiscriminating, without an own opinion, characterless.*

The young teacher Wilm Hosenfeld continued to regularly write about what moved him, stirred in him, angered him, and brought him joy. These are vivid accounts of a restless mind. On November 21, 1921, he wrote:

> *Yesterday, the priest was here. How they* [the children] *are well-behaved then, how they diminish before him in submissiveness and faultlessness. And all of that is a mask. I do not punish with the cane and also don't give out too much extra work as punishment, and it is often impossible to get their attention. But once I have dispensed some punishment everything is as it should be, at least on the outside. . . .*

Nevertheless, there were also some favorable outcomes. When Hosenfeld presented Johann Wolfgang von Goethe's poem "Erlkönig" ("Elf King") to his students in December 1921, he impressed them with stories about the evolution and setting of the poem; the room turned breathlessly silent. The children understood what he told them and said it had been very nice. It was Hosenfeld's intention to get the children to speak. He wanted them to tell him what was on their minds, to describe nature, and to perceive everyday life through their own eyes, not through the lens of grownups.

He showed them how to plant fruit trees and how to refine them using grafting. One day, Hosenfeld brought his workbench to the classroom. He wanted the children to use it to make something. His older colleagues could only shake their heads. They could not—or would not—understand what he was trying to achieve. The principal was not amused and supervised Hosenfeld's lessons unannounced, obviously with the intention of slowing down his zeal. Hosenfeld sensed the distrust and wrote: *He* [the principal] *is businesslike and cold and plays the boss card, and even though he may want to conceal it, it pops out of him through all buttonholes. He should have an eye for new and extraordinary things that a teacher is trying to do in his school, even if he doesn't immediately have a heart for them.* The principal's inspection visits missed their mark—Hosenfeld was not swayed from his course to reform the education system.

One of Hosenfeld's role models was the Swiss educator Johann Heinrich Pestalozzi. He admired that Pestalozzi always looked out for the good of others rather than his own. Pestalozzi also never lost sight of his goals. *What do we do for others, if we were not to receive payment for it?* Hosenfeld asked after reading a book about Pestalozzi. *What do we do for the sake of the work, the good deed, the noble aim?* Hosenfeld also quoted Pestalozzi in his writings: *"No power in life develops from instruction through words, but instead only through action, love through love, faith through faith, thought through thought, doing through doing."*

The continued education of young adults was one of Hosenfeld's primary concerns. Advancements in this area had been made prior to World War I, which were then undone. Vocational schools, as we know them today, were officially introduced in 1920, but the offerings in rural areas were limited or simply nonexistent. Hosenfeld initially organized an evening course in Kassel on fruit farming. He expanded his offerings to include history and literature once he noticed an interest for them. It is important to learn more, he always emphasized, especially in the country.

After the disappointing experience with the Wandervogel group in Rudolphshan, Hosenfeld realized that creating new projects without consulting the clergy and community representatives would again lead to failure. Kassel's proximity to Frankfurt enabled Hosenfeld to exchange educational ideas with like-minded teachers and Wandervogel members. In fact, during the winter of 1923, he successfully established a school for continuing education in the village. It offered evening courses once a week. Young adults between the ages of 15 and 25 could choose from courses in economics, history, civics, German, and literature.

After some tedious preliminary work, Wilm Hosenfeld started a type of vocational school and adult education center. The positive feedback encouraged Hosenfeld to continue and plan beyond Kassel, in order to embed advanced education schools as a model in the state of Hesse. Some evenings, he would read a newspaper article aloud, for example about the Rentenmark, the currency introduced in 1923 to contain hyperinflation (and that was replaced one year later by the Reichsmark). In this way, Hosenfeld would launch a question-and-answer session. *But I want to mentally rouse these lads and guide their thoughts in another direction*, he wrote in his journal. *They are stuck all day in their work, whatever that may be. One makes brooms, the other chops wood in the forest, the other is a craftsman, and so on. It is all work that requires manual labor while the mind is idle.*

Some manuscripts from Hosenfeld's talks underline his efforts to educate children and youth, as well as his attempts to secure the participation of parents. Schooling of the mind was part of the voyage into a new age that began with the Weimar Republic, the first-ever democracy on German soil. In one of Hosenfeld's speeches from the spring of 1924, there was mention made of *a change in fortune for our fatherland. The old Reich with its might and power had collapsed. A new state with new power would arise. Let us be awake to experience this time, let us listen into the inner workings.* It may sound emotional today, but then it was an affirmation of the Weimar Republic, which was not a sure thing in the turbulent 1920s.

During the enrollment of a new class in the spring of 1924, Hosenfeld asked parents to trust him and to not regard the school as a hostile monster. The first duty of the teacher is to encourage children and to respond to their abilities and needs. Hosenfeld felt that parents *should not become impatient, scold, and criticize, "Oh, you are so dumb, nothing will ever become of you," and other similar remarks. Nothing is achieved through this. Quite the opposite; the child will be drained of courage and then much is lost.* [I would] *rather praise than criticize.*

***

During his nearly six years there, Kassel was a challenging work environment for Wilm Hosenfeld. Still, it was there he first had a chance to put his ideas on modern schooling and adult education methods into practice. In the spring of 1927, he took up an opportunity to run his own school, where he would be able to carry out his ideas on a more consistent basis. Thus, Hosenfeld and his family moved to Thalau, southeast of Fulda.

Thalau, a rather poor farming village of about 400 residents, was not far from Mackenzell, where his parents lived. The school building, a solid-timbered house built in 1909, was adjacent to the church. The teacher's residence was on the floor above the classrooms, where up to 90 children were taught. Hosenfeld had the support of a second teacher. Apart from that, he was his own master.

What no one could have known when they first arrived in Thalau was that this village would become the immediate center of the family's life, and remain so into the 1950s for Annemarie Hosenfeld and her children. Anemone, Wilm and Annemarie's second child and oldest daughter, had been born in Kassel in 1924; three more children were born in Thalau: Detlev in 1927, Jorinde in 1932, and Uta in 1937. The children kept Annemarie increasingly occupied. There was little time left for her interests in art, music, and literature.

Although Annemarie had a domestic helper, the work never ended. Taking care of the children was one thing. There was also a large garden belonging to the school, and a barn for chickens, goats, and a pig, which was fattened and butchered. Alongside his work at school

Wilm Hosenfeld with Annemarie, his children, and some of his students in front of the Thalau schoolhouse in 1929. Pictured are Anemone (*left of Wilm*), Detlev (*with Annemarie*), and Helmut (*holding a stick*).

and with the adult education program, Wilm Hosenfeld was busy with life in the village. He led the choir, organized festive events, and was the church organist. At home, he took care of the garden and had a special hobby: beekeeping. Most years, the beehives yielded so much honey he was able to supply friends and relatives with it.

Hosenfeld occasionally brought his children to the classroom, though they had not yet reached school age. This both relieved his wife's burden and loosened classroom lessons. Jorinde Krejcige (née Hosenfeld) recalled the early days at school. "When I was three or four years old, our father had sometimes taken me along to the classroom," she said. "I was allowed to sit with the big girls or next to him at the desk. Beneath the desk stood a crate filled with sand. There were little trees, tiny houses, farms, and so on. He used this to explain the village, the neighboring villages, and the countryside. The children would then be allowed to build it [the village]. During the break, we went upstairs to Mother, had breakfast together with her, and then she would send me back down to the classroom." Jorinde relayed that her father played guitar or piano during music lessons, singing folk songs with the children. There was also a flute group, and two girls played the violin.

Her brother Detlev spoke in glowing terms of a lovely childhood in Thalau. "We had so much freedom," he said. "Also, the beautiful surrounding countryside. Going sledding or skiing in the winter. In the summer, we went swimming in a lake near the Wasserkuppe Mountain, a favorite spot for gliders. The pets, the vast garden. Across the way, there was a lovely meadow with fruit trees."

The children may have felt happy and secure in Thalau, but it was a big change for their mother. In the beginning, Annemarie had difficulty adapting. She was not thrilled about her husband's transfer to a village even smaller than Kassel. She initially found the farmers to be unwelcoming and reserved. From the farmers' perspective, they probably saw the wife of the village teacher as presumptuous. Either way, it took a while before both sides drew closer together.

In many respects, Thalau was the opposite of Worpswede. The differences between peasant life in the state of Hesse and the animated nature of artists and painters in northern Germany became ever more apparent to Annemarie—even more so than had been evident in Rossbach and Kassel. To a certain extent, the frequent visits of relatives and friends offset this feeling. Visitors came from Worpswede, Mackenzell, Fulda, and many other places. The Hosenfelds' guest book from the 1920s contains sketches, drawings, and entire essays about the hours and days spent together. Although sometimes the workload of cleaning, cooking, and baking became too much for her, Annemarie cultivated a participatory household, in which her children learned from an early age to pitch in and help their parents.

Wilm Hosenfeld with his students in Thalau in 1934. Some boys are wearing Hitler Youth uniforms.

She was able to speak to her husband about everything. But Wilm Hosenfeld was very busy and often away. He organized commemoration ceremonies, such as for Constitution Day in August 1929, which marked 10 years since the adoption of the Weimar Constitution. For the occasion, Hosenfeld spoke about reconstruction in Germany and the oppressive war debts, ending with the appeal: "Our hearts shall belong to this new state!"

One particular cause important to Hosenfeld was keeping alive the memory of World War I. When he spoke about injured and killed comrades, his own experiences on the front came back to him. In a speech on Memorial Day in February 1932, he said, "This is long ago, but in the night, when the noise of our work-filled day has subsided, they stand again before us, this one with a shattered skull, that one with a perfectly round hole in the chest, this one barely recognizable, pale and dirty all of them. We cannot rid ourselves of these pictures; they will always return, always and forever! And we will always be amazed that we were spared, that it did not take us as well."

Pictures of the war clung to Hosenfeld. But he did not make a radical break from the murderous events. Only much later, under the weight of his experiences during World War II, was he able to denounce the large scale of death in war as senseless.

Wilm Hosenfeld with five-year-old Detlev in 1932.

PART II:
CRITICAL FOLLOWERS

National Socialism

When Adolf Hitler came to power on January 30, 1933, Wilm Hosenfeld did not believe, like so many did, that the leader of the National Socialist German Workers' Party (the National Socialists or the Nazi Party) would stay in office only a short time before handing over control of the government. In his Memorial Day speech on February 20, 1932, Hosenfeld lamented the inner turmoil of the German nation and the political fervor that was stirring up the people. No one was fully capable of seeing what the change in government truly meant. Hosenfeld had always publicly defended the Weimar democracy. As a progressive teacher, he was probably a typical centrist voter, a follower of the political wing of the Catholic church. In the eyes of many Germans, the Weimar Republic had been anything but a success, if only because of the large-scale unemployment. Many thought Hitler would perhaps be able to overcome domestic political differences and bring about an economic upswing.

Furthermore, Hitler's sharp attacks on the 1920 Treaty of Versailles, which placed overwhelming burdens on the German Reich, fell on fertile soil. The reparations were to be cast off so Germany could once more look to the future with hope. This message was well received by a majority of the population. As far as Wilm Hosenfeld was concerned, parts of his populist-nationalistic worldview were definitely compatible with the *Blut und Boden* ("blood and soil") ideology of the Nazis, which focused on ethnicity based on the bloodlines and territory of the population. The wave of propaganda with which the National Socialists overran the country most likely had an effect on Hosenfeld as well. In any case, he did not distance himself from it.

On April 15, 1933, Wilm Hosenfeld joined the *Sturmabteilung* (SA)—also known as "Storm Troopers" or "Brownshirts" because of the color of their uniforms—which was the original paramilitary wing of the Nazi Party. Hosenfeld felt a connection to the SA because, among other reasons, former World War I soldiers were also members. Was he aware of the clubbing attacks and brawls this squad carried out against communists, social democrats, and unionists in cities like Berlin? In his secluded village in the Rhön Mountains, these incidents were unlikely to be discussed. Everything was peaceful in Thalau. However, newspapers told another story.

Following the dissolution of the Catholic Teachers' Association, Hosenfeld joined the National Socialist Teachers' Association (NSLB). Whether he could have avoided membership is unclear. The expectations on the part of Germany's new ruler certainly would have been high. Hosenfeld saw teaching as his true calling and wanted to continue in that line of work. There was also, of course, an understandable financial consideration because he was responsible for a large family.

Wilm Hosenfeld, in a full SA uniform, with Helmut (*left*) and Detlev (*right*) in 1934. The boys are wearing Hitler Youth uniforms.

However, this did not stop Hosenfeld from criticizing the plans of the Nazi regime to bring youth education under its wing. He disagreed with the principle that "youth should be led by the youth," because he saw it as a diminishment of the influence of school and the parental home.

***

There was a somewhat different catalyst that led to Wilm Hosenfeld joining the Nazi Party in 1935. During a teachers' meeting, many of his colleagues loyal to the regime believed he had crossed a line into insubordination. He announced the book *The Myth of the Twentieth Century* by Alfred Rosenberg had been scientifically refuted. Rosenberg was a kind of chief ideologist for the Nazis because he wanted to replace Christian teachings with a religion based on a racial "blood and soil" myth. As punishment for his statements, Hosenfeld was stripped of his adult education center, which also meant a reduction in income. A teacher had to travel to Thalau to take over the classes. Hosenfeld saw this as a bitter and unfair reprimand. Perhaps this incident explains his membership in the Nazi Party. He may have wanted to outwardly dispel any doubts about his loyalty to the Nazi movement.

Following his deposition, Hosenfeld was more disappointed and disenchanted than ever. Upon joining the Nazi Party at the Kurhessen province regional administrative offices, he appealed the decision to relieve him of his duties at the adult education center. The district leader for the Fulda region responded on November 16, 1936, that Hosenfeld could not yet be employed for the "teaching of ideological lessons on a National Socialist basis." Yet, this was not a dismissal. "Instead, I want to give each person enough time to accept National Socialism and lay all inhibitions aside," the district leader also noted. "I respect your honesty and openness when you admit—and it is also confirmed by others—that you are still struggling to take this step."

Sounding more like a threat, the district leader explicitly refrained from launching disciplinary proceedings. In such a case, Hosenfeld's membership in the Nazi Party would have been terminated after a year and probably ended his career. There was a lot at stake for him, and he knew from then on he would be under observation.

Wilm Hosenfeld took part in the Nazis' ostentatious rituals with their absolute claim to power. In September 1936, he traveled as an SA assault leader to the national party convention in Nuremberg to participate in the Rally of Honor. Hosenfeld took his place among the approximately 500,000 others in the marching columns on parade. He was accompanied by his younger brother Rudolf. There is very little mention in Hosenfeld's writings about the convention. He merely referred to the display of weapons: *The modern weapons are shown in action. Tanks and anti-tank weapons. Air force. The spectacle upsets me. Woe unto us if it becomes necessary to wage war with such weapons.*

Nazi soldiers during the Nuremberg rally in 1938.

Hosenfeld rarely found words of praise for Hitler. This may have been because Annemarie resolutely rejected the political ascendant from the start. She found Hitler's hate speeches, his salivating shouts, his distorted facial expressions, and his false gestures simply abhorrent. Wilm Hosenfeld, on the other hand, had a weakness for the ceremonial. For example, on November 9, 1937, he was moved while listening—together with his students—to a radio broadcast of a ceremony commemorating the 14th anniversary of the so-called Beer

Hall Putsch (Munich Putsch), Hitler's failed coup attempt in 1923 to overthrow the Weimar Republic.

In depicting the ceremony in his journal, Hosenfeld uncritically adopted bombastic Nazi vocabulary. He wrote of the *Blutfahne* ("Blood Flag")—the swastika flag—that had supposedly been stained with blood during the putsch, and about the putsch participants decorated with the Blood Order medal. While "Horst-Wessel-Lied" ("The Horst Wessel Song"), the Nazi Party anthem, played, the names of the fallen National Socialists were read aloud. *His name* [Horst Wessel] *is the last one*, Hosenfeld wrote in his journal. *No, these heroes did not die; they live. Their names will be called out across all of Germany. They will march along. And my heart marches with them. I belong here. I feel it.* According to Hosenfeld's accounts, the schoolchildren listening with him were similarly impressed by this almost mythical worship of the dead and of the "heroes."

Only after World War II was well underway did Hosenfeld realize the clear political calculation behind this hero worship with its drum rolls and fanfares. It was all meant to prepare the public, and particularly the youth, for great sacrifice. Hosenfeld was also led astray by another central tenet of Nazi ideology: the delusion of superiority of the German race and inferiority of other races and religions, especially the Jews. Only later did he understand what horrific destructive intent stood behind this ideology. At a graduation ceremony in early April 1938, he called youths to him and said, "You, young men and women, don't disregard the laws of blood when you are choosing your future spouse. Because the laws of blood are the most decisive for health and mental disposition, the character of your descendants. The National Socialist state opens our eyes to the question of genetic makeup."

Was this a concession to the current climate or mere lip service? The latter is unlikely. In a sketch for a biology lesson, Hosenfeld outlined the objectives of the Nazis' official racist policies: *to fight against the decline in the birth rate, inadequate hereditary quality, and the mixing of races.*

Hosenfeld was also preoccupied with folklore, which was in vogue during the Nazi period. He had been interested in this field of study for a long time and created school lessons from it: tales and narratives with which he attempted to awaken children's interests. Whenever Annemarie believed her husband aligned himself too much with the Nazi regime, she expressed sharp criticism. Wilm Hosenfeld wrote about this in his journal:

> . . . *She can see my errors clearly, lately even Helmut is judging me. That is a good deterrent. I already have some experience. If she could just convince herself to work actively with me and help me, instead of always just judging, then I could achieve much more and I would be happier while doing it. Especially the folklore work in the village is a thankful task that earns the work of the teacher recognition.*

Nonetheless, he was a fairly critical follower of the Nazis. In fact, Hosenfeld really could rub them the wrong way. There were some things he did not like at all, such as not being able to take initiative and plan activities. It was now the party, with its subsidiary organizations, that was responsible for keeping its members in constant action: meetings of the Nazi Teachers' Association, SA leader discussions and tournaments, roll calls, and marches and endless speeches.

Eventually, Hosenfeld felt his need to be seen doing something was a dead end. *Whenever I'm part of a larger collective, I get weary and feel alone*, he wrote after an SA leader discussion in Schmalnau, near Fulda, on May 5, 1938. Three days later, he wrote: *SA sports day. Fulda. I took part in it. It has again put me off of the whole thing. I do not have any more joy doing it. I am ever more aware of the senselessness of it.*

The feeling of not belonging stayed with Hosenfeld. In the same journal entry about the Munich Putsch of 1923, his enthusiasm seamlessly transformed into a sober realization. He wrote: *I belong here. I feel it. I have always been here. It is my fate that I'm not wanted. That is a great injustice that is done to us Catholics. If we don't surrender our religious conviction, we are not complete National Socialists.*

***

Hosenfeld was concerned his influence on the education of children and youth was declining. *We teachers play a pitiful role in leading the youth*, he noted. *I believe that seldom before we have been pushed aside as we are now.* The tightly led Hitler Youth was soon going to ideologically and organizationally capture all German youths. Helmut Hosenfeld was a Hitler Youth leader. Other youth organizations were banned.

Even more alarming to Hosenfeld was the constant pressure on the Catholic church. A concordat on July 20, 1933, between the German Reich and the Vatican, intended to find an arrangement that allowed Catholic denominational schools and monasteries to continue operating on German soil. But Hitler had no interest in sharing his educational influence with one of the country's two largest churches.

Hosenfeld intently followed the German bishops' letters of protest about the Nazi regime's church policy. In the encyclical *Mit brennender Sorge* (*With Burning Concern*), issued in March 1937, Pope Pius XI condemned the persecution of Catholics in Germany, the leadership cult around Hitler, and the racist policies. The Nazi regime exacted its revenge by publicly disclosing in courts the sexual offenses committed in monasteries.

During meetings of the Nazi Teachers' Association, Hosenfeld found himself in an awkward position. He felt he should stand up and plainly express his support for Catholic denominational schools according to his beliefs. After one such meeting on May 5, 1937, he dejectedly observed: *The Catholic teachers are all leaving. Everyone is trying to duck. Not a single one stands up like a man for his faith. Also not me. The cowards would abandon me, and why should I fight for a lost cause.* Hosenfeld also clearly recognized the scare tactics the Nazis used at this time. *The party uses lies, distortion, and defamation, and, when that is not enough, terror*, he wrote.

On another occasion, Hosenfeld remained demonstratively seated when, after a Hitler speech was transmitted in a pub, the guests arose and shouted out, "*Sieg Heil!*" ("Hail Hitler!").

This map shows several of the territories the Third Reich and its
allies annexed in the late 1930s.

He painfully missed the open exchange of ideas, which he so
loved. Instead, Hosenfeld found himself in a climate of fear and
mistrust, as he discovered after a conference of the Nazi Teachers'
Association in Gersfeld on February 5, 1938. *I have the need to speak
occasionally with colleagues about school issues,* he wrote in his journal. *But
with whom? There is hardly one amongst them whom I can trust. A comradely
bond among ourselves is as good as nonexistent. No one trusts the other. Expressing
an honest opinion is dangerous.*

Despite his disillusionment, at the time Hosenfeld did not consider
turning his back on the Nazi regime or cutting his ties. His mood
often fluctuated between despondency and enthusiasm. Hosenfeld
fully supported the annexation of Austria into the German Reich,
carried out in March 1938. Around the same time, he delivered a
speech as part of the Memorial Day celebration in Thalau in which
he described the annexation as the fulfillment of the hundred-year-old
dream of a greater German Reich.

In autumn 1938, Hosenfeld's grave concerns were reignited by the artificially triggered crisis around the Sudetenland, the western border of Czechoslovakia where many ethnic Germans lived. He attentively listened to the speech Hitler gave on September 26 at the Berlin Sports Palace. Hitler emphasized his claim to the Sudetenland in an aggressive tone. Hosenfeld noted concerns in his journal:

> *Threat of war! This evening Hitler* [delivered a] *speech. We did not like it. He speaks without end, arrogantly, one can say it is not elegant or reflective. Expressions such as "democratic liar" are unbecoming of a great statesman that represents a large nation. He does not want to back down. We fear that there will be war.*

This note demonstrates that in Hosenfeld's assessment of the threat of war he was in agreement with his wife. The artificially escalated situation underscored for him that with one stroke of the pen Hitler could lead Germany into war. The people would not be able to stop him, Hosenfeld noted in his journal on September 27; it would not even be asked. *Much different than democracy with its parliament,* Hosenfeld wrote. Hosenfeld's concern *about his and his family's fate, and to an almost greater extent, the fate of the nation,* increased each day. He knew the consequences of war through his own experiences. *We race to the loudspeaker whenever the radio broadcasts news. Annemarie is so depressed that the smallest emotion leads her to cry,* Hosenfeld wrote.

It was only when England, France, and Italy gave in and released the Sudetenland in the Munich Agreement of September 29 that the Hosenfelds were able to breathe a sigh of relief. The threat of war had been averted, or so it seemed to Wilm Hosenfeld, who did not want to believe in the possibility of a major conflict. That Hitler was disappointed by the concessions of the three Western powers was not something the two of them could have known; the dictator would have liked to demonstrate his military force. Hitler made up for it six months later when Germany occupied the rest of Czechoslovakia.

Events came in quick succession in the autumn of 1938. On November 9, *Kristallnacht* ("Crystal Night," also referred to as the "Night of Broken Glass" because of the shards of glass on the sidewalks from Jewish shops that had been attacked and plundered), with its assaults and arson attacks on Jewish businesses, synagogues, homes, and other establishments, left Hosenfeld speechless. He had not thought that such violence and killing was possible. *Pogrom of the Jews throughout Germany. It is a terrible situation in the Reich, without law and order and outward displays of hypocrisy and lies*, Hosenfeld wrote in his journal. Out of disgust at the continuing hate-filled tirades in *Der Stürmer* (*Striker*) newspaper, he canceled his subscription to the propaganda-filled publication, which he had only started a few months earlier.

Unlike her husband, Annemarie foresaw what was coming, although she always suppressed her fears. She knew that on one hand her husband inwardly rejected war, but on the other, he was absolutely prepared to wear his uniform if the fatherland called. She would soon have to live with this quandary during the long war years.

Wilm Hosenfeld was deemed fit for limited military service in April 1937. He commented in his journal, *But I feel fully fit.* Hosenfeld had already taken part in air defense exercises. As an SA squad leader, he commanded larger formations that underwent regular drills. *That's*

A Jewish business the morning after *Kristallnacht* in 1938.

fun, he wrote in his journal on April 25, 1937. *I enjoy leading a large unit.* Over two years later, on June 4, 1939, Hitler visited the town of Kassel. Hosenfeld was tasked with leading the SA Flag 418 unit and securing the barricades. The operation was militarily organized, and only after it was completed did things lighten up. Hosenfeld wrote from Kassel to his oldest son Helmut, who was on labor-service duty: *When I am among comrades like that, then I am basically lonely. I'm often amazed how most people cease existing as an individual and turn into a social being when a mug of beer or something similar is involved.*

On August 26, 1939, Hosenfeld received his induction order in Thalau. Hitler had ordered the mobilization of German troops. He said goodbye to his wife the same day. Annemarie was despondent. Her husband was 44. *Why did he have to go to war again?* she asked herself. Several hours later, Hosenfeld collected his gear from the artillery barracks storehouse in Fulda: rifle, gas mask, bayonet, etc. From then on, he was a member of the Third Company of the Home Guard Battalion.

On the day of his departure, Hosenfeld wrote a sentence to his wife, one he would repeat many times in one form or another in the coming years. *You don't have to worry about me,* he wrote. *It's just a shame that we are not together.* Hosenfeld was still convinced Hitler was not going to allow the situation to escalate. *I don't believe there will be a war, despite all* [the] *ominous signs. I have the feeling that Hitler wants to just flex the muscles of the entire vast mobilization apparatus. Ultimately, he will seize every opportunity to negotiate.*

Hosenfeld was characterized by a naïveté, as he once self-critically admitted. In May 1918, shortly after his release from active military duty, he noted in his journal: *I always seek out the best and most beautiful in all people. I consider everyone to be good and noble, and* [I] *create an ideal image* [of them]. Hosenfeld's wonderful ability to approach people, to accept them, and to initially see only the good in them had a downside: he possessed a trusting nature that occasionally carried over into politics, only to later be regretted. *My overly open nature is a mistake, for which I later experienced much unpleasantness, trouble, disappointment, and pain,* he wrote in his journal.

As with most Germans, Hosenfeld did not recognize until the country was on the threshold of World War II that Hitler had systematically planned the war since his ascension to power and was determined to ignite it at the first opportunity. Sergeant Wilm Hosenfeld, a twice-wounded veteran of World War I, participated in World War II from the start through the bitter end. He was not positioned on the front, as he had always wanted, but was rather part of the "rear guard," as the secondary sector of the Wehrmacht was called.

Wilm Hosenfeld with Helmut in 1939. Note Wilm's "Hitler moustache."

Many people in Poland were in a similar position to the Germans. They just did not want to believe war was imminent, even though the tone from the German side was aggressive and danger appeared clear and present. The Poles did not imagine that a single war-mad statesman could simply push a button and set into motion an enormous military force to destroy Poland. Certainly, precautions were taken to protect against such an attack: windows were darkened, gas masks were at hand, and troops stood at alert.

But then again, the restaurants and bars were well attended. Orchestras played on, and people danced and celebrated, almost more exuberantly than usual. During the day everything proceeded normally. People in Warsaw took the streetcars to work, the same as they did any other work day. Musicians rehearsed pieces for their next live performance on Polish Radio. Up to the end of August 1939, Władysław Szpilman, the 27-year-old aspiring pianist, spent many hours working hard in the studio. On the last evening of August, Szpilman returned, tired and exhausted, to his parents' house on Śliska Street in Warsaw and soon went to sleep. At daybreak, explosions could be heard in the distance. He thought of the frequent field exercises, turned on his side, and read a few pages of a book. Suddenly, his mother stood at the door, and in an almost stammering voice, said, "Get up! War . . . it has started."

2

Polish Prisoners of War

With the start of World War II, Poland was subjected to a pincer from which there was no escape. From the west, divisions of the German Wehrmacht, supported by the navy and air force, stormed into the country on September 1, 1939. The Red Army of the Soviet Union marched in from the other side and occupied the eastern part of Poland. The so-called Hitler-Stalin Pact, signed on August 23, 1939, included a secret supplementary protocol wherein both powers had staked out their areas of interest in east-central Europe and the Baltic region. Joseph Stalin became the ally and accomplice of Adolf Hitler, and he gave Hitler carte blanche to carry out his conquests. The two politicians had set up a rigged game and their first victim was Poland.

Wilm Hosenfeld's premature exit from military service in 1918 denied him the chance to achieve something he had always secretly wished for: to be an officer. Even so, Hosenfeld did not lightheartedly put on a Wehrmacht uniform.

He had been in charge of the school in Thalau for 12 years. It was also in Thalau where Hosenfeld left behind his wife and five children. His oldest son, Helmut, was by then conducting his Reich Labor Service duties in Kirtorf, Germany, in central Hesse. This "Honorable Service to the German Nation" was compulsory for all 18- to 25-year-olds at the time.

The parting at the Fulda train station was difficult for everyone. Hosenfeld had carefully arranged things for the school, as well as the family. As a matter of course, Annemarie had deferred to his organizing hands. Although she discussed pending questions with

The Hosenfeld family in Thalau in 1938.

him, the final decisions were always his. In a letter to her husband on September 10, Annemarie described the parting scene in Fulda:

> *When the train pulled away, I walked through the darkness of the town with my three sobbing children. In the darkened train we drove home, unprotected, and left alone from now on. Jorinde slept in my lap. My soul was with you, and I pray that I receive strength. Hand-in-hand I went home with the children, and as their pain, their crying, became less, I found comfort for us.*

Annemarie attempted to distract herself and come to terms with her new life, but she found it difficult. Who could fill the void that her departed husband left behind? *Every room in our house, every path in the garden, every tree and flower speak of you, of your kindness to us*, she wrote. *I have never seen a more proud, noble, and sweet man, and so I am happy even in sadness.*

She had barely finished the letter when she heard reports on the radio about air raids in Warsaw. She knew her husband was heading east, but did not know exactly where he was going. The optimism she had just regained was now gone again. To make matters worse, Annemarie received bad news from her hometown of Worpswede. Her mother had suffered a second stroke and was near death in a Bremen hospice. After hesitating several days, Annemarie finally heeded her father's urgent request and traveled to northern Germany.

Seeing her mother shocked Annemarie: her face was distorted, her body in the throes of death. She and her sister, Gertrud, alternated spending time at their mother's bedside. Shortly before her death, their mother regained consciousness and recognized them. She was thus able to peacefully die.

Annemarie saw definite signs of war in Bremen. Communication trenches were spread throughout parks and public places. Before returning to Thalau, she visited St. Johannis Church, where she had been married 19 years earlier. She wrote to her husband on September 23: *You can imagine how that moved me. But it gave me comfort. I have to live and be healthy. Nobody knows what the coming days will bring. I want to return home. My love for you and the children carries me. Wilm, pray for peace, pray for us.*

***

There could be little talk of peace, however. The great military strength of the German forces overran its neighboring country. Despite brave resistance, Poland was forced to capitulate within weeks. One of the biggest problems, even during combat operations, was how to accommodate the prisoners of war (POWs). Sergeant Wilm Hosenfeld was one of those tasked with finding a solution. The advance group to which he belonged drove in a military vehicle the final 60 miles to their destination of Pabianice, south of the industrial city of Łódź.

On the way, German soldiers encountered lines of refugees. Hosenfeld already sensed the whole wretchedness of the war, which had struck the Poles first. He described the scenery in his journal:

> *. . . on overloaded carriages they sit, being pulled along by a gaunt horse, men, women, always accompanied by a flock of children, these*

are the most enviable. Many walk on foot, often barefoot; they have been on the road for days, have nothing to eat. Then you see mothers holding children in their arms, children running after them, carrying heavy bundles. Some pull handcarts filled high, baby carriages and such always next to the road in the dust that the cars swirl up.

Polish soldiers being marched to a POW camp in Pabianice in September 1939.

In Pabianice, Hosenfeld was responsible for setting up a Polish POW camp on the grounds of a closed-down factory. The 60,000-person city showed signs of fighting. Hosenfeld wrote: . . . [There are] *shot-up buildings and burnt-out ruins whose hollow windows were looking to the sky like dead and empty eyes.* His first order of business was to secure quarters for himself and his comrades. Hosenfeld and a troop of men went from house to house and requisitioned accommodation. The inhabitants had to give up their space, move into different rooms, or find somewhere else to live. Hosenfeld found accommodation with a German merchant who had sent his family to Zittau, Germany, when the war broke out. Hosenfeld had everything, as he wrote to his wife: *bedroom, bath, kitchen, a fully set table. Only you, my dear darling, sweet Annemarie, and the dear kids, are missing.*

All of Hosenfeld's organizational talents were required to arrange the sheltering of the POWs who streamed into Pabianice by the thousands. Many had been marching for days and were famished and completely exhausted. Upon arrival, a selection process took place. Polish officers were separated from their troops, ethnic Germans were separated from the Poles, and Jews were segregated from everyone. Jews were immediately required to perform heavy physical work, like digging the trenches being installed to defend Pabianice. The ethnic Germans received release papers, performed assistance services, and could otherwise move freely about. Hosenfeld described Pabianice in his journal:

> *Ever more masses were delivered to the camp at night. The figures appeared out of the dark, emaciated and slowly trudging, in their soiled green-brown shirts; most in long coats of the same color, that would hang down to the boots, ripped, dirty, the faces tired and gray, dulled to their fate. And so they swell up out of the dark and step into my field of vision for a moment, indistinct, shadowy, like a vision, and then disappear again in the darkness of the camp.*

At first, there was great chaos on the large factory grounds, with its brick buildings and warehouses. More than 10,000 POWs arrived in several waves through the end of September 1939. Hosenfeld took charge to secure the camp barbed wire and machine-gun posts. He also procured large cooking pots and food. Within a short period of time, he and his comrades built a large-scale kitchen with 30 kettles and obtained horse meat, beef and pork, potatoes, and sauerkraut. The prisoners received three meals a day. In his journal, Hosenfeld wrote: . . . *the weather has gotten cold and rainy, and these poor Polish prisoners, who spend days circled in by an iron ring of German troops lying in the dirt and cold and tired and starved, have no other wish than to hit the sack somewhere.*

To his son Helmut, Wilm Hosenfeld wrote: *You wouldn't believe how starved these masses were. Gradually, they are hungry no more. Prisoners are housed in the machine rooms and other parts of the buildings. It's a shame to see these poor people, but we are powerless to* [relieve] *their suffering. Hopefully, an epidemic does not break out.* He also showed compassion to the plight of the Jews, who were harassed and abused. *Such treatment disgusts me,* Hosenfeld wrote.

The prisoners quickly came to understand that Hosenfeld was anything but cold-hearted. *I think people can tell that I am suffering along with them,* he wrote in a letter to Annemarie. *Wherever I am, they surround me and tell me their needs. I don't bark at them and try to help wherever I can.* Two young women searching for their husbands convinced Hosenfeld to let them into the camp. He defied all regulations and allowed them into the grounds through a side entrance. *But their search was without success,* Hosenfeld wrote. *They thanked me . . . and wanted to embrace me, as I wanted to embrace them, but my eyes were filled with tears, and I left them standing there. With others, I had the luck to find their loved ones.*

One day, a woman approached him outside of the camp and explained she could no longer cope with the workload of her house and farm on her own. She implored him to release her husband from the POW camp. Hosenfeld asked for his name: it was Stanisław Cieciora. He told the woman to return in three days and she would be able to take her husband home. Hosenfeld kept his word. The Polish couple thanked him with a friendship that lasted throughout the war.

Hosenfeld's hands-on, uncomplicated manner evidently impressed his superiors. After only a few weeks, he was temporarily put in command of the camp. Hosenfeld was pleased the prisoners willingly kept the grounds tidy and harvested potatoes and grain in the fields, albeit under guard. *Life has triumphed over war,* he wrote in his journal. *Bless the order! Bless the work!*

With many people in his immediate vicinity, Hosenfeld, in a sense, felt back in his element. Even though he belonged to the German occupation force, he was still able to help. It was easy for Hosenfeld to connect with Polish children and adults alike. They were not his enemies. In a letter to his youngest daughter, Uta, he said: *Sometimes*

I take the Polish children in my arms and think of my small girls. He also sent Uta a postcard to say he knew she was praying for him. He gave a young boy—who worked the water pump at a public place where Hosenfeld was able to wash the dust off of his face—a coin, and the boy was very happy.

Some Poles spoke German. Otherwise, there were ethnic Germans who were used as interpreters. Somehow, communication

A postcard Wilm Hosenfeld sent Uta in 1939. It reads, "This little Polish boy prays also for the father like you, when you are going into your bed . . . "

was always possible. During services at the parish church in Pabianice, Hosenfeld mingled with the worshipers. In his journal, he wrote:

> *How extraordinary to kneel at the altar rails amidst Polish women and mothers, and to bow before the sacrament together with them. We smite our chest together, and in different languages, speak the [prayer,] "Jesus, for You I live," and there is no hate between us. Rather, I sense how they include the German soldier in their hearts and prayers and mean me well.*

He permitted the prisoners to hold prayer services and masses in the camp. Hosenfeld wrote that *this unified religious attitude* of the Polish Catholics impressed him. He lamented *the faithless, fragmented worldview of the Germans.*

Hosenfeld was, of course, aware of the fraternization ban imposed on every Wehrmacht soldier. But he ignored it. His respect for the Poles increased with every encounter. *Poland will probably disappear from the map, but the Polish people will not disappear*, Hosenfeld wrote. He surmised Poland would reach a compromise with Germany and perhaps the two countries would even have a shared future.

***

There was a continued, significant divergence between Hosenfeld's personal behavior and his political stance against the Nazi regime. At the beginning of the invasion of Poland, he drew historically unsupportable parallels to the start of World War I. He believed Kaiser Wilhelm II had attempted, up until the last hour, to keep peace. But since 1902, England had engaged in a *ruthless course of encirclement.* In the same way, he ascribed a desire for peace to Hitler, because he believed Hitler's demands to England (a protective power of Poland) were acceptable and modest.

Neither the reference to 1914 nor the claim of Hitler's peaceful intentions were correct. Imperial Germany had convinced itself of encirclement to justify its military buildup and war-mongering; the decision to invade Poland had been made months earlier. Hitler was only concerned with how he would express himself in confidential discussions with the generals.

Hosenfeld bought into the German propaganda and in a letter raised the appeal to his son Helmut: *All ideological and domestic political contrasts must step back. Everyone has to be a German who stands* [up] *for his nation.* His reverence for Hitler grew at the end of September 1939 when victory over Poland was certain. In the same letter, Hosenfeld continued his praise:

> *Never has a German statesman played a larger role than the Führer today. Just think, if the Führer applies the strength of the German people in their entirety, so that what was today organized for war can be put to use after the war for peace, and works of peace can be built with the same determination with which today's war is being waged. What a great and exhilarating future is then before us.*

Of course, with historical hindsight, we know this was purely wishful thinking. The massive energy of the German nation that Hitler mobilized had the objective to annihilate and destroy. But at the time, millions of Germans thought as Hosenfeld did. They trusted the criminal gang that had maneuvered itself to the top of the state. Many people allowed themselves to be willingly seduced and enticed into committing crimes as well. This was the dividing line for Hosenfeld. Never once during the years of war did he allow himself to be persuaded to take part in attacks on the Poles. His ethical and moral compass remained intact.

Hosenfeld endured intellectual excursions into the world of politics based on propaganda and without actual knowledge of the facts and background. This, however, did not impact his personal actions. Hosenfeld allowed no one to dictate what he should or should not do. He confided his observations in his journal or in his letters.

Hosenfeld's days were otherwise spent with the demands in Pabianice and problems Annemarie reported from Thalau. The family had money worries. She even had to borrow money for the trip to Worpswede when her mother was dying. Clothes for the children, school, food—everything cost money, and their garden and livestock provided little relief.

Detlev, the second-oldest son, took care of things at home as his father had previously done. "My carefree and almost idyllic childhood in the large schoolhouse with the attic rooms that father had converted just for us, the garden, and the nearby meadow abruptly ended as soon as the war started," Detlev recalled. "Since practicality was not a strength of our mother, I had many responsibilities at home. I took care of the rabbits and the bees." All this in addition to school. Beginning in 1940, Detlev attended the secondary school in Fulda. He rode his bike to the train station in Schmalnau, and from there, continued on the train to Fulda. There was very little time for activities.

Reflecting on his mother, Detlev said he most admired Annemarie's interests in art and literature, which she had brought from her childhood home in Worpswede. He also emphasized her musical talent. "She could sing wonderfully," Detlev said. But the daily routine during the war demanded a lot of Annemarie. For example, Detlev said that much effort was required just to bake bread. "She used a handcart to bring the dough to the bakehouse, which was located on the other side of the village," he said. "Then she baked. It took a while before she would return." Detlev and his sister Jorinde believe their mother was overwhelmed with her situation during the first months of the war. First, there was separation from the man she loved more than anything and whom she constantly missed. The management of the household, the wellbeing of the children, and decisions about this and that—everything was her responsibility. *If I only knew which of the chickens should be butchered*, Annemarie wrote in one letter.

It took a while before Annemarie became friendly with some of the farmers in Thalau. In her eyes, most of them were stubborn and selfish, and she wanted nothing to do with them. In a letter to her husband, she claimed the people in the village had long since forgotten about him; he should be under no illusions about the people of Thalau or even his former students. In Annemarie's opinion, the people in northern Germany, near her childhood home, were much more loyal and sincere.

Her attitude changed, though, as more young men from Thalau were enlisted into the military. Some did not return because they had gone missing or were killed in action. Concern for the soldiers—one of whom was also her oldest son, Helmut—brought the villagers together. Eventually, Annemarie reconciled with them.

3

Terror at Every Turn

In the weeks after the outbreak of war, the written correspondence between Thalau and Pabianice was slow. Both Wilm and Annemarie Hosenfeld wrote letters, but the mail was left unattended somewhere for days on end. The mail service returned to normal again in October 1939. The letters between Wilm and Annemarie (whom he affectionately called "Annemie") formed an unbreakable connection. They could both voice their deepest feelings for one another. Quite often, these were love letters, in which they professed their missing physical closeness, or exchanged memories of happier days gone by. Telephone calls were rare, except on special occasions or prior to a home leave to arrange when and where to meet.

Since they sometimes wrote to each other every two or three days, their letters would often crisscross. Hosenfeld numbered his letters. The sum of his letters was great. Hosenfeld's comrades were astonished that he kept to himself in his free time instead of spending it with them. Annemarie's accounts kept him up-to-date about the situation at home and the children's development. It was not uncommon for her lines to carry a sad, distraught tone—she could not resign herself to the separation. Thus, it was up to Wilm to console her and help her through the difficult phases. Every now and then he would contradict her. In a letter dated October 6, he wrote:

> *You have indeed often complained that you have an especially hard time. That is not true. You are merely suffering more; even with the most minor events that would not trouble someone else nearly as much, you*

*are shaken to your core. God does not give you more than you should
carry in His judgment. That is why I know that despite everything,
I will see my dear, sweet, happy Annemarie again. Carrying you in
my heart, your Wilm*

The letters—like Wilm Hosenfeld's journal entries, preserved in
their entirety—were important to the couple, but also a source of
some misunderstandings and a trigger of huge worries. An apparently innocuous remark by Hosenfeld, according to which he liked
to hug a Polish girl, was taken by his wife in such a way that she
admonished him to fidelity and warned against erotic adventures.
At one point, filled with desperation, Annemarie wrote: *Where are
you, my husband, in the foreign country? Maybe on guard duty, perhaps in a
strange bed. My tears flow onto the white paper—one day peace will come! One
day my beloved will return home! Someday, so say the children. One day . . . all
fairy tales begin.*

Over time, however, Annemarie grew more confident. A different
tone sometimes emerged in her letters. In one dated November 6, she
informed her husband about the career prospects of their oldest daughter, Anemone. She was to take up nursing, enroll in a typing course, and
learn stenography. *Please, write to me of your opinion immediately, and should
you agree with me. Then, write a sensible letter to Anemone. I will undertake nothing
without your consent.* Annemarie then referenced his most recent letter:
number 38. She would read it over and over again. Annemarie wrote:

*With a divine recklessness, I forget all my worries with the children,
the household, and also the larger concerns about the fatherland, about
all of our dear soldiers (there is something brewing in the West, people
are saying), and lie down in bed and belong to my dearest. Is that
the prototype of a letter to a soldier? A German woman should, a
German woman must—oh, that Fulda newspaper, the hyenas from
the women's league! . . . Write to me once about the beautiful women
you are meeting. In the theater? In social circles? In the cinema? On
the street? Are you meeting with them? Do they know that you have us?*

Annemarie seldom commented on the war in her letters, even though she had a firm opinion of it. She did not expect a quick end to the war. Hope arose that Hitler would be content with his rapid victory over Poland, having previously added Austria and Czechoslovakia to the territory under his control. She attentively followed the events, spoke with other solders' wives, and listened to the BBC or the Swiss radio station in Beromünster. (The Nazi government forbade both of these stations.)

Detlev connected the radio in the living room to a speaker in the kitchen so Annemarie could listen to the Nazi leaders' speeches, programs from abroad, or concerts. She knew, for example, that Belgium and the Netherlands made a peace proposal to Germany and Hitler had rejected it. (Holland declared itself neutral, as it had in World War I.) *The war is senseless,* she wrote in one of her letters. *In the West, the giant armies lie opposite for months. This tension is nerve-wracking.*

When Wilm informed Annemarie on October 8 that his company commander had recommended him for promotion to officer, her reaction was cautious: *If it is possible, try not to be promoted to officer. Otherwise, there is the chance that you will be deployed to the West. The cruel continuation of this horrible war seems to me a certainty. . . .* Her husband responded that he would receive a higher salary as an officer. A transfer was not inevitably connected to the promotion. He could not understand the madness, he wrote, if the war were to become a reality in the West as well. Annemarie, who had shortly before received the Mother's Cross (*Mutterkreuz*) in bronze, wholeheartedly agreed with her husband. In her letter of October 18, she wrote:

> *For what does Herr* [Mr.] *Hitler need our children? As cannon fodder! And if you wish to have another boy or girl, my husband, I will carry it with a hundred delights, but it shall never be born in this "wonderful" German fatherland. I am not bitter, because I have not lost anyone, but I am saddened by the fate of the others of whom one now often hears.*

Hosenfeld responded on November 10. He figured she had written the letter after hearing one of Hitler's speeches. The address had shaken him as well, he replied. *I only listened for a short time, but gather from it that the Führer wants the war,* Hosenfeld wrote. *The hope of peace vanishes ever more, the calamity continues on its way.*

On November 17, Annemarie received a visitor: a staff sergeant who was a comrade of her husband. She was eager to hear something new about Poland from him, but was bitterly disappointed. The soldier raved about Hitler and National Socialism and even gave her *ideological instructions*, which she indignantly rejected. She took the unpleasant meeting as an opportunity to present her position on the Nazi regime to her husband. The fact the staff sergeant had virtually idolized Hitler was unacceptable to her. She asked her husband if he was of the same opinion: *Then, despite all of our love, we will not understand one another. Do you have confidence in this leadership?* She again accused him of wanting to be an officer at all costs. Annemarie said she liked him a hundred times more as a sergeant than a lieutenant. He should leave such ambition to younger soldiers. *Your mission in life is a different one,* Annemarie wrote.

Annemarie severely criticized her husband's position on the Wehrmacht and Nazi politics. In one letter, she wrote:

> *Why do your comrades always assert that you have a burning desire to be a soldier? Is that really enough for you, to spend a short vacation here and then to happily be a soldier again in Poland? Wilm, I cannot believe that. I do not want to believe it! Then, I think about how fanatical you are about the SA. You had to play soldier. You only had to read war books. You secretly reported for drills as a reserve officer.*

It would be difficult to handle three or more years of separation. Under such circumstances, Annemarie explained, she was not the right woman for him. In one letter, she added: *I consider this war as senseless. Every government that does not understand how to secure peace for its people is no good, because the people want peace.*

Hosenfeld addressed his wife's accusation by saying she worried too much. As a soldier, he was doing no more than was required of him. What his innermost thoughts were, no one knew. *I will tell you only this, that I am sometimes ashamed to be a German soldier*, he wrote. He could not share all his thoughts in the letter. Annemarie knew him, though—Wilm was in agreement with her on all questions. In fact, his position changed under the pressure of events in his immediate vicinity.

In Pabianice, Hosenfeld continued to act as a benefactor and help others. When a package arrived from Thalau, he shared its contents—among other things, apples and nuts—with three Polish prisoners who worked as doctors and assistant physicians in the hospital sickbay. He listened as they told him how they had suffered in the war and which of their relatives were missing or dead.

Hosenfeld was able to arrange with the local commander for the release of other Polish POWs. A woman whose husband and two sons were released squeezed a 20-złoty bill into his hand as a thank you. Hosenfeld immediately gave it back to her and asked that she read a mass for him instead. Another woman reached for her perfume bottle and sprayed him with it. Hosenfeld was unable to defend himself. Days later, he still smelled the perfume.

***

At the end of October 1939 the POW camp was disbanded. Everything happened quickly. The prisoners were marched in columns to the station, where trains waited to transport them to Germany. The Wehrmacht required additional soldiers for the imminent campaign in the West, which would come to be known as the Battle of France. Consequently, there was a shortage of industrial and agricultural workers. Polish prisoners and forced laborers filled the gaps; officers remained imprisoned.

For Sergeant Hosenfeld and his comrades, it was a time of uncertainty. The command changed. Initially, they had orders to act against poachers and timber thieves in a forest about 20 miles from Pabianice.

Children saluting Nazi soldiers in Nuremberg in 1938. The sign reads, "City circle / Jews are our misfortune."

On the way there, Hosenfeld marveled at the helpfulness of the Poles. When his vehicle got stuck up to its axles in a swamp, a farmer pulled it out of the muck with his horse and cart.

During a stopover in a village, children who had just come from school flocked to the German soldiers. Hosenfeld described the scene in his journal: *It seemed strange to me, when all of a sudden I was in the midst of the laughing, happy group of children, who stood around us curious and not shy at all, chattering with us as if we understood everything.* Such situations led him to get a dictionary and learn Polish.

While his comrades found accommodation in a forester's lodge, Hosenfeld returned to Pabianice. Since the POW camp had been disbanded, he was no longer under constant time pressure. He devoted even more time to his letters and journal entries. Hosenfeld took the streetcar to Łódź for shopping and made new contacts among the people. He met a Polish woman who sought his help because the Gestapo had just arrested her husband.

During Hosenfeld's efforts to help the woman, he discovered this was in no way an isolated case. Instead, previously prepared "wanted" lists resulted in a wave of arrests throughout the country. Ethnic Germans denounced Poles to the German secret police in order to avenge supposed injustices. Moreover—and especially outrageous— the German security service (*Sicherheitsdienst* or SD) and task forces were systematically going after Polish upper-class intellectuals. On November 10, Hosenfeld wrote to his wife: *A powerless anger, a paralyzing horror, is moving from house to house wherever a Pole lives who stands above the average. This is not about revenge; it has the appearance that they* [the Nazis] *want to exterminate the intelligence. . . .*

Hosenfeld experienced the first wave of terror in Germany's destructive campaign of Poland. He was stunned, even though he did not know the full extent of the thousands killed. *How much I enjoyed being a soldier, but today I want to rip the gray uniform to shreds*, Hosenfeld wrote. *We are to hold the shield behind which these crimes against humanity are committed?* With "shield" he meant the Wehrmacht, which he considered innocent—an error, as he would later discover.

***

The war against Poland was over, but the signs of violence, destruction, and extermination increased ever more. On November 16, 1939, Hosenfeld noted in Pabianice:

> *Since I have seen the atrocities of the SS* [*Schutzstaffel*; a paramilitary wing of the Nazi Party], *I am certain that we must not be allowed to win this war and that we cannot win it because we lack the moral strength to do so. When the spirit of brutal violence triumphs, it will destroy all opposing forces within the Reich. All abominations that played out in the basements of the GPU* [Soviet secret police] *are now upon us.*

Hosenfeld encountered terror at every turn and refused to avert his eyes from it. In November, he learned that in Łódź, Jews, carrying their luggage and distinguishable by an armband even children were forced to wear, were herded to a train station. They were crammed into cattle cars and taken away, allegedly for resettlement in Russia.

Hosenfeld was outraged at the rough treatment carried out by the German railway staff. Jews were less respected than livestock, he wrote. By chance, Hosenfeld overheard an officer ask a Gestapo agent, in response to the wave of arrests, if he thought such methods were conducive to winning the support of these people for reconstruction. The Gestapo agent replied that if he actually thought even one would return, they would all be shot trying to escape.

A few days later, Hosenfeld and his advance guard reached the small town of Kałuszyn, located 30 miles east of Warsaw, where they were to procure accommodation for his company. However, there were hardly any intact houses left. During their offensive a few weeks prior, the Wehrmacht had virtually turned the entire city into rubble and ash and deported the Jewish residents. Hosenfeld and his soldiers stayed in a parsonage, where refugees fleeing Soviet-occupied eastern Poland had previously found shelter. He informed Annemarie that he asked the vicar to hear his confession, even though the vicar barely understood German. Hosenfeld used his knowledge of Latin to help bridge the language gap.

The next stop was the city of Węgrów, 150 miles from Pabianice. There, the Wehrmacht appropriated Polish army barracks that were unscathed from the offensive. The city itself was a landscape of rubble and ruin. A German military band played marches and melodies from operas and operettas in the middle of burnt-out and destroyed buildings. Polish children and old men listened as the band played. Wilm Hosenfeld was aware of the absurdity of the situation. What the residents urgently needed more than an outdoor concert was food and coal for the coming winter.

Sergeant Hosenfeld was on hand at the Węgrów station to see a train of refugees arrive from the Polish territories. These areas had been annexed and were subject to "Germanization." The local inhabitants were being expelled to make space for German settlers in the newly created Nazi provinces (*Reichsgaue*) of Danzig-West Prussia and Wartheland. Hosenfeld observed the scene in his journal:

> *The poor people tumbled out of the wagons, which were filled to the bursting point, carrying their pitiful possessions, staggering old men and women, men, and many, many children. A small girl sat in a baby carriage, nearly crushed by the bundles and blankets and things, but it was such a sweet, delightful child with bright, happy eyes of a cherub that I did not want to look away.*

In the moment, he felt helpless and pulled out candies from his pocket and gave them to the child.

Hosenfeld usually described such impressions in letters to his wife. In his journal, he also wrote of the helpless anger he felt when he saw the refugees. A woman desperately searched for warm water for her small child. An old man asked him where they should go. A farmer reported he had just come from the forest with his horse and carriage. The Germans had given him 10 minutes to collect his wife, children, grandparents, and only the most necessary baggage. The family was completely destitute; they had nothing to eat and did not know where to go. Hosenfeld wrote:

> *. . . And I cannot help them. The tragedy cuts into my heart. This is the reality of the resettlement, about which such lofty words are spoken. The people are shoving into the train station building, seeking shelter from the cold. A large, gaunt man with a black fur hat on his fine head looks at me with earnest eyes. He must see me as one of the monsters, or does he think that I have a good heart? I would have liked to have spoken with him, but I balk at addressing him. He is one of the intellectuals whom they want to exterminate.*

Hosenfeld further asked himself in his journal:

Why are these people torn from their homes when no one knows where to house them? They stand in the cold for one day, sit on the bundles, their pathetic possessions. They are given nothing to eat. This is systematic; these people are to become sick, miserable, helpless, they are meant to perish. What the war has spared will be killed in this heinous way. Where does this hellish plan come from, who can treat people this way?

Initially, he blamed only the Nazi regime for the tragedy. But after reflecting on it, he wrote: *And yet we are all guilty, no, we were all lied to and tricked. A deep sadness covers my soul.*

Hosenfeld wrote several letters and longer narratives between December 13 and 16. He could barely endure watching the plight of the refugees without being able to help them. In his bags, Hosenfeld had bread and cheese, but of course it was not enough for that many people.

He always looked to strike up a conversation and gather additional details. Three women had given birth during the train ride. One woman had attempted to slash her wrists. In one of the cars there was a dead body. While Hosenfeld spoke with people, the next train packed with refugees pulled into the Węgrów station. *How many destinies, how much suffering does each train of these outcasts bring with it?* Hosenfeld wrote. *I meet many soldiers, railway men, officers. They are full of compassion and outrage. One of them told me, "It is shameful to be a German."*

***

Annemarie was shocked by what her husband reported concerning the expulsion of the Polish people and harassment of the Jews. She voiced her fear that the same would happen in Germany. The public was being misled. *I believe that it is not God's will that we are increasingly racing toward this disaster; we must rebel*, Annemarie wrote. As she often did when in despair, Annemarie went to church to arrange her thoughts and find solace. When the organist played Handel's "Largo" during one service, she lost her composure and bitterly wept.

Annemarie's letters leave no doubt she was distraught over the progress of the war. She wrote: *What fools were they who saw the war as a solution to a dispute among nations.* She did not believe a word of the propaganda. At the end of November she summed up her hopes and fears in a letter to her husband:

> *I can well imagine that someday you will come to us on vacation. But that you will be with us as before, that you will no longer be a soldier, that I do not believe anymore. You should not know about my inner conflicts if you were to come home today. I can no longer cry, I can no longer pray, I can no longer hope. . . .*

An eagerly awaited message in early December 1939 pulled Annemarie Hosenfeld out of her somber mood. Wilm announced he would be spending the Christmas holidays in Thalau. The reunion with his wife and children would be a joyous, but short, time. It was not the end of all worries, but at least it afforded the opportunity for personal conversation, instead of writing letters.

The ruins of Węgrów, Poland, a small city 30 miles east of Warsaw.

4

First Home Leave

Perhaps expectations were too high, especially those of Annemarie Hosenfeld. She had been excitedly looking forward to her husband's arrival shortly before Christmas 1939. In any case, there was a scene before Wilm's departure on January 4, 1940, during which the couple exchanged heated words. Annemarie would later admit in her letters that she regretted this. The pain of parting burdened them more than when Wilm left at the beginning of the war. Annemarie accompanied her husband to Fulda, where they took a room in the Hotel *Hessischer Hof* for a few hours. At two o'clock in the morning, the express train to Dresden departed Fulda. Annemarie vividly described her emotions:

> *How slowly the train drove out of the station concourse. I stood and stood, until the red light disappeared in the distance. No one was on the platform. I stepped, as if in a dream, down the steps and mechanically went into the ugly waiting area and saw our two chairs still standing exactly as we had left them. It was half past three. I sat down and the endless loneliness came over me. . . .*

Hosenfeld had a similar reaction. During the train ride, he felt how much he missed his wife and children, especially his two youngest daughters, Jorinde and Uta. *I remained standing in the corridor of the train for a long time and stared at the window and almost physically felt the grief,* he wrote. *And the train carried me ever farther, relentlessly farther away.* He took advantage of a long layover in Dresden to distract himself. Hosenfeld visited the dog kennels and also bought clothes and shoes for the children. He wanted to send these items home from Węgrów. Many necessities—not only food—were in short supply in Germany. Another nightly train ride took Hosenfeld to Sokołów Podlaski in eastern Poland. From there, a horse-drawn sleigh transported him to Węgrów.

Wilm and Annemarie Hosenfeld during a home leave in 1939.

Sergeant Hosenfeld had by then been moved back to his company. He and several officers occupied a former teacher's house in Węgrów. In the first weeks of the new year field exercises and lessons were planned, including gas protection training courses and the like. Due to the bitter cold and snow, with temperatures down to -5°F, soldiers could not stay outside for long. Hosenfeld thought of skiing like he did back home, but was missing the skis.

The harsh winter made things difficult for the inhabitants of Węgrów, particularly the Jewish residents who were disadvantaged and discriminated against. Coal stockpiles dwindled, as did the grain and potato reserves. Electricity was shut off at night. The German soldiers, however, suffered no hardships.

Hungry children were always nearby, hoping to receive some left-overs after meals. *Jewish children are also there every day*, Wilm Hosenfeld informed Annemarie. *They work, whatever they can get their hands on, just so that they get something to eat.* An older Jewish man also made himself useful by working various jobs, for which he received food for himself and his family. As soon as the old man saw a German soldier, he removed his fur hat and greeted him with a "Heil Hitler!" Hosenfeld, who often spoke with the man, let himself be photographed with "Kompanie Johann," as the man was called. He sent the picture home to Thalau.

Wilm Hosenfeld (*left*) with "Kompanie Johann" in Węgrów in early 1940.

Hosenfeld exchanged letters not only with Annemarie, but also with his children. Their eldest daughter, Anemone, wrote to her father that the Poles were the worst enemies of Germany. He replied, gently but precisely, on February 29, 1940:

> . . . *I like them very much. It's nice that they love their fatherland. The atrocities* [of the Germans] *were horrible and cannot be understood. I was recently with a Polish family. I had brought some German illustrated magazines with me. There were pictures of the war in there, among others a picture showing a fallen Polish soldier. The girl cried and said, "Maybe that is my brother. We have not heard from him and we don't know if he is alive or dead." Many people don't know about the fate of their soldiers. That is difficult.*

Hosenfeld was in contact with a number of Polish families. He maintained a close friendship with several of them, which endured the war. From the start of the war, Hosenfeld attempted to help Poles whenever the opportunity arose. Hosenfeld was thus able to free Joachim (Achim) Prut, a former Polish officer, from the custody of the Gestapo. His wife had turned to Hosenfeld in Pabianice following a wave of arrests in Poland. Details about Prut's release are unknown.

Hosenfeld visited the Prut family in Pabianice March 9 through 13. The train ride took him through Warsaw, where he was caught up in the flow of refugees coming from eastern Poland, at the time occupied by the Russians. The trains were incredibly overloaded. Many travelers were forced to stay behind on the platform. *The German military always has priority*, Hosenfeld wrote. *We could have spread out. According to regulations, we were even supposed to be alone, but we allowed people into the compartment with us. The soldiers are especially accommodating with women and young ladies.*

A young Polish woman sat next to Hosenfeld, and he soon struck up a conversation with her. She was 31 years old and married. Hosenfeld described her in his journal as attractive and sensual. She took his hat and placed it on her head. *I sensed her approach with every fiber of my being*, Hosenfeld wrote. *My long abstinence and attraction to women made it difficult to resist. When I got off, she waved to me. Had I told her to come with me, she would have interrupted her trip.*

In Pabianice, Hosenfeld met an utterly frightened Prut family. On one hand, they were extremely grateful for Joachim's release. But the fear of being arrested again or deported weighed on their minds. These people lived in an agonizing uncertainty. There was nothing in which they could take pleasure. The fear of being sent away paralyzed every expression of life. During a visit to the administrative authorities in Pabianice, Hosenfeld witnessed a civil servant—an ethnic German—hit and kick a Jewish man lying on the floor.

***

Upon his return to Węgrów, Hosenfeld took advantage of his ample free time to pursue his favorite pastimes: writing and reading.

In his letters, he described other sergeants and officers from whom he usually kept his distance. Hosenfeld could seldom be convinced to take part in a chess match or join in a game of cards. He wrote about a captain who was his immediate superior:

> *He is the typical Nazi, full of prejudice against those with differing opinions, exceedingly polite, but fake and ingratiating. Subservient with superiors, and brutal against subordinates, undisciplined, lets himself go anytime he can. I am in secret opposition, which he notices. Although he still treats me correctly, I can feel the prick of the thorns against me.*

He occasionally used a typewriter for his letters. Practicing on the machine added a little variety to his daily routine, which Hosenfeld found increasingly monotonous. He surprised Annemarie with the suggestion that Thalau's mayor should petition him to fill its teaching position. Then, he could end his military career. Annemarie was skeptical. She passed on the request, and the mayor endorsed it. But the petition was met with little enthusiasm by the relevant school council in Fulda. After several weeks of back and forth, the request was eventually denied.

While preparations for the Battle of France were already running at full speed in Germany, Hosenfeld, stationed in the snow-covered east Polish city of Węgrów, still wondered if the war would actually expand. Following a speech by Hitler at the Berlin Sports Palace on January 30, 1940, in which he launched threats against Great Britain and France, Hosenfeld suspected a huge blow would be struck against those countries in the spring. But he was not sure. *The state of the war has shifted in favor of us,* he wrote to his father-in-law, Karl Krummacher, on March 16. *It is possible that peaceful solutions can still occur. I don't believe that it will come to a German offensive in the West.*

A meeting took place between Adolf Hitler and Benito Mussolini on March 18 at the Brenner Pass on the Austria–Italy border. Hosenfeld held out hope that political tensions might lead to negotiations. He believed Germany was in a good position. Hosenfeld wrote: *It is a great historical hour for our nation, and we will not surrender the trump cards that we hold in our hand without a beneficial return, the Führer will see to that.*

***

In the spring of 1940, Annemarie directed her husband's attention away from the great political issues to more mundane everyday matters in Thalau. It had also been a harsh winter in the Rhön Mountains with unexpected cold. Streets and paths were covered in snow; water pipes were frozen. Skis and sleds were used to bring letters and packages to the post office. Sometimes, when soldiers from Hosenfeld's company were on home leave, Annemarie would give them mail for him. Since other women in Germany also used this method, a kind of shuttle service for letters and packages developed parallel to the home leaves and army postal service. The military prohibited the practice in the spring of 1940, but it could not really be stopped.

Toward the end of February, Thalau and the surrounding areas freed themselves from the embrace of winter, and the heralds of spring appeared. It started to thaw, as Annemarie described in one letter: . . . *All of a sudden the giant mass of snow was gone and wide strips appear out of all that white on the brown fields. On top of that, a blue spring sky. You could forget that there is a war going on. The yearning for spring awakens, the longing for sun and carefreeness.* She had almost all good things to report about the children. Helmut, who was by then continuing his medical studies in Frankfurt, successfully passed his midterm exams. He was still spared from the conscription to military service. Detlev was coming along well in school, particularly in the subjects of English and German. Uta, the youngest, was turning into a happy and vivacious child. She always was in the mood for jokes and antics, and occasionally received a "spanking" from Annemarie as a last resort. Jorinde was kind and charming: . . . *I can always look at the fine, small face* [of Jorinde] *with its big eyes that somehow appear bright and other times appear dark*, Annemarie wrote.

The children challenged their mother, but at the same time, provided her with stability and pleasure. And yet, in almost every letter she nonetheless complained that Hosenfeld was not there at her side: *You cannot know how much I long for you. I suffer unspeakably from the separation. I cannot write anymore; all this crying weakens me.* At another point, she wrote: *I have to fend off so many black shadows and nightmare visions, cry so many tears, before I can laugh in the arms of my dearest again.*

Annemarie could not—and would not—completely ignore the political happenings. In Thalau, young men were constantly being called for military service. Increasingly, families were required to take soldiers into their homes. The unease carried over to Annemarie. *One can hear about the preparation for the spring war in the West everywhere,* she wrote. *I am often stricken with fear, so that I lie as if frozen stiff in bed and can hear my heart beating as loud as a hammer. Wilm, Helmut, Helmut, Wilm! I cannot think any further. I grow dull against other sorrow and hardship.*

Despite the Wehrmacht's announcement of a ban on home leave, Hosenfeld was allowed his second trip home at the end of March. His second-youngest daughter, Jorinde, was to take part in her first communion on "White Sunday." In Catholic families, this is a special day. The marriage of Wilm Hosenfeld's younger brother Rudolf was also taking place around the same time.

Before heading home, however, Hosenfeld spent Easter in Węgrów. Being unable to spend significant church holidays in the company of his family always put Hosenfeld in a melancholy mood. He would then seek solace in liturgy. During the Easter service in the monastery church, he again joined the Polish locals. Hosenfeld observed the service in his journal:

> *It shook me, when the young church members struck up the Credo on the organ and the hallelujah sounded so joyful and free and heartfelt through the space. . . . Between the singing church members stood young women and girls, who would direct a furtive glance at the fine faces, and then glance back at me, before focusing on their prayer book again.*

Hosenfeld arrived in Fulda on the morning of March 31, following a nighttime train journey through Berlin. He missed a train there and did not expect anyone to pick him up at the station in Fulda. To his great surprise and joy, his wife stood on the platform. Together, they drove to Thalau, where the children welcomed him. Annemarie had expressed her expectation for this home leave in a long letter:

> *Our time of fighting has passed. I believe that the time apart has matured us. I don't want to have to fight for you. I now want to have the certainty that you are mine, and in this knowledge I will become strong and calm and steady. We both know the weaknesses of the other, as well as our qualities. Just as you are, that is how I carry your picture in my heart, that is how I love you and am proud of you.*

***

The Battle of France was well underway when Hosenfeld returned to his post in mid-April 1940. However, the Wehrmacht was not yet marching against its Western European neighbors as expected, but initially against Denmark and Norway. The offensive had been postponed several times due to unfavorable weather conditions; on April 9, 1940, it finally began. Since Denmark did not fight back for long, German forces concentrated on Norway. Following the occupation of the port cities of Oslo, Bergen, and Trondheim, the Norwegians fiercely resisted over several weeks—which the German propaganda kept a secret. So it was that Hosenfeld had the impression both countries would be conquered with a wave of the hand, followed by England and Scotland.

The wintry inaction finally came to an end in Węgrów. It was Sergeant Hosenfeld's responsibility to prepare newly conscripted troops for the war in an intensive training program. He wrote: *I enjoy the training of new recruits, although it is very demanding throughout the entire day. They are not young people anymore; most are married, have their own careers, are working, and have a professional life. It touches me how they are willing and ready to do everything in order to please their superiors.*

Hosenfeld often spent what little free time he had at the casino with his commanding officer, who wanted to be entertained. It was unusual to get up and leave the table before the officer did.

On April 24, Hosenfeld was informed he had been promoted to lieutenant. This had been his wish for a long time; due to his injury in World War I, he had not yet achieved it. Now, largely without his own efforts, it had finally come about. The requirements for the position had long been fulfilled. Hosenfeld only mentioned the promotion to his wife as an aside, even though the news must have given him a sense of gratification. He was aware she would receive the news with mixed feelings. *Should I congratulate you on your promotion?* Annemarie asked. *Life is temporarily somewhat more pleasant for you, and as you move ever farther away, I can only be sad about that.*

It was no secret to Hosenfeld that some of his comrades begrudged him the officer's rank. He confided in his journal: *I notice that I am being strongly criticized. I am too active; I should be more reserved and not attract attention.* Hosenfeld was accustomed to leading field exercises from a horse. He could voice his commands while riding and simultaneously enjoy the blossoming of spring. It was with some concern, however, he observed his company increasingly sealing itself off from the Polish public. The soldiers' quarters were secured with tall wire fences. At the same time, Hosenfeld had the impression more Poles than ever displayed a hostile attitude. Until then, many hoped Germany would lose the war, but the Wehrmacht's successes in Denmark and Norway had frustrated those expectations.

The Poles' disappointment surely multiplied in the following weeks due to the blitzkriegs carried out by the Wehrmacht. On May 10, 1940, attacks on Belgium, the Netherlands, Luxembourg, and France all began. The goal was to force France to capitulate within a few weeks. Hitler wanted to avoid at all costs another war on two fronts, which had been Germany's downfall in 1918. Following a victory over France, Hitler hoped to come to an arrangement with Great Britain and then march together against the Soviet Union. Hosenfeld at first assessed the invasion of neutral countries such as Belgium and the Netherlands with restraint: *It has now come to a fight of life and death after all. I cannot let go of the thought about what is happening in the West. It lies like an incubus on my soul.*

But soon Hosenfeld was no longer able to suppress his admiration for the speed of the conquests. *It is downright unbelievable, with which speed the German troops advance*, he wrote. *The French and Belgians also appear not to have much appetite for war.* Hosenfeld continued to regard Hitler as a genius who had drafted strategic plans and personally led the operation, just as the propaganda untruthfully maintained. *What organization!* he noted. *Fabulous! And this feat of arms in the West! Boy, oh boy, who wouldn't like to be a part of that!*

Hosenfeld then curbed his enthusiasm because it became clear to him what his active participation on the front would mean to his family, particularly now with Annemarie in the hospital. The mental stress she constantly felt left its mark on her. Annemarie suffered a miscarriage. Because the pain would not subside, she was forced to undergo surgery in Fulda on May 21, after which her condition improved. Hosenfeld had asked permission for a special leave so he could be by Annemarie's side, but was denied the request. Now, he did not want to further upset her. In a letter, he wrote: . . . *My spirit of adventure, if I should call it that, is losing its appeal when I think of you and the children. I do not have to justify myself to you. You know my attitude toward duty and honor, and I do not have to justify myself to any other person. It is fine by me if the war ends here.*

Annemarie was anything but thrilled about the Wehrmacht's advance in the West. While in the hospital, she heard on the radio of heavy losses suffered by an infantry unit from Fulda. *Who can then still be happy about victories!* Annemarie wrote to her husband from her hospital bed. *I am sitting in the sun at the bay window and look onto flowering chestnuts, lilacs, and hawthorn bushes. Children are playing in the garden. And out there in France and Belgium our German soldiers are bleeding to death, daily thousands of flowering people are dying.* She had previously made her opinion about the war's progress clear: *We hear news every day and pray every night that nice prayer from the little field songbook for the soldiers. I cannot be glad about the magnificent victories. Women and mothers can never forget that endless amounts of blood must flow.* On one hand, Annemarie could understand that her husband enjoyed being a soldier. *But haven't you done enough for your fatherland?* she wrote. *If it must be, I will endure it, because God allows it. Voluntarily? I cannot understand that.*

***

Hosenfeld was far away from the great events of the war; he accepted his situation. He had no choice. His superiors made decisions about his future use—he neither knew them nor was he in a position to influence them. *I sit in my lonely little room,* Hosenfeld wrote. *The lad has started the fire, the rain rustles against the zinc pots that cover the roof, and the wind howls strongly along the house. I look over the gray landscape, toward the west, to you.*

At the end of May 1940, he was transferred from Węgrów to the small town of Jadów, around 20 miles farther east toward Białystok. Jadów was predominantly inhabited by Jews. There, Hosenfeld led a company for several weeks. *Every morning I ride in front of the company to the area where we have our field duty training and take in the surroundings,* he wrote. Exercising in the open field took Hosenfeld's mind off of concerns about his wife and the events of the war in the West. Along with the training, he had time for conversations. He spoke to a sergeant from Stuttgart, Germany, about the poems of Rainer Maria Rilke and the paintings of Paula Modersohn-Becker, both of whom he was familiar with because of Annemarie. By early July, he more often used free time to swim.

Around the same time, to his great disappointment Hosenfeld was informed he had lost command of the company and would be reassigned to a guard unit. This meant he would be leaving the active troops, about which he was not happy. Now there was virtually nothing holding him in Poland. He wrote to Annemarie: *You see, my dear wife, I want to discuss this with you. . . . Just now I have learned that the guard unit I am assigned to is being moved to Warsaw. That is a small consolation.* It was a momentary consolation, and at the same time, a fateful decision concerning the future years of the war: Lieutenant Wilm Hosenfeld was being assigned to the center of a war of extermination. While a member of the Wehrmacht, he was a witness to its destruction. The Wehrmacht was primarily responsible for the biggest crime of the 20th century: the annihilation of millions of non-combative people.

Pages from Wilm Hosenfeld's 1940 Węgrów journal.

5

A Change of Location

The 1930s began with hope for Władysław Szpilman. He was born in 1911 in Sosnowiec, Poland, in the Silesia region. Szpilman began his piano studies in Warsaw and continued at the Academy of Arts in Berlin. His teachers were Leonid Kreutzer and Artur Schnabel. Szpilman possessed not only talent, but also a healthy amount of ambition. He took additional lessons with Franz Schreker and was soon able to compose his own pieces. In addition to classical music, he was interested in upscale popular music with its French and American influences.

Szpilman was immersed in Berlin's music scene at the end of January 1933. When Hitler seized power, Szpilman, a Jew, had no choice but to return to Poland. At the Chopin Academy of Music in Warsaw, Aleksander Michałowski took over his additional training until Szpilman was hired by the Polish Radio in 1935. He soon made a name for himself due to his versatility and improvisational abilities. In those days of live radio broadcasts, two- or three-minute breaks occasionally had to be bridged while microphones and musicians were being positioned for the next piece. The transitions were ideal experience for the young pianist, and even if listeners noticed the interludes, they would have perceived them as pleasant.

Before long, Szpilman was in great demand as an artist, accompanying soloists and even entire orchestras and effortlessly switching between jazz, chansons, and classical. The pianist belonged to the Polish musical delegation that performed Karol Szymanowski's Symphony no. 4 to an international audience at the 1937 Paris World's Fair. *My father also composed the music for a number of motion pictures, as well as many pieces, chansons, and songs that were very popular,* Andrzej Szpilman, Władysław's son, later wrote. *Before the war, he was already performing with the world-famous violinist Bronisław Gimpel, along with future stars Henryk Szeryng and Ida Haendel.*

Whenever he was not on tour, Władysław Szpilman lived at his parents' home on the third floor of an apartment building on Śliska Street in Warsaw, along with his brother, Henryk, and two sisters, Regina and Halina. Their father was a passionate violinist. Music grew in importance for the Szpilman family during the years of oppression because it provided escape from the destructive fury of the occupiers.

Following Poland's capitulation at the end of September 1939, the German police and SS regarded Jews as fair game for bullying. Before long, the first raids and random arrests occurred. Slaps in the face, kickings, and other abuses in public areas were common. Day by day, Jews lost all of their rights. They were not allowed to go out in the evening, were forbidden to ride on trains and public transport, and were not permitted to own a telephone. New orders and bans systematically restricted their freedom and daily life. The occupying forces appropriated money, valuables, and real estate that belonged to Jews. In desperation, many Jews left Warsaw. Vacant houses and buildings spoke of an exodus the Germans methodically promoted.

In light of these events, the Szpilman family made a far-reaching decision: they decided not to flee. The parents wanted to hold out in Warsaw with their four adult children as long as possible, with the expectation that their situation would one day improve—at the latest, when the Americans joined the war, for which they eagerly hoped.

***

Władysław Szpilman last performed live on Polish Radio on September 23, 1939, as the building was being shelled. At 3:15 p.m. the station ceased broadcasting. Initially, Szpilman and his siblings, Henryk, Regina, and Halina, were glad their parents had decided to stay. They couldn't imagine leaving everything—the apartment, the piano, the furniture—behind. Some Jews who fled to Soviet-occupied eastern Poland had even returned to Warsaw.

However, the Szpilman family's situation did not improve. The Germans continuously intensified their harassment. Władysław and Henryk Szpilman were outraged at the order that Jewish men had to bow before every German soldier. As soon as they saw a gray uniform in the distance, they turned onto a side street so they did not have to greet the soldiers. Their father, on the other hand, complied with the order. He did not avoid the occupying soldiers, but instead greeted them with a friendly smile and a deep bow, quite often triggering a feeling of insecurity in the process. It was simply irony the Germans did not detect.

The requirement to bow was degrading, and not everyone was able to deal with it as elegantly as the old man. Even more so was the Germans' rule for Jews to wear a white armband with the Star of David. In this way, the occupying forces stigmatized and branded a segment of the population that had, for centuries, substantially shaped the art and culture of Poland.

But this was not enough for the occupying forces. It was downright alarming when trains carrying Jews supposedly earmarked for the "Germanization" of regions in western Poland started arriving in Warsaw during the winters of 1939 and 1940. What was the meaning of that? Rumors about the construction of a ghetto started to circulate in the city. People were crammed into railcars in freezing temperatures. Szpilman later wrote in his memoir: *There were transports where barely half the people were still alive, suffering from horrible frostbite. The other half consisted of corpses; frozen stiff, they stood between the living and only fell to the ground once those alive moved.*

The establishment of a "Jewish residential district," as the Nazis referred to the approximately one-square-mile area in the center of Warsaw, was justified for hygienic reasons. What cynicism! The area was enclosed by a wall, *so that typhoid fever and other Jewish illnesses would not spread to the other parts of the city.*

During the summer of 1940, ever more people streamed into the quarter. Non-Jewish residents were forced to vacate their homes. Within an already overcrowded part of Warsaw, half a million people were now forced to live. The dark streets teemed with figures wearing white armbands. Everyone was agitated, running frantically back and forth like animals in a cage not acclimated to one another. At first, the Szpilman family comforted one another in that they did not have to relocate. The street where they lived was already in the ghetto, a bitter consolation in a sea of desperation. During the night of November 15, 1940, the gates of the ten-foot-high ghetto wall were closed. The SS took over guard duty. There was no longer a chance for Jews to escape.

Forced laborers building the Warsaw Ghetto wall.

***

Wilm Hosenfeld's transfer from Jadów—the furthest post in eastern Poland—to Warsaw in the summer of 1940 was not a smooth one. Wanting to take advantage of the last nice days there, he went out riding alone, which was strictly forbidden. It was a sunny day and he wanted to watch the Polish farmers during their hay harvest. Hosenfeld did not always explicitly follow regulations. By the time he returned it was dark, and his superior had organized a search operation, which he then called off at the last minute.

The transfer to Warsaw delayed Hosenfeld's plans for a home leave. Originally, he wanted to travel to Thalau at the beginning of July. To the great disappointment of his wife, the home leave was postponed to the second half of the month.

In one of her letters, Annemarie prepared her husband for what awaited him in Thalau: all sorts of work in the garden, where vegetables and fruits had grown in ample amounts and had, to some extent, already been harvested. She wrote:

> We have been eating salad and radishes for a long time, and I have harvested almost an entire patch of spinach. Soon, I can also cook the turnip cabbage. The peas, the first variety, are growing well. I have made a pile of bush beans. The potatoes are chopped. The raspberries have taken well. The bees have been busy as well. The spinning of the honeycombs produced more than 120 pounds of honey.

Hosenfeld looked forward to working in the garden, and he started almost as soon as he arrived. The children also helped. For two weeks, they were again one big family, though not always a harmonious one. There was friction and occasional arguing during this home leave as well. Annemarie sometimes had the feeling her concerns and fears were not seriously considered. She believed her suffering due to the war was much greater than her husband's because she was singlehandedly responsible for five children, the household, and the garden.

The older children noticed the tension between their parents. Wilm Hosenfeld tried to explain the cause of friction in a letter to his son Helmut: *Mother and I have completely different characters; we are not able to carry on as calmly and easily as a married couple who have such a big son and a daughter of sixteen years of age and three more small children should have learned to do by now. That will never be the case.* He then made a drastic comparison to illustrate their differences: *Mother is a fiery young thoroughbred that bolts along when it has had enough of its shackles, and I am a slow and steady plow horse that wants to purposefully and reliably go on its way. It is to be expected that the cart that both of them pull occasionally be knocked about.*

Annemarie also recognized distinct contrasts following her husband's home leave. In one letter, she observed: *The shadows that clouded our last time together have not disappeared. I love you, deeper and more dearly, and with a greater willingness for sacrifice than before, but I can clearly see how different we are and how much we have grown apart in this year.* In another part of the letter she confessed she had butted against his vanity. There was talk of a wall rising up between them.

***

Hosenfeld reported for duty in Warsaw on August 1, 1940. The contrast to the Jewish-populated towns of Jadów and Węgrów in east Poland could not have been greater. The wounds the war inflicted upon the Polish capital a year earlier had not begun to heal. When he saw the rubble, Hosenfeld felt anger at the senseless destruction. By now, the Wehrmacht had firmly established itself in Warsaw and was in possession of the government and administrative buildings, as well as chic hotels. The occupiers exercised control and violence across the city. The German military dominated the streets. The Poles took heed at every street crossing so as to literally avoid ending up under a military vehicle. Warsaw was pulsating again, albeit under a foreign rhythm.

Hosenfeld was flooded with new impressions, which he committed to his journal even more often than before. He wrote more letters to Helmut, expecting him to be more understanding in military matters than Annemarie.

Hosenfeld was impressed by the dashing officers of the German air force. More high-ranking military staff now crossed his path. After a meeting at the historic Radziviłł Palace, the former seat of the Polish government, he wrote:

I felt so small among the top brass, colonels, majors, even an air force general sat at my table. A lieutenant colonel is the man in charge. How confident and assured these soldiers are, without any trace of inhibition or anything weighing them down. They are soldiers, and only soldiers. That is not me. My contribution lies elsewhere, but that's unimportant. That is why the likes of us are burdened and insecure. Nothing would be better than to be able to return to the old mission in life.

Hosenfeld was aware that he, a reserve officer, did not belong to this category of soldier. Intellectually, he had long since distanced himself from them.

Wilm Hosenfeld (*center*) with a group of high-ranking Nazi officers at the Warsaw sports complex.

For the time being, there could be no talk of a return to his career as a teacher. A new and multifaceted scope of duties awaited Hosenfeld. As an officer in a guard company, he was responsible for overseeing the security of Warsaw military installations and warehouses that contained supplies and replenishments like fuel depots. He got along well with the soldiers on the ground. Hosenfeld praised, but also reprimanded when necessary. He always found encouraging words for his comrades, and on occasion, played a round of cards with them, especially during his nightly inspections when the hours dragged.

Occasionally, Hosenfeld served as the commander's deputy ordinance officer, where he could put his diverse experience to use. Among other tasks, he was used as a courier. On one occasion, while traveling in a special train compartment, he transported secret documents to Berlin.

Eventually, he grew into a job that became his main field of activity: organizing and supervising sports competitions for German soldiers who needed to train and physically toughen up before redeployment. For this purpose, the Germans seized the sports facilities on Łazienkowska Street in the southern part of Warsaw near the Vistula River. Not far from there was a group of buildings with army barracks, from which the Polish army had been expelled. This was where the guard regiment was now stationed. At first, Hosenfeld also resided in the barracks, but he later moved to the sports facility.

He experienced his first sporting event in Warsaw on August 18, 1940. Soldiers from the four districts of the General Government—Warsaw, Kraków, Lublin, and Radom—participated in the competitions. Hosenfeld observed the games from the VIP box. The SA group leader and district head of Warsaw, Ludwig Fischer, welcomed him with a handshake. A few weeks later, Fischer established the Warsaw Ghetto.

Hosenfeld did not lack in variety. He attended meetings in the sports stadium, rode out to the Vistula River, watched concerts in the Café "Club" (exclusively reserved for Germans), and even dined in the elegant Hotel Europa, located in the city center and directly adjacent to the offices of the military commander. Before the war, foreign diplomats often stayed there. Now, officers traveling through Warsaw stayed at the hotel, where, in Hosenfeld's words, they were housed like princes. He had never before seen such a grandiose building, but he was not deceived. *Speaking with officers, it came to light how life was envisaged on a purely external basis*, Hosenfeld wrote. *The pleasure of life, outward recognition,* [and] *success are motivating forces that provide incentives to perform.*

This map shows the division of Poland and other territories that Germany and the Soviet Union drew up in their "nonaggression" pact signed on August 23, 1939. With the agreement, Adolf Hitler and Joseph Stalin essentially rewrote national borders to benefit their own crusades.

Hosenfeld would not be denied contact with Poles in Warsaw. He visited a Polish family whom he had met some months before during a train ride. He kept a watchful, caring eye on people. He encountered them daily on the street and looked into their faces. In his journal, Hosenfeld wrote:

> *Outwardly, life takes its course, but one can feel and see how the chains hurt the Poles; the most depressing for this nation must be not*

being able to predict when things will one day change. It's my opinion
that Germans are acting too much as rulers. Communication is not
wanted; the Pole is to remain servile, as was once emphasized from
a position of authority.

The arrogance of the occupiers can be traced to the preceding
series of Wehrmacht victories in the Battle of France. Some officers
considered the German troops invincible. They chose not to see that
Great Britain was putting up significant resistance following France's
defeat. The intensified air and naval war against England that Hitler
ordered at the beginning of August 1940 was missing its mark. It was
not yet possible to think about German troops landing there.

***

Around the end of August 1940, Wilm Hosenfeld received an
assignment that repeatedly occupied him during the ensuing weeks. It
also took him back to east Poland, to the German-occupied province
of Wartheland and to East Prussia. Hosenfeld was assigned to be a
liaison officer in the preparation of a film about the fate of Germans
in the Volhynia region (between Poland, Belarus, and Ukraine) prior
to World War II. His job was to lead a team from the film crew and
help identify potential filming locations and venues. Hosenfeld was
also tasked with appropriating Wehrmacht artisans to build the film
sets. His writings do not indicate why he received this assignment;
however, it is likely his organizational talent, outgoing nature, and
soldierly attitude played a role.

Third Reich Minister of Propaganda Joseph Goebbels commissioned the Wien-Film Company with the production. The director was
Gustav Ucicky, a German-Austrian who had made a name for himself
with a string of popular films. Photographers, camera crew members,
and set designers were all part of the group. Wilm Hosenfeld's first
trip with the film crew took place across several days through Mińsk
Mazowiecki, Węgrów, and Wyszków. The reconnaissance apparently

was not successful. Many photos were taken, but there was no idea where the stage set for the propaganda film should be built. The director considered a marketplace in a historic setting.

The search continued at the start of September. This time, the trip took them through Łódź to Poznań, from there to Thorn, and finally to Sensburg in East Prussia. While in Łódź, Hosenfeld left the group and drove to Pabianice to check on the Prut family. They still lived in uncertainty and fear of deportation.

Wilm Hosenfeld (*right*) with the Prut family in September 1940. Joachim (Achim) Prut is pictured in the center.

Hosenfeld got to know the architect Walter Röhrig, who would later design the movie sets. Whenever possible, he kept his distance from the others because, for the most part, the evenings were filled with heavy drinking. Eventually, the marketplace in Chorzele, south of Allenstein, was chosen for the shooting location. The film, *Heimkehr* (*Homecoming*), was mostly shot at Wiener Studios and featured a well-known cast including Paula Wessely, Attila Hörbiger, and Carl Raddatz.

Hosenfeld sent his wife almost daily reports about his travels and bought her a rosary made out of coral as a memento. *For days now we have been rushing across the east German and Polish landscape,* he wrote. *At a moment's notice the picture changes, but it always stays the same—vast spaces, sky, country roads, villages, people, cities.* In Rudczanny at the Niedersee Lake in East Prussia, he encountered people who had fled there to escape the Allied air raids on Berlin. They were mostly women with their children who felt safe, but faced an uncertain future.

On September 5, 1940, Hosenfeld returned to Warsaw, happy to carry out his usual tasks. *This afternoon I had my horse saddled and rode alone for two hours along the Vistula River,* he wrote in his journal. *The current flows broad and calm, a steamboat with a towing crane moves upstream next to me, the birds scream in the bushes at the water's edge, the noise of people is far away. I am alone with my horse and my thoughts.*

Even though Hosenfeld wrote to Annemarie nearly every day during his travels, promised her a nice souvenir, and affirmed his yearning for her in almost every letter, she was not impressed by his role as the liaison officer on the film project. She wrote:

> *I don't like it. You are a soldier now, that is why we have to do without you. I consider this task to be unimportant in a war, unworthy of an old officer.* Gerd [Annemarie's brother] *told me how France is destroyed. I saw pictures of the destroyed houses in Bremen. Would it not be more correct to have soldiers assist with the reconstruction there, instead of rebuilding a Polish marketplace for the purpose of a film?*

It was unnecessary to shoot trendy films in such times, Annemarie argued. Young German girls were being forced to work in underground bunkers and manufacture munitions. *But such fat bon vivants can travel the world searching for film motifs!* Annemarie lamented. *If your comrades envy you for this position, you can gladly pass it on to them!*

Because of the Allied air raids, the war drew ever closer to the Hosenfelds' home. Bremen, Berlin, and other cities came into the crosshairs of the bombers. It was the Allied response to the German aerial campaign against England. For several weeks starting in September 1940, the Luftwaffe flew nightly attacks against London with hardly a pause. The raids were meant to demoralize and destroy industrial plants. But the British resistance could not be broken.

On September 27, the "Axis Pact" (commonly known as the Tripartite Pact or Berlin Pact) between Germany, Italy, and Japan was announced. Annemarie asked Wilm what she should think of it. She wrote: *I believe that America will now be less inclined to participate. Many soldiers from our local area have come to Poland. What is the significance of these massive troop redeployments to Poland?*

Most people could not have imagined Hitler was well on his way to opening another front in the war—in this case against the mammoth Soviet Union (still referred to as Russia in the German language). Wilm Hosenfeld also did not seriously expect an offensive against Stalin's giant realm, even though he still considered Hitler to be in a strong position and was impressed by his threatening gestures. At the same time, he bemoaned the consequences of the war and desperately searched for the sense in all the suffering and destruction. Hosenfeld wrote:

> *Every day, death collects its grim harvest among the young men, every day brings further devastation and disaster over enemy cities. The war always demands new victims. God is silent. The hearts of the people are hardened. He leaves them to their ruin. History is a single graveyard of hate and the triumph of misery that people cause themselves.*

Almost magically, Hosenfeld was repeatedly drawn to the Tomb of the Unknown Soldier in Warsaw. It was near the office of the military commander, where Hosenfeld would begin his nightly patrols. He wrote about the memorial in his journal:

> *. . . I make my rounds with the night guards and step into the soft light at the Tomb of the Unknown Soldier and greet the dead enemy as if he were a brother. The red flowers glow in the blue light, no, they do not glow, they lie there as if moistened by tears; they wither and mourn and in their representation of impermanence they show*

*the face of death more clearly than they did when I saw them a few
hours ago, still vibrantly fresh.*

While preparations for the invasion of the Soviet Union were
being drawn up, plans for a much more ghastly and barbaric campaign
were taking form: the extermination of European Jews. Poland and
its capital city would play a special role in these plans.

***

Wilm Hosenfeld visited the notorious Pawiak prison in Warsaw
with the film crew in August 1940. Located in the northwest part of
the city, the prison mostly housed political prisoners, including many
Jews. Pawiak was under the control of the German security police
(*Sicherheitspolizei* or SiPo), known for its brutality. Torture and murder
were daily occurrences at the prison. During their walk through the
halls of the prison, the film crew saw what they were meant to see:
packages with bread and bacon. The prisoners, including children,
apparently did not receive anything. Hosenfeld felt great pity for the
pale and emaciated figures he saw there. An eight-year-old Jewish
boy told him they wished for a larger piece of bread.

Judging by his writings and letters from September to December
1940, it appears at first Hosenfeld barely noticed the creation of the
Warsaw Ghetto. According to witnesses, he nonetheless had contact
during this time with Jewish and non-Jewish families in Poland. On
September 30, Hosenfeld wrote in his journal: . . . *the Polish daughter-in-
law of the Jew Frau* [Mrs.] *Sachs will take over the move. All Jews will go into
the ghetto.* Hosenfeld had met the woman with her husband, Hans Sachs,
and their son during a train ride. Along with their closest relatives,
the Sachs had been deported from Łódź and desperately tried to get
seats on the train for themselves and their luggage. Hosenfeld had
helped them and given the boy a harmonica.

On November 16, while visiting with the Luckhaus family,
Hosenfeld again met Mrs. Sachs. By then, her husband worked as an

engineer in Russia and could not return, Hosenfeld noted in a letter. She gave Hosenfeld a doll for his daughter Uta, about whom he had spoken on the train. He was surprised and looked at her questioningly. Hosenfeld later wrote about the experience:

> *She also very much wished for a little girl, but she now had to divorce her husband. From her bag, she pulled out the photo of her husband and cried. I found out the entire story from Luckhaus. Her father had been an Austrian officer in the First World War, had fought in Italy, and was the director of a primary school in Łódź. The mother had been the director of a school for girls. She herself was a student of sports. One brother had been killed in Warsaw, another was being held [as a] prisoner of the Germans. The parents had all their belongings taken away, leaving them completely destitute. They had been deported across the border to the Governorate. There they live in wretched conditions in some village and have the small daughter with them. Through coincidence, I meet this woman again and hear her life's story. What a tragedy!*

The situation of the Luckhaus couple also saddened Hosenfeld. *He is a German, but does not feel a sense of belonging and suffers under the misfortune of the Polish, the nation that his wife belongs to,* he wrote. *The woman hates the Germans with a patriotic zeal and the fervor of an oppressed and subjugated believer robbed of her freedom.*

Eduard Luckhaus was a former athlete and sports teacher. As an ethnic German, he found employment in the sports department of the Warsaw district administration. He was often in contact with Hosenfeld on official business; Luckhaus trusted him and opened his heart to him. Luckhaus still felt the effects of the German siege of Warsaw one year prior. His wife, Krystyna; their child; and he had lived in an extensively destroyed part of town. They had survived amid great danger and now faced an uncertain future.

Through research conducted by the historian Thomas Vogel, we know Eduard Luckhaus was later drafted into the Wehrmacht.

His wife, also a sports teacher, belonged to the relief corps of the Polish army. She helped persecuted Poles and was in contact with the Polish underground army that launched the 1944 uprising against the German occupiers.

Another family with whom a bond of friendship existed during the war involved Annemarie. Zofia Cieciora was one of the Polish women in Pabianice who, with the help of Wilm Hosenfeld, had managed to free her husband, Stanisław, from the POW camp. The couples exchanged letters and packages and met at the Cieciora residence on a country estate in Samter, near Poznań. Antoni Cieciora, Stanisław's brother, was a priest involved in the Polish underground. His name was on a Gestapo "wanted" list and his life was in extreme danger. It took some time, but Hosenfeld found a solution: he gave Antoni the alias "Cichocki" and employed him as a Polish teacher at the sports and vocational training school he ran.

In November 1940, Zofia wanted to help the Hosenfeld family by sending a Polish girl as a domestic helper to Thalau. After her previous helper had resigned, Annemarie searched for a replacement in Germany. Her search was unsuccessful, however; due to the war, finding workers was nearly impossible. As a result, Annemarie urgently asked her husband to be on the lookout for someone in Poland. This turned out to be quite difficult because chilling stories circulated in Poland about how Polish foreign workers were being treated in Germany. Zofia offered to send a young waitress whom she personally knew and who was willing to go. However, due to German bureaucracy, the plan failed—the German labor agency would have had to provide consent.

***

In the letters he sent to Thalau in November and December 1940, Hosenfeld seemed dejected and morose. *Sometimes I sit at the table brooding and don't want to talk to anyone. . . . I remain empty,* he wrote. *I run through the city like a stranger who is out of place here.* At another point, he wrote: *I was out early exercising with the company. The fog wraps around my soul, or something else, I don't know what it is. I am so tired and indifferent.* His depression may also have been connected to physical problems that had plagued him for weeks. Hosenfeld repeatedly suffered from bad headaches, impaired vision, and difficulty speaking. Medical examinations failed to explain the cause of these symptoms.

The doctor recommended Hosenfeld at least temporarily stop smoking and do without horseback riding. Thus, he resorted to taking his bicycle more often when he moved around the city, or he simply walked. Hosenfeld was not concerned with the risks involved. He saw more than other officers who rode through Warsaw in cars.

The medical examinations continued for weeks, but the findings were inconclusive. *I look too healthy*, was Hosenfeld's laconic opinion. The events in his environment also did not help improve his wellbeing. The ethnic Germans, with their nationalist sentiments constantly on display, ground on his nerves—*even though their children can barely speak a word of German*, he noted. Anger again took hold of Hosenfeld when two young Poles who attempted to stop a German soldier from raping a Polish girl were sentenced to a firing squad. *One must not think, otherwise you would lose all desire for being a soldier*, he wrote. *What kind of a legal view is that!* The two Poles were presumably shot.

This sustained depressive mood strengthened Hosenfeld's wish to end his Warsaw service, and at most, to perform his duty at a military barracks in Germany. He did not want to be committed to a hospital. Instead, Hosenfeld requested home leave, which was approved for the second half of December. This was his third vacation of 1940, given he had also spent two weeks in Thalau in October. Two trips home during the year was the standard rule.

6

The Warsaw Ghetto

The two-week home leave was good for Wilm Hosenfeld. His health problems subsided. In contrast to Warsaw, where violence carried out against Poles followed him wherever he went, life in Thalau with his family was downright idyllic. He described a *big wash day* in his journal: *Everyone helps. Putting everything in order is a great joy to me. I clean the attic, put up strings for hanging the laundry on, seal the basement windows, clean the washroom, and wring the large laundry pieces together with Helmut, since they are too large for the small hands of Annemarie. What peaceful work.*

Detlev and Anemone were still in school in mid-December 1940—vacation started shortly before Christmas. Hosenfeld made their breakfast and helped them on their way. He wrote: *I'm sorry to have to send the two of them out into the cold, but the efforts will harden them.* Jorinde Krejci recalled how her father looked after her when he was also on home leave in 1943. "At that time, I attended secondary school in Fulda; it was a long way to get there—two kilometers [about one and one-quarter mile] on foot and eighteen kilometers [about eleven miles] with the train," she said. "It was winter and the snow was high. I woke up at six, got dressed, and went into the kitchen, which was the only room that was already warm. Father had heated the oven, cooked milk, and prepared the breakfast. He emptied the ash drawer outside. When he came back, he said, 'Don't you want to stay home today? The snow is so high. Just stay here!' I was touched by his concern and said, 'But Father, I have to go to school.'"

This time, the holidays harmoniously passed, except for the parting at the train station in Fulda. Annemarie was again overcome with sorrow at their separation and bitterly complained.

***

Back in Warsaw, the brutal reality of the German occupation quickly caught up with Hosenfeld again. Krystyna Luckhaus informed him that in early January 1941 around 300 patients from a psychiatric institution in Chełm, Poland, her hometown, had been murdered by the SS and Gestapo. During a meeting with a German entrepreneur operating in Poland, Hosenfeld heard about the fate of a young Polish doctor who was pulled from his bed in the middle of the night, sent to Auschwitz, and killed four weeks later. The original Auschwitz concentration camp served as a central collection point for Polish intellectuals and members of the resistance beginning in the summer of 1940. By the end of the war, around 70,000 people had been murdered there. The second Auschwitz location, the Birkenau extermination camp, opened in 1941.

Such stories became more prevalent and weighed heavily on Hosenfeld's mood. He had tried for weeks to be declared unfit for service and be returned to Germany. A neurologist who examined him several times told him not to get his hopes up. *I asked the doctor in a roundabout manner what he wanted to do with me*, Hosenfeld wrote. *He felt that I would probably be released as being fit for garrison duty. But first he wants to use a special device* [on me]. *I am also not riding with the others anymore. He wanted to bring me into the hospital, but I refused.* Everything happened just as the neurologist had predicted. He declared Hosenfeld "fit for garrison and field duty," which meant nothing, other than that he would have to continue serving in his current role in Warsaw. *That does not only destroy your hopes, dear wife, but it also weighs me down to such a degree that I have no desire for anything*, he wrote to Annemarie. *More than anything, though, my concern is for you and the thought that you may not be able to handle the burden and the separation anymore.*

Several of the letters Annemarie sent to Warsaw in the early weeks of the new year reinforced his concerns. Hosenfeld desperately searched for a solution, but found none. In addition, his wife had to deal with more bad news. Helmut, who had been studying medicine, received his induction order, although it was to be effective in three months' time. What Annemarie hoped to postpone had now become a reality. In a letter to Wilm, she wrote: *Now my boy must become a soldier. We have to let him go to an unknown fate, maybe to his death.* This was too much for her. On January 20, 1941, she wrote:

> *I cannot pray anymore. The day comes, the day goes. I no longer expect anything from anyone. The children do not have a dear mother, almost nothing touches me any longer. Maybe I'm physically at the end of my strength. I could have cried yesterday.* [I was] *touched that other people wanted to be good to me, the relatives, the foreign officer.*

This letter, like some others, was a snapshot of her absolute despair. Time and again, she had to overcome her desperation in order to endure everyday life in Thalau. The "foreign officer" she referred to in the letter was a first lieutenant whom she had met by chance in Fulda. He invited her to the cinema and a café and apparently tried to court her. Annemarie let it happen. She related the meeting to her husband: *We enjoyed a nice afternoon. He told me about the campaign on France, captivating and clear, and I listened to him with pleasure. He has a certain resemblance to you, I value that in him, and then again he is also like Gerd* [her brother]. As they parted, he even kissed her. *I know that you absolutely cannot be jealous*, Annemarie wrote. *But still, a strange man should not kiss me.*

There is no sign Wilm Hosenfeld directly reacted to this letter. Instead, several lines he wrote to Annemarie may be interpreted as admonition: *I hope that you are fully roused again, strong and brave, and understand and withstand the repulsive nature of our time.* At the same time, he expressed his understanding of her wish to break free of her constraints and, in his words, to feel the *pulse of the time.*

Despite the separation brought about by the war, Hosenfeld's family remained his focal point. He would have seen a dissolution of his family as his greatest personal defeat. That is why, even from Warsaw, he made such an effort to hold things together. He sent letters and presents to his children on special occasions, for example. On January 25, he wrote to his eldest daughter, Anemone, on the occasion of her 17th birthday:

> *When I see the children on the street, sometimes they go to school, and then I follow them and listen to them talking, even though I don't understand what they are saying. Instinctively, I think, those could be our little girls. One thing always satisfies, and that is the thought that you are doing well, that you are safe from the war and don't have to experience the terrible suffering of so many families, as I see here at every turn.*

Hosenfeld often met schoolchildren. His work occasionally took him to two German schools in Warsaw. He also visited Polish private schools to ascertain accommodation space for the Wehrmacht. In one instance, Hosenfeld's visit caused a panic because the director, a nun, thought he was a Gestapo official. He managed to quickly calm her down.

Second lieutenant Wilm Hosenfeld with Polish children in September 1940.

***

By describing his routine and various activities in detail, Hosenfeld allowed his wife to experience his daily life. As duty officer, he was responsible for everything and everyone. In one letter, Hosenfeld wrote:

> *The telephone rings constantly. Here a soldier has an accident and requires an ambulance; there a deserter is arrested. One department asks if today is a public holiday and if the teams have leave until 12 o'clock. Another wants to exchange German money into Polish currency and asks where he can do this. The courier wants the courier mail. I've been called and have to pick up classified documents at the army supreme command. A senior executive officer contacts me from Kraków; he wants an accommodation prepared, as do 15 soldiers. A general of the medical corps had an accident between x-y, send a car immediately. Two drunk soldiers are in a bar and destroying everything. Notify the field police. . . .*

Hosenfeld also wrote about his visits to the cinema. Regarding a film about Otto von Bismarck, he commented the movie was ideal for world-history classes. *I liked it very much*, Hosenfeld wrote. *Do you know what I really don't like anymore about these patriotic films? The militarism, the belligerence. And how I would have been captivated by that in the past. The weekly newsreels, with their extensive coverage of the war, don't interest me anymore.*

Concerning the film *Victory in the West*, which glorified the Battle of France with material from weekly newsreels, Hosenfeld wrote in his journal: *Nothing significant that one doesn't already know about the war. The entire thing is a stringing together of film documents. [It is] one-sided; the awfulness of war was not shown for reasons of propaganda.* His initial admiration for the string of victories in the West made way for a certain reflectiveness. Hosenfeld also distanced himself from Hitler, as demonstrated by his reaction to the chancellor's speech on February 24, 1941, at the Public Brewery in Munich.

Hosenfeld disapproved of Hitler's self-admiration and belittlement of Germany's previous rulers. *This was arrogant and unfair*, Hosenfeld wrote. *The German nation is now stuck in a straitjacket from which it cannot free itself. This is the only reason that the so-called great unity is possible. One should not be fooled and believe that it is an ideal consensus or even an increased one.* This insight, however, did not keep him from believing Hitler's Germany would be victorious. Hosenfeld thought political matters in Europe would be arranged in such a manner that a long period of peace would follow.

In a letter to Helmut, Wilm Hosenfeld noted that of all the things Hitler wrote about in his book, *Mein Kampf* (*My Struggle*), a surprisingly large number had already been realized. He expected *a confrontation with the Russian government*, hence with communism, in the future. Furthermore, Hosenfeld wrote, the issue of the Jews would be solved. *After Hitler, there will no longer be a Jew in Europe*, he observed. A shocking sentence, the meaning of which became more apparent to him with each passing month.

However, Hosenfeld's allegiance and faith in a Nazi victory only started to waver when he became aware of the extent of the crimes committed in his immediate surroundings. On March 3, he saw inside the Warsaw Ghetto for the first time. The Wehrmacht had a storeroom with beds, mattresses, tables, and chairs in one of the cordoned-off neighborhoods. Hosenfeld arranged to have needed furniture transported to a school in the Praga district, where new accommodations for soldiers were being set up. What he saw in the ghetto deeply shocked him. *Terrible conditions, an absolute indictment against us*, Hosenfeld wrote. *The people vegetate and starve. Like in an anthill, they crawl through filthy streets. In tatters and poverty-stricken.* [The] *Jewish Ghetto Police resorts to drastic measures.*

***

The people in the ghetto were cut off from their previous lives and now found themselves caught in a surreal world, one that initially had

Wilm Hosenfeld on horseback leading troops through the streets of Warsaw.

the appearance of normalcy. Jews had been able to go to restaurants and cafés. There were theater performances and cinema showings. Those who still had money or other valuables enjoyed themselves for as long as possible. At the same time, a paralyzing uncertainty about the future held sway. The thought that something terrible would happen was a perpetual nightmare, Władysław Szpilman wrote. In the "Small Ghetto," where the Szpilman family lived, conditions were initially halfway tolerable. Intellectuals and wealthy bourgeoisie mostly lived there. As Szpilman wrote, the "Small Ghetto" *was proportionately less lice-infected with pests exterminated, compared to the Large Ghetto.*

The actual horrors played out elsewhere, namely in the "Large Ghetto." There, in northern Warsaw, the narrow, fetid alleys and streets were overcrowded with, as Wilm Hosenfeld described, *seething masses of poor Jews who lived in wretchedness, in filthy and cramped spaces.* Raids and arbitrary arrests were common throughout the Jewish district. Young men were taken from their homes by the SS and Gestapo and sent to construction sites, where Jews almost always had to do the dirtiest and most dangerous work. Władysław Szpilman tried to avoid such laborious jobs since he was concerned about his hands. A single injury or broken wrist would have ultimately ended his already jeopardized career.

Having access to information was extremely important in the ghetto. Szpilman described the fate of a man whom he regularly visited because the man always had the latest news. Jehuda Zyskind, both a master of the art of living and an optimist, smuggled media publications into the ghetto. He was also in contact with underground groups, which he supplied with writings. Zyskind was a giant of a man and worked as a janitor, driver, salesman, smuggler, and street organizer. Whenever Szpilman had a bleak outlook on the future, became despondent about life in the ghetto, and could no longer see reason in his existence, Zyskind, in just a few sentences, gave him reason for optimism. Jehuda Zyskind, who had so often bolstered Szpilman's courage, was murdered during the winter of 1942. Szpilman wrote of the incident: *Stacks of secret material were lying on the table, and Jehuda and [his] wife and children were sorting them. They were all, including the small three-year-old Symche, shot right there and then.*

The Szpilman family's material situation deteriorated after only a few months. Everything, including jewelry and the piano, was sold on the black market in order to secure their survival. Although he experienced life in the ghetto as a millstone he had to move every day to continue living, Szpilman prodded himself along. He had to earn money to ensure the survival of his family. *I began my wartime career as a pianist in the Café "Nowoczesna," which was situated directly in the center of the ghetto on Nowolipki Street*, Szpilman wrote. The route to the café led through narrow alleys and along part of the ghetto wall. He encountered squalid people, beggars, and smugglers at every turn.

So-called smuggler kings, who were still able to afford luxury items, had the run of the café. Szpilman's music was of little interest to anyone. Sometimes, he was even asked to stop playing. People had important things to discuss and could barely hear their own words.

The pianist jumped at the first opportunity to move to a different venue. At the new venue, a café on Sienna Street, Jewish intellectuals who frequented the establishment appreciated Szpilman's music.

Regulars at the café included painters, scientists, and teachers. This was also where Szpilman first met Janusz Korczak, the author and educator who had previously founded orphanages and garnered a favorable reputation with his book and donation campaigns on behalf of orphaned children. Korczak continued his mission in the ghetto, into which he had voluntarily gone. *Back then, when we spoke with him in the sauna, we had not yet suspected that his magnificent life, with such a bright passion, would end,* Szpilman wrote. Korczak later died alongside his children.

One day, Szpilman witnessed a young boy trying to crawl back into the ghetto through an opening in the wall. The child had already pushed his things through the hole. However, he got caught on a piece of the wall and started screaming. Szpilman pulled on the small body with all his strength. On the other side of the wall, a police officer had noticed the child and beat him. When the musician finally managed to free the child, he died in Szpilman's arms. The officer had shattered the boy's spine.

Jews forced to move into the Warsaw Ghetto.

***

Polish children also suffered from hunger and terrible poverty outside the ghetto. Hosenfeld's quarters were located on the ground floor of a military compound. The windows were barred with iron rods. Early in the morning, children came to his window and begged for food. Sometimes it became too much for Hosenfeld and he tried to chase them away. But he then thought of his own children and cut off a piece of bread and gave it to two girls. *I could not resist them,* Hosenfeld wrote. When he was out and about on Sundays, he would sometimes take several slices along, so he would not be empty-handed if any children approached him.

When he saw beggars, Hosenfeld was not able to simply walk past them. Many people came and went near the Vistula Bridge that led to the Wehrmacht hospital. There, he saw a blind man asking pedestrians for help. With the blind man was, as Hosenfeld described, a boy with *terrible scars on his face*, a woman with a small child on her lap, and another person with two small girls who were singing hymns. All of them were obviously in great distress and hoping for alms.

In early March 1941, Warsaw was the scene of a situation Hosenfeld found upsetting. The Polish director and actor Igo Sym had been courted by the occupation force and commissioned to build a German-language theater in Warsaw. He was shot dead in his home on March 7, apparently by a member of the Polish underground army. Sym was viewed as a Nazi collaborator. He had helped prepare for the film *Heimkehr* and was responsible for hiring the actors. This is where Hosenfeld got to know him. Two days after Sym's murder, Hosenfeld wrote to his wife: *Thereupon, several hundred hostages were taken with the threat that they would be shot if the perpetrator would not step forward by this evening.* Reich Minister of Propaganda Joseph Goebbels, who had commissioned the film, intervened. Most likely on his orders, 21 of the hostages were shot.

The revenge act was discussed a few days later in Eduard Luckhaus's office in the Brühl Palace at Warsaw district administration headquarters. A first lieutenant present was of the opinion that too few Poles had been shot for the murder of Igo Sym. In comparable situations, the English and French had reacted much more harshly. Hosenfeld noted in his journal: *These are such naïve brains. If we put ourselves on this low level, then the nations would attain the nouveau of cannibals. The nations would have to take turns exterminating one another.*

***

During the spring of 1941, signs that Germany was preparing to attack the Soviet Union increased. Hosenfeld was aware of the changes in his surroundings: among other things, the massing of troops and simultaneous withdrawal of parts of his battalion. Hosenfeld took this to mean there would be war with the Soviet Union in the summer. *Since this is expected to last for a longer time, we will want to secure an economic basis with the Ukraine and the Donets Basin,* he wrote. *Russia remains a constant threat to us, ignoring contractual agreements by not delivering what was agreed upon* [and] *reorganizing its army. And* [it] *stands in opposition to us, anyway.* Once again, Hosenfeld's attitude mirrored the German propaganda. The Soviet Union neither represented a threat to Germany nor did it break agreements. On the contrary, it was the German side that did not deliver industrial goods as agreed.

There were additional pieces of news aside from indicators of a forthcoming Eastern campaign. Hosenfeld was appointed to sports officer at Warsaw military headquarters. In addition to control over the guard duty and various organizational assignments, he was now officially in charge of the sports facilities.

As an aside, he found out that the Wien-Film Company had, as planned, completed building the set for *Heimkehr*. When filming was finally due to start, a thaw set in and the picturesque snowy panorama melted away. Actors and the entire crew left without having started their work. Over 100,000 Reichsmark (approximately $40,161) were wasted.

The prospect of another home leave in the second half of March was a much more positive situation. The news from Thalau sounded as though Hosenfeld no longer had to constantly worry. Annemarie was of a better mindset, although she had to overcome several difficult weeks when Jorinde and Uta ran high fevers. This resulted in many sleepless nights for their mother. Sometimes, Annemarie longed for Worpswede, for her mostly carefree childhood. *Life is wondrous,* Annemarie wrote in a letter to her husband. *I'm in no mood to work. I want to be a young girl again and run through the fields with bare legs and lie in the sun and dream away the days and in the evenings sit with men and listen to music and poems.*

But the reality in her part of the world was a different one. In the same letter, dated March 7, she reported on the funeral of an old man from Thalau who had been greatly respected by the locals. She wrote:

> *The people sang and prayed, the relatives cried, and amid all of that peace you could hear the incessant thunder of cannons. Strong-boned, sluggish with rough facial characteristics, these peasant people stood there. I would have liked to draw them, these austere, plain, hard workers! How foreign and fragile I am amid them and already [have] lived with them for 14 years!*

7

Sports and Gas Officer

The spring of 1941 gave Annemarie Hosenfeld new energy. She was not able to completely blank out the war—some days the news stories about the successes of the German military in North Africa and the Balkans came thick and fast. Nonetheless, she loved seeing nature come back into bloom. In a letter to her husband, she wrote: *I am finding much more pleasure in the work outside. . . . The birds are chirping, my small girls are playing near me, the sky is blue and sunny, and above all, there lies an endless peace. The fruit trees carry thick buds and all the bushes are already covered in a thick green.*

The letters she continued to regularly send to Warsaw also described the pranks the children played on her and the fun they had together. A new domestic helper was once again available to Annemarie. She needed this assistance because her father, Karl Krummacher, came to Thalau for a three-week visit in May. The artist contributed to the merriment and entertainment of the household by telling the children stories of Worpswede. He was happy to read aloud one of his texts to neighboring families. However, he was also a demanding person and did not mince words. He reproached his daughter that the marriage had made her intellectually stiff. *But what good would it do him, of all people, if I were able to entertain him with literary recitals,* Annemarie wrote. *The room would be cold, the shoes not clean, and he would have to do without his porridge and all the other things.*

However, she sometimes did long for intellectual endeavors and, for example, the opportunity to describe the people and landscapes in her immediate surroundings. The intensity of experiencing things often amazed Annemarie. A snatch of nature would be enough to enchant her. *A field with marsh marigolds and a blue sky, and I am intoxicated with joy for a few hours,* she wrote. *Not always, certainly not always.*

She applied her writing talent in the many letters she composed during the war. On one hand, she would always find new ways to lament her separation from Wilm Hosenfeld: *How distant and foreign your current life is to me; how bitter it is for me not to be able to share anything with you. I don't know what fate still demands of me. Sometimes I think that I died long ago and a ghost image lives in my body, a body that is searching for a soul, but the soul is gone.* On the other, she expressed her endless love and unquenched longing for him in moving words. A few lines from him were enough to raise her from a gloomy mood. In one letter, she wrote: *You really made me very happy with your dear, dear letter. I also want to be with you, to take your face in my hands and kiss your warm lips and your soft, dark hair and your eyes and tell you that your home is always with me.* The couple had to resign themselves to the possibility the war and their separation would last for years. *Resignation is the right word because I do not make this sacrifice voluntarily or with pleasure or with understanding,* Annemarie wrote.

Annemarie intently followed the events around her. Military convoys were on the streets in and around Thalau. She witnessed how the school doctor examined a boy in light of a possible forced sterilization permitted under Nazi law for the "prevention of genetically diseased offspring." A female teacher tried to protect the child from the procedure; she said that while he was not particularly smart, he would be very hardworking later in his life. The physician asked the boy to name the capital of Italy. When there was no answer, he instructed the nurse to schedule the boy for sterilization.

In several letters she wrote in May 1941, Annemarie commented on her acquaintance with the first lieutenant she had met a few weeks earlier in Fulda. The relationship with Hans Müller (his name has been changed here) should have long since ended. Müller usually arranged to meet Annemarie in Fulda where they would go to concerts and theater performances. Her two eldest children, Helmut and Anemone, were not pleased about their mother's contact with the officer and voiced their feelings. *He is not a typical person*, Annemarie wrote about Müller. *He is sensitive and good; he is manly and honest.* In a letter dated May 19, she promised her husband she would always be forthright with him. She could certainly understand he did not want to hear anything about Müller. And if Annemarie's children objected that their mother had a friendship with another man, then she would do without it. *Don't be angry with me*, she wrote to her husband. *You really have no reason to be because I wrote him that this meant we would never again see each other, and he will respect that. It was not easy for me to hurt him.*

Barely three weeks later, she asked her husband to approve the friendship. Annemarie wrote:

> *He is in Fulda and yesterday evening we went to a concert. I met several friends there. I get along very well with him and am getting to know him as a mature and good person with diverse interests. Very often we speak about you, and he would very much like to get to know you. . . . Dear Wilm, can you not understand that I enjoy being with a person who understands me and can relate to me? Did you not also have friends in Poland,* [the] *Pruts and Luckhaus*[es] *and so on. Can you not understand that sometimes you need a person to prop you up?*

In a letter to Helmut, Wilm Hosenfeld attempted to dispel any fears that his parents were drifting apart. *For instance, I have told Mother that I have various friends here, among them a woman, whom I highly regard, without taking it any further,* he wrote. *This was very difficult for Mother and she worried that it would endanger our domestic bliss. Mother's relationship with the first lieutenant was equally irrelevant.* Hosenfeld further assured Helmut that love for his wife had actually increased through the separation. There were few marriages as harmonious and happy as theirs, he insisted. Occasional conflicts were nothing unusual given their opposite characters and contrasting dispositions.

***

A rift never developed between his parents, as Helmut had worried, nor was there a lasting alienation. In any case, there was no shortage of other events to claim the Hosenfelds' full attention, including the spectacular flight to Scotland of Rudolf Hess, who was third in command in Nazi Germany. He claimed he had been sent by Hitler to make a peace offering. Hess was immediately arrested. He was later convicted and sentenced to life imprisonment at the Nuremberg Trials. Hess's flight caused quite an uproar everywhere. Annemarie reported that people in Fulda were arrested for making careless statements about the event. She considered Hess to be a decent, sympathetic person.

When initial reports mentioned a crash, Hosenfeld immediately had his doubts. He discussed the event with other officers in the casino and joked that Hess probably wanted to go to England. This was soon confirmed. The version of the story told by Hitler, that Hess was mentally disturbed, seemed suspicious. Hosenfeld wrote: *Someone who is mentally disturbed is not capable of flying to Scotland, and a person with a clear mind must tell himself that he is causing tremendous damage to his fatherland without achieving anything.*

While discussions about Hess's mysterious flight continued, preparations for the campaign on the Eastern Front were in full swing. Hosenfeld no longer had any doubts an attack on the Soviet Union was merely a few weeks away. On the way to his guard post, Hosenfeld noticed increasingly more troops crossing the Vistula Bridge on their way east. *I got out and spent one hour watching the men passing by*, he wrote. *What lies ahead for them? I would have liked to go with them.*

For days, he heard the rumbling of military vehicles and hoofbeats of horses. Hosenfeld could hardly escape the sight of the troop columns. He observed:

> *I walk next to the marching soldiers. I want to shake the hands of these brave fellows. They have already marched 30 kilometers* [about 19 miles]*, and they are supposed to continue marching through the*

night. From his accent, I recognize the sergeant on the horse as coming from Hesse. Next to him is a saddled horse with no rider. With one leap I would be in the saddle.

The fact the soldiers were entering a war whose initial aim was complete destruction was not something Hosenfeld could have known in the spring of 1941. Although he had plenty of duties, as he watched the troop deployments he felt there was nothing holding him in Warsaw. From Hosenfeld's perspective, the only two possibilities were a return to Thalau or a deployment to the front, *so that I can find a deeper meaning for the separation from you, one whose effort, marching, and deprivation awaits us.* Because he was still physically fit, the 45-year-old did not consider himself too old for such a task. Hosenfeld wrote to Annemarie:

I can never remove the thorn of having to live and experience without you. When I look across the wide water, and the white sails and ships appear, the seagulls and swallows fly overhead, in the willow bush a nightingale sings. How wonderful it would be to sit here with you and to feel your hand in mine and to hear our hearts beating together! But like this, everything appears bleak and soulless.

One reason Hosenfeld did not get a chance to serve on the front was because his superiors would not let him go. They wrote glowing references, but did not want to do without his organizational skills and military competence in Warsaw. The battalion commander thusly justified Hosenfeld's promotion to first lieutenant: [He is a] *mentally alert and versatile officer, who has proven himself as a recruit instructor, platoon leader, and deputy company commander.* Hosenfeld's regimental commander similarly appraised him: *Military skills very good. Energetic, confident demeanor in front of the troops. Good instructor. Has proven himself as deputy company commander.*

The regimental commander particularly wanted to keep Hosenfeld in Warsaw because of the sports program. Hosenfeld organized numerous competitions for the national day of sports on May 25, 1941. Sports teams composed of the SS, police, and Hitler Youth all participated. Concerning the day's speeches held in the stadium, he wrote: *The addresses do not touch the heart. The police colonel cannot do it, and neither can the member of the Hitler Youth.*

In a letter to his wife on May 31, Hosenfeld described his responsibilities as sports officer:

> *The sports association of the headquarters covers about 20 different units, all of which I look after. They are in and around Warsaw. In addition, I am responsible for the management and supervision of the sports facilities. Above all, though, the actual sporting activity is my responsibility, so track and field, football, handball, tennis, swimming, water sports. There is endless running around, in between reporting to the commander or a deputy. . . . Tomorrow is the opening of the swimming pool and the boathouse, combined with the competitions.*

The boathouse was located near the Vistula River. Rowing and sailing were part of the program Hosenfeld gradually established, which was soon used by many soldiers.

Hosenfeld clashed with the sports commissioner of the General Government, Dr. Niffka, who was his point of contact with the German civilian authority in occupied Poland. Niffka asked Hosenfeld to ensure the Polish national insignia was removed from the sports stadium. He was of the opinion that all traces of the Polish state should be removed, including memorials to the composer Frédéric Chopin and the poet Adam Mickiewicz. Hosenfeld responded the Germans should honor the intellectual accomplishments of a nation, even if they were at war with that country. It would be more fitting for a cultured nation to respect monuments instead of destroying them. Anything else would represent a return to barbarianism. Hosenfeld commented in his journal: *The people believe that the war can be won with such arrogance.* His writings do not indicate if he was successful in convincing Niffka to keep the Polish insignia intact.

Hosenfeld's criticism of the Nazi system increased in clarity and severity. He was appalled by the German film *Ohm Krüger* (*Uncle Krüger*), one of the most popular movies of the 1940s. The theme of the film was the brutal war of the British against the South African Boers. Hosenfeld questioned what gave Germany the right to make such a clearly anti-British propaganda film. He wrote:

> *Isn't the extermination campaign against the Polish, not to mention the Jews, exactly the same? It is safe to say that everything that is of use to us, regardless if it is a lie or hypocrisy, can be used for war propaganda. It will no doubt achieve its desired result with the majority of the German masses, to paint the English as monsters. But why did the Führer make such great efforts to secure the friendship with England? Were these not the same English back in 1933, 1938? The Bolsheviks have remained the same as well.*

A war of extermination against the Poles and Jews—this journal entry could not have been clearer.

Wehrmacht soldiers playing soccer at a Warsaw sports complex in 1941.

***

In his new role as gas defense officer, which he carried out alongside his sports responsibilities, Hosenfeld went to Pabianice for a training course in the last week of May 1941. As he got off the streetcar he ran into the daughter of the Prut family, who invited him home to her parents. The reunion with his friends was so affectionate and lighthearted he made the spontaneous decision to stay.

Hosenfeld was supposed to reside on the factory grounds he had previously converted into a Polish POW camp during his time there. The buildings were now used to house resettled Volhynia Germans, whose fate had been exploited for propaganda in the film *Heimkehr*. These ethnic Germans, who had settled in Volhynia (the former Polish, and current Ukrainian, region) were waiting for new accommodations in the Wartheland region.

When Hosenfeld went to the camp he was overcome with his memories of the prisoners who had begged for bread at the gate before he organized food for them. He also recalled the church services in the camp that had deeply touched him. The Polish gatekeeper immediately recognized Hosenfeld. The man and his wife were happy to see him, and enthusiastically greeted him. The sight of the Volhynia Germans who lived in the factory buildings nevertheless depressed Hosenfeld. These people, who were now considered ethnic Germans, were obviously poorly cared for and deeply worried about their future.

Walking through Pabianice, Hosenfeld noticed most of the businesses had been taken over by Germans. *There are still enough Polish here, but, as everywhere else, they are not doing well*, he wrote. *They timidly move aside.* Hosenfeld's path took him through the ghetto with its approximately 8,000 Jews. An old man with a coarse, almost disfigured, face took his suitcase while a Jewish police officer showed him the way. *Hundreds of Jews passed us, always pulling their caps from their head, some already removed it 10 steps before and then performed a humble bow*, Hosenfeld wrote. *They are happy to be allowed to work; they make aviator uniforms,* [and] *they also receive food and are paid.* Whoever did not obey, though, was taken to the ghetto in Łódź, named "Ghetto Litzmannstadt" after the German general Karl Litzmann, a Hitler supporter.

The German occupiers amassed around 200,000 Jews in Łódź. The conditions there were as catastrophic as in the Warsaw Ghetto. A transfer to Łódź meant death through work, a fact that had long since made the rounds. This is why, during his walk through the ghetto in Pabianice, Hosenfeld had the impression the Jews were satisfied with their lot. The Pabianice Ghetto itself existed only until May 1942. Most of its inhabitants ended up in the Chełmno extermination camp. Those remaining were Jews still capable of work. They were transported from Pabianice to Łódź for forced labor before eventually being killed.

***

When Hosenfeld returned to his post, Warsaw resembled an occupied city. Getting through streets and in public places was nearly impossible. Military vehicles blocked traffic everywhere. Even the trams got stuck in the city center. Hosenfeld endeavored to keep the sports operation running. Some days there were so many things to do he had difficulty managing everything. Hosenfeld's helpfulness resulted in many things landing on his desk, things for which he was not even responsible, like requests for sportswear and equipment. These were matters for the civilian administration.

My journal is full of empty pages, Hosenfeld wrote. *Today,* [June 12, 1941] *I see that it is Corpus Christi! How far removed is this world that extolled by these words. Like a distant, beautiful magic, an almost unreal dream of a better world raises the memory of this day in me.* Soon thereafter, he held a photo of his daughter Jorinde in his hand, in which she is wearing a white dress during the Corpus Christi procession. The picture moved Hosenfeld to tears. When his son Detlev informed him of the meager prospects of the honey harvest, he responded: *I am happy that the garden and all the fruit trees are in such beautiful bloom. How I would love to be home now, working in the garden and the bee house, but there is no possibility of vacation at the moment. Nobody knows what the future will bring for us. Everything is up for grabs.*

Wilm Hosenfeld wrote to his son Helmut about a long discussion he had with a lance corporal who wanted to join the SS. Hosenfeld urgently advised the 19-year-old against it, and wrote how regretful it was that young people were so filled with hatred. Young people, Hosenfeld insisted, no longer had a clear understanding of events and could not distinguish right from wrong. He also gave Helmut, who was still in basic training, advice for the "army business": he should never show his inner superiority and instead always explicitly answer with "yes." Hosenfeld understood his son's wish to take up arms as soon as possible, but added there were more important things. He wrote: *Take advantage of the opportunities that are consistent with your profession and may be useful to you in becoming a good doctor.*

The worldwide uncertainty and tension that had built up in anticipation of a German invasion of Russia was finally unleashed when the Wehrmacht began its attack on June 22, 1941. *War with Russia!* Hosenfeld wrote on that day. Instead of the often alleged peaceful solution, Hitler's wish of military confrontation had been granted. *A radical solution must be found and this can only happen through violent means,* Hosenfeld wrote. He described the military situation in a letter to Helmut. The time had come, Hosenfeld believed, to put an end to both Bolshevism and the last great continental power. He was certain England would remain the bitterest of German enemies and the United States would soon declare war. The subjugation of the Soviet Union opened up the possibility to reshape the Eastern Region. *I am just now sitting at the radio and listening to the propaganda company reports about the first battles. Our invasion is an enormous assault and the Russians have been awaiting it for weeks.*

Hosenfeld was, however, wrong. Stalin had in fact received reliable information from various sources about an impending German invasion. But he paid these warnings no heed, relying instead on the "nonaggression" pact signed in August 1939 in which the two countries agreed to take no military action against each other for the next 10 years. It is also conceivable Stalin did not want to provide Hitler with any grounds for military action. Additionally, the Soviet dictator had ordered the execution of thousands of his own officers in 1937 after receiving misinformation that the high command of the Red Army was planning a coup. Thus, the leadership of the Soviet armed forces was extensively weakened. Regardless, the advance of over 3 million German soldiers caught the Soviet Union unprepared, leading to heavy losses inflicted on the 2.9 million-strong Red Army during the initial months of battle.

The thunder of cannons on the front lines could be clearly heard in Warsaw. Hosenfeld expected Soviet air raids on the Polish capital, and he did not have to wait long for the first bombings. *I see clouds of smoke rising from the veranda*, he wrote. *Right after that two Russian planes come again. Very high. The first wounded have already arrived here. Now that war has also arrived.* Near the airport, a packed streetcar was hit by a bomb. More than 80 passengers immediately died. In terror, the Polish residents recalled the German air attacks of September 1939. Special bulletins about the Wehrmacht's quick advance led Hosenfeld to believe the military operation would last only several weeks. In a letter, he told Helmut that he would, in all probability, not be needed for the Eastern campaign because of the speed by which the German troops advanced.

***

By now, Hosenfeld had come to accept the war on the Eastern Front would take place without him. Instead, he trained soldiers to compete for the German Reich Sports Badge, which included tests in running, discus and javelin throwing, swimming, and other disciplines. At the end of June 1941, he traveled to Berlin to participate in a training course for sports judges at the Reich Academy for Physical Education. On his first day, Hosenfeld visited the facilities built for the 1936 Summer Olympics, including the mighty Olympic stadium and the "House of Sports" with the Reich Academy for Physical Education. *That is a vast complex, wonderfully equipped. During the next days, I will come to know all of this closely*, he wrote to his daughter Anemone.

On July 4, Annemarie arrived in Berlin. Her husband had informed her about the training course early on and suggested she set aside some money for the trip. The training program allowed enough free time for them to spend time together on outings. They went to the cinema and theater and visited monuments, among them the memorial to the fallen soldiers of World War I on *Unter den Linden* Boulevard. Wreaths had been placed at the monument for the German soldiers who had died on the Eastern Front. The atmosphere of the memorial, erected in 1931, awakened Hosenfeld's memories of the battles he had participated in between 1914 and 1917.

Hosenfeld completed his training sessions and theoretical lessons before noon each day. During breaks, the impressive early successes on the Eastern Front were eagerly discussed. The Supreme High Command of the Wehrmacht still exaggerated the achievements, leading to a sense of elation among the course participants. Some were already drawing up plans for the future layout of Europe under one single great power: Hitler's Germany. Hosenfeld was of the opinion this was neither unusual nor new. *Napoleon had similar plans*, Hosenfeld wrote, *but today we have a different power and larger impact forces.*

Annemarie stayed in Berlin for a week. Then, their paths diverged once more. She left Berlin heading west back to Thalau, with her husband going east to Warsaw.

***

Back in Warsaw, Hosenfeld busied himself with preparations for the Fighting Games of the Wehrmacht, which were due to take place later in the summer. He had only just started when he had to leave for a three-week training course at the military gas defense school in Celle, Germany. Because of his own experiences with gas attacks in World War I, Hitler placed a special emphasis on gas defense.

Hosenfeld found this rather annoying. He had no interest in gasmasks and various chemical warfare agents in crisis situations. Although he had not volunteered for this additional task, the trip to Celle on July 23, 1941, afforded Wilm the opportunity to see his family. His wife decided to visit him and planned to bring along Detlev, Jorinde, and Uta—all of whom he longed to see. The four of them arrived in Celle at the end of July. The night before their arrival, Hosenfeld again experienced dizzy spells, which he only confided to his journal. The family was together for almost two weeks. Then, Annemarie and the children returned home to Thalau.

Wilm, Detlev, and Annemarie Hosenfeld (*front, left to right*) bidding farewell to Helmut (*second row, left*) in August 1941.

Wilm Hosenfeld changed his travel plans when he found out during a phone conversation that Helmut, who was in Erfurt, would soon be transferred to the Eastern Front. The two of them immediately met. Annemarie also came with Detlev. They said their goodbyes on

August 14, 1941. Annemarie stuck a rose into the barrel of Helmut's rifle and said in a pleading, almost commanding tone, "Helmut, you will not shoot at people with this rifle!" Hosenfeld noted: *How happy we are that we are still able to be with the big boy for these short hours. We accompanied him to the transport train. I still see his dear face in front of me, how he is sitting at the carriage door. When the train pulls away I want to run after it and see him one more time. I am filled with a great pain.*

Hosenfeld then allowed himself two days in Thalau before returning to Warsaw. He used the time to harvest honey with Detlev. The peaceful work was good for him. During his return trip, Hosenfeld realized the extent of the new psychological stress in store for his wife. Annemarie had raised the question of what sense there was in some soldiers taking part in sporting activities while others were shot dead. He made an effort during the subsequent weeks to convince her that nothing would happen to their son on the Eastern Front, that Helmut would safely return home. In the meantime, the upcoming Wehrmacht Sports Week in Warsaw was postponed indefinitely. The regular sports operation continued without change.

— 8 —

Tolerance and Compassion

Amid all of Wilm Hosenfeld's activities in Warsaw—which by now were many—management of the sports school began to take center stage during the summer of 1941. He was the gas defense officer and remained responsible for the guard duty. He was busy in the operations room at headquarters on a regular basis, and because of the air raids on Warsaw, was supposed to provide suggestions for an effective air defense strategy. His superior, Major General Walter von Unruh, constantly assigned him new tasks. Apparently, the major general valued Hosenfeld's organizational talent and enthusiasm.

Apart from that, the sports competitions afforded some variety and improved the reputation of the commander's office. Headquarters staff members participated in the swimming and athletic competitions held on August 23 and 24. Hosenfeld was a judge for both events. Receptions were also hosted by representatives of the civilian administration of the General Government. Hosenfeld informed his wife that, as a sports officer, he spent time with people from the highest circles. *Previously, I was somewhat inhibited, but now I can move about as a matter of course*, he wrote. *When one is a bit critical, you see behind the wallpaper right away and become more self-confident.* Hosenfeld also told his son Helmut: *I now have a real school, just as I always wished for.*

In autumn 1941, officers and teams were given the opportunity to participate in a sports training course. Preparations for the course were elaborate. Hosenfeld found a sports teacher to instruct the practical aspects of the course. He also brought in scientists and doctors from Germany for the teacher's seminar and presented several lectures himself. This was the first-ever training course of its kind in the General Government, and it caused quite a stir. After receiving inquiries from Kraków and other Polish cities, Hosenfeld had the idea to offer such courses elsewhere, too.

***

As much as the sports activities demanded of him, Hosenfeld's attention was especially focused on the German troops' advance against the Soviet Union. After all, his son Helmut was serving on the Eastern Front. By mid-September 1941, Hosenfeld's initial excitement for the Wehrmacht's successes gave way to skepticism. He had underestimated the fighting morale of the Red Army, instead expecting an overthrow of the communist system. The triumph of the German forces on the Western Front against small countries and war-weary France had led Hosenfeld to an incorrect conclusion, he realized. *In Russia, we are meeting an enemy that is numerically superior and well-equipped,* Hosenfeld wrote. *On top of that, the enormous area comes to his [Russia's] aid. If the outcome is not decided in our favor by fall, we will lose the fight in the East.*

Hosenfeld told his wife the war would last for a long time—a quick resolution in the East should not be expected. Of course, he continued to try to calm her fears. *You do not have to worry so much,* he wrote. *I am going through the same as you. At night you are a different person, and when you are lying in bed the most terrible thoughts come over you.*

Annemarie regularly kept him informed about people from the village or their relatives and friends who had perished. Such news would lead to sleepless nights for her. She also asked her husband how the pastoral letter written by the German Catholic military bishop, Franz Justus Rarkowski, should be understood. Rarkowski had described the war against the Soviet Union as a necessary crusade. Hosenfeld replied that he dismissed the term "crusade." After all, the National Socialists were persecuting Christians in their own country. Hosenfeld did not consider the countries invaded by Germany to be enemies. He wrote:

I have no hate against neither the Polish nor the Russians. How quickly all of that drops away, once you stand across from the people. There are captured Russians who were brought by a transport convoy. The soldiers treated them as if they were their workmates. Except for the uniforms, there would be no difference.

Hosenfeld's attitude toward the "enemy" and the people persecuted by the Nazi leadership was governed by respect, tolerance, and deep compassion. Following a short visit with the Prut family in Pabianice, he wrote in his journal: *He* [Joachim Prut] *does not believe in or want a German victory. His pride as a Polish officer suffered too much humiliation, and he is flush with burning patriotism. Our personal relationship is not affected by that. I experience ever greater hospitableness.*

In the summer of 1941, Hosenfeld had not yet reached the point of questioning the Nazi system as a whole and viewing it as the agent for the war and crimes being committed. His concern was to help the affected people, if only through small gestures of compassion. On a trip with Colonel von Hohenau to a country estate outside Warsaw, Hosenfeld noticed the SS was employing Jews from the Warsaw Ghetto. They were treated like slaves with the threat of return to the ghetto if they made the smallest mistake. *The boy who took my horse after I had been riding had such a sympathetic face; I gave him a złoty and he thanked me in his best German,* Hosenfeld wrote. *I always feel sympathy toward these people.*

After buying fruit at a Warsaw market, Hosenfeld witnessed an event similar to what Szpilman had experienced on the inside of the ghetto wall. A Jewish boy had crawled through a hole in the wall to smuggle potatoes into the ghetto. A police officer spotted the boy before he was able to crawl to the other side, threw him to the ground, and battered him. Hosenfeld wrote: *I saw the thin, bare legs under his long, baggy coat and the frightened face of the child. The thought came to me that this could be my Detlev. I wanted to get out and give the apples to the boy. I was ashamed that I belong to those who are responsible for such misfortune or who allow it to happen without helping.*

During a two-week vacation in Thalau at the beginning of October, Hosenfeld was informed about another incident that alarmed him. A young Polish forced laborer had been working on a farm in the Rhön Mountains for two years, where she had a reputation as a good worker. One day she forgot to wear the violet "P" emblem on her blouse, which identified her as a Pole. Because of this minor infraction, a German auxiliary police officer beat her to a bloody pulp. The farmer and his wife stood and watched. Hosenfeld wrote: *The most noble impulses of kindness to others and humanity are being exorcized from our youth.* This was only one example of, as Hosenfeld described, *the primitive level of human civilized behavior we have fallen to.*

An important source of information about wartime events and the crimes being committed in the name of Germany were wounded soldiers returning from the Eastern Front. They were being treated in Warsaw hospitals, from where they would return to the front once doctors declared them again fit for duty. In his discussions with them, Hosenfeld heard details about the extent of German casualties, facts systematically withheld from the propaganda. A lance corporal, for instance, told him the threat from partisan fighters in the contested areas had significantly increased. There were acts of sabotage, battles, and mass murders on an almost daily basis. The dreadful shootings of Jews filled Hosenfeld with disgust. Five thousand, including women and children, were shot dead in Gomel, Belarus. *That has nothing to do with war anymore,* he wrote. *This has me feeling paralyzed. Will we and our children suffer the vengeance for this one day?*

In one journal entry, Hosenfeld wrote: *Argument at the lunch table about shootings of Jews and prisoners.* This brief sentence confirms he did not keep this knowledge to himself, and that in conversation with his comrades, Hosenfeld strongly condemned the murder of civilians, Jews, and POWs. Wilm Hosenfeld was not overly cautious. His wife called to his attention that censors had opened some of his letters, but this did not persuade him to be more low-key. He admitted he was concerned about the future. He witnessed a lot of brutality, ignorance, lies, and whitewashing. The war was weighed down by injustice. Propagandists acted as though they were heroes of the written word.

Regarding a speech by Reich Minister of Propaganda Joseph Goebbels, who had once more presaged a Wehrmacht victory over the Soviet Union, Hosenfeld commented: *When one contemplates the misery here in the country and considers that we are not able to master it, that we only govern through terror, hardship, and hunger, then one comes to the realization that this cannot end well.* Had any of his remarks been read by the counterintelligence or Gestapo, they would have been classified as defeatism and Hosenfeld would have been subjected to severe punishment handed down by a military court.

Hosenfeld also made critical comments about the situation in the hospitals in Warsaw. There were not enough doctors, nurses, or medicines. The medical treatment and care of the wounded was completely inadequate. He asked himself, if the care was already insufficient at this stage, how would it be on the Eastern Front, where subzero temperatures were by now normal?

Wehrmacht troops positioned during an offensive on the Eastern Front in 1941. The German soldier on the right is guarding captured Soviet prisoners.

***

Wilm Hosenfeld was now more often being posted to the regional war office across from the main train station in Warsaw. It was here that fighters from the Eastern Front arrived, while fresh replacement troops were sent in the opposite direction. In the process, there were always standstills, causing much congestion. Some of the units from the Eastern Front brought vehicles that needed repair. This meant a longer waiting period for the soldiers. Hosenfeld sent many of them home on vacation without much ado. The young men were, of course, very happy in such cases. For others, he organized a system of supervision so they would not be tempted to do anything foolish, which, in his words, *usually ended at the military court*. His superior, Major General Unruh, was appreciative things ran smoothly at the regional war office.

Swastika flags are wafting from lampposts in the Polish capital, Hosenfeld began a letter to his wife on December 3, 1941. He was referencing German Cultural Week in Warsaw. The occupying forces had organized a number of events to represent German cultural heritage. The program included readings, films, and theater performances. Artists and authors who were on the Nazi regime's good side also appeared. Heinrich George, a popular film and theater actor, recited poetry. Hosenfeld took little pleasure in the cultural week: *I find it has all too many slogans, too much pretension and façade.*

He did, however, watch one of the films. *Ich klage an* (*I Accuse*) was a movie directed by Wolfgang Liebeneiner that had been completed earlier in the year. It used clever plot devices to make a sympathetic case for the Nazis' euthanasia program. Hosenfeld offered an assessment of the film in his journal:

> *From the standpoint of the actors and the technical aspect, this was an excellent film. But now, when millions of young lives are being destroyed by war, supposedly for the greater good, why is there a need for a film that wants to establish the authorization of doctors*

to shorten an incurable life? How unimportant that is in the middle of war. Who will spend their thoughts on that, to surrender so many people, our comrades and our enemies, to death? The fact that captured Russians are being treated so shamefully, even in our home country, letting them almost starve, that is so appalling, inhuman, and so simple-mindedly stupid, that one can only be deeply ashamed that we are allowing this to happen.

Hosenfeld learned from some sources that hundreds of thousands of Soviet POWs had been deliberately left to starve. Annemarie also heard about the prisoners. She wrote: *In Gersfeld, Russians are systematically starving. I'd rather that they cut our butter and bread rations further than to take this endless guilt upon us.*

Similar to her husband, Annemarie was occasionally racked by pure desperation at the massive injustice war brought down upon entire nations. She lamented:

Is there nobody who wants to stand up and show these blinded people the misery! Does nobody have a heart anymore! Can this world never be ruled by love, understanding, goodness, and trust to one another? How willing we all are to sacrifice, to deprive ourselves, so that the brother next to us can also live in peace. Who taught us to hate others whom we don't even know?

Some days, Hosenfeld held a morning service for the soldiers who waited in Warsaw. In plain language, he offered them thoughts about the essentials of life, thoughts they could take along on their way, before returning to the front. In doing so, Hosenfeld noticed the mostly young men were spiritually starved and thankfully listened to him. Away from war and destruction, he, at least temporarily, had the effect of a peacemaker. He felt almost like a pastor, Hosenfeld wrote. He said that next time he was home, he wanted to take literature back to Warsaw with him so he would have material for future morning services.

On December 8, 1941, he faced a new challenge: the second sports training course for officers and teams, which was to last until

December 19. Then, news of the Japanese attack on the American marine base of Pearl Harbor in Hawaii burst onto the scene. The United States reacted by declaring war on Japan. Germany, in turn, declared war on the United States. A new front had been opened—but how many now? Hosenfeld immediately understood what this meant. *The Americans had been instrumental in the outcome of the previous war*, he wrote. *This time they will also decide it to our misfortune.* In Hosenfeld's notebook, which he used for short entries, he revealed another realization: *For Germany, this war is an enormous anti-selection: the best men remain on the battlefield, the scum is preserved. With that, the opposite of what National Socialism and its racist teachings wanted to achieve will occur.*

He wrote to Annemarie that he had been horrified to hear of Hitler's declaration of war against the US. What she and many other Germans feared had now materialized. He had grave concerns about Helmut; however, there was nothing Wilm could do for him. All the same, he fought against a sense of doom that had taken hold of him. If it weren't for his obligation to duty, he would sit in a corner and stare at the wall.

Hosenfeld ended 1941 with his family in Thalau. The general had granted him another home leave; he was the only officer in the entire battalion that had been allowed to go, even though his previous home leave was only two months prior. This exception was no doubt a recognition of Hosenfeld's exceptional service.

— 9 —

Holding the National Socialists Accountable

With the US entry into the war, Wilm Hosenfeld was able to see the defeat of the Wehrmacht earlier and clearer than others. The number of countries with which the Axis Powers were at war had now risen to 26. Nonetheless, Hosenfeld, as a patriot and Christian, yearned for a victory over Stalin and Bolshevism. But conditions were rapidly deteriorating. At the end of 1941, German troops were entrenched near Moscow. They lacked the strength for a decisive attack. It was apparent the Eastern campaign had been poorly prepared. The top military command had not planned for a winter war. The replenishment of weapons, munitions, and fuel was increasingly more difficult. Soldiers suffered the effects of extreme cold. Winter clothing was scarce. The frozen ground made it impossible to dig trenches and shelters.

Reich Minister of Propaganda Joseph Goebbels appealed to the general public to donate warm clothing, blankets, and skis for the soldiers. The collection drive was to begin on December 27 and continue into the first week of January 1942. Packages were quickly assembled in Thalau. Annemarie had the astute foresight to have already sent self-knitted gloves, wristlets, and other wool items to Helmut. She had wanted to provide her son with ski gear as well, but her husband did not agree. *We are providing* [for] *two soldiers, and in my opinion, we are doing enough*, he wrote. In the end, though, she got her wish and also sent the skis.

The year 1942 started off with a surprise for Hosenfeld. He had just gotten used to his duties in Warsaw again when Helmut phoned him from the Praga district, introducing himself as "Private Hosenfeld." Along with two comrades, Helmut was on his way to Kassel, where they were scheduled to take part in a medical training course. Hosenfeld drove into the city to meet them and brought them to the command headquarters. They all spent three days together. The father and son had much to talk about. Helmut described the events on the front, while his father talked about his activities and the sites in Poland. Hosenfeld arranged a dinner with his friends the Schoenes. *The boys really appreciated the sincere hospitality and the great interest about the events of the war,* he observed in his journal. *They were the center of attention all evening and allowed themselves to be served and spoiled like well-behaved children.*

In a letter to his wife, Hosenfeld was enthusiastic about the visit, which had brought him happiness and delight. He wrote in his journal: *We separated like two dear, old comrades. Not as father and son. The gray cloth makes equals of us.* It was probably not only the uniform that had elicited such a heartfelt connection. Hosenfeld gave each of his children a feeling of deep attachment and devotion, even if he could not be with them. Days later, he still lamented he had forgotten to give his son cookies and apples for his journey.

Annemarie was overjoyed to welcome Helmut home to Thalau. *He stood in the kitchen, still wearing his coat, cap, and waist belt. What a joyful reunion!* she wrote. Helmut spoke about the exhausting trip, his time in Warsaw, and again and again about his father. *He enjoyed everything while he was with you,* Annemarie wrote to her husband. *The wonderful sports facilities, your apartment, your job, and also the people that you deal with . . . hold on to him.* She was happy that father and son had the chance to be close. *You can give this son so much and you must be there for him!*

Helmut looked after his siblings while he was in Thalau. He played often with Jorinde and Uta. In the evenings, he studied the Pythagorean theorem and other math assignments with Detlev. Helmut did not think about himself, Annemarie wrote to Wilm, but instead wondered if he did enough to help his siblings.

Wilm and Helmut Hosenfeld in Warsaw in January 1942.

***

In contrast to the hectic pace of the previous year, there was little for Hosenfeld to do at company headquarters for the time being. Due to the harsh winter, the sports operations moved slowly. The training of an "infiltration commando team," which operated independently from the front lines and was active in open terrain, provided some variety in his duties. Hosenfeld took advantage of the idle state of his office to write lengthier entries in his journal, which he always carried in his coat pocket. (Hosenfeld mailed the journal to Thalau in August 1944.) At one point, he criticized the selfishness of the Germans. During the fur and wool collection for the winter relief program, the Germans had taken fur coats, fur collars, and other valuable items from Polish women to keep for themselves.

Reflecting on revolutionary wars, Hosenfeld confronted the ideology and contradictions of the Nazi regime. Similar to the Jacobins in the French Revolution and Bolsheviks in the Russian Revolution, the goal of the Nazis was the eradication and destruction of dissenters. In his journal, Hosenfeld wrote: *Now and then they shoot a certain number, also native Germans, but they cover it up from the public, they confine them in concentration camps, and let them slowly waste away there.* The Nazi system was closely linked with big business, keeping capitalism afloat while preaching socialism. It afforded the right to personal and religious freedoms, while at the same time, it persecuted Christian churches. It spoke of the Führer, and the right of hardworking, personal development—though everything was contingent upon a person being a member of the Nazi Party. *Hitler offers the world peace while simultaneously building up arms at an incredible rate*, Hosenfeld wrote. Hitler announced it was not his intention to assimilate other nations into the German state, but, as Hosenfeld wrote, *what does he do with the Czechs, the Polish,* [and] *the Serbians?*

Hosenfeld's admiration of the Führer had long since dissipated. He disapproved of the malicious attacks on intellectuals, the bourgeoisie, and followers of the German Centre Party, as well as Hitler's tirades against US President Franklin D. Roosevelt and British Prime Minister Winston Churchill. On January 30, 1942, on the anniversary of his ascension to power, Hitler had insulted the leaders as "windbags and drunkards," "miserable lunatics," and "liars." Annemarie also criticized the speech for its verbal abuse and narcissism. Apart from that, she felt: *We can be tremendously proud of our nation. They all do their duty, these German people, and they work and fight and grit their teeth and are willing time and time again to make sacrifices.*

In this context, Wilm Hosenfeld was mindful the National Socialists disregarded their own tenets. The little person was expected to make sacrifices for the overall good of the community in wartime. Even people with physical disabilities were conscripted into the Wehrmacht. Hosenfeld wrote:

> *. . . and in the offices of the party and with the police you see the most*
> *healthy young people working, far removed from the line of fire. What*
> *are they being saved for? They take the property of the Polish and*
> *Jews, make it their own to enjoy, and take pleasure from* [it]. *Some*
> *have nothing to eat, they live in want, and are cold, while others do*
> *not hesitate to take everything for themselves and dissipate in luxury.*

He felt it was an impossible situation that high-ranking military members and civil servants, as well as their wives, had a sufficient number of horses for personal enjoyment while there was an acute shortage on the front.

Overall, Hosenfeld used Hitler's speech to take account of National Socialism. In a letter dated January 22, sent for Anemone's 18th birthday, he again complained about the suffering inflicted on people around him. He also described what he saw outside:

> *Convoys of heavy trucks roll past my window, heading east. Over*
> *there, the smoke-blackened ruins of people's former homes stare at me.*
> *In between them the people of the city are walking, thickly wrapped*
> *against the winter, cold and hungry. Heavy boots of soldiers thudding*
> *on the pavement. The wind carries a distant soldier's song to me. I*
> *sit lonely between the unloving walls.*

Occasionally, Hosenfeld would take part in funerals for fallen soldiers. According to him, up to 20 dead troops were buried in Warsaw each day. Funerals had almost become routine. In one entry, he wrote:

> *Long, deep pits are dug out, the frozen upper layer has to be blown up.*
> *The coffins are successively carried in. The music plays, a delegation*
> *of soldiers shoots the honor salute, first one pastor speaks, then the*
> *other. They don't know anymore what they should say. Behind one*
> *coffin stand the relatives, behind the other, several comrades. Most*
> *coffins are unaccompanied.*

Hosenfeld was very skeptical about reports coming out around this time. One would only find out a city had been taken by the enemy if it was successfully recaptured. Hosenfeld wrote that soldiers ridiculed press announcements about military victories in the war against the Soviets. In fact, everything had been abandoned and the Germans had fled from the Red Army. *The laurels were picked too soon and now hang as wilting wreaths around the head of the dismissed commander-in-chief, Field Marshal von Brauchitsch,* Hosenfeld wrote. *Other field marshals stepped back under this burden.* Because the Wehrmacht failed in its goal to capture Moscow, Hitler removed all military leaders and personally took command.

***

A new sports training course for 60 soldiers from various units, including seven SS junior squad leaders, took place in late January 1942. The program included skiing and skating, swimming, gymnastics, boxing, table tennis, and singing, which Hosenfeld also considered important. He discovered talented participants—pianists, violinists, and guitarists, for example—whom he selectively employed for the course. Songs of the Wandervogel and Landsknecht groups were sung in the rooms of the sports school. Hosenfeld's own speeches were also well-received. *One simply had to be sure of something and deliver it with conviction, then the people would follow,* he explained. *During the talks I don't make any grand statements, but persuade through examples and clear and plain speech. Often, I use question and answer to encourage participation.*

Hosenfeld set up a gymnastics course for the female assistants working in the intelligence division of the Wehrmacht. In vain, he attempted to convince individual women to lead a group or to rehearse a folk dance. Although most of them had been active in the League of German Girls, they demonstrated little aptitude for athletic and cultural matters. Finally, Hosenfeld hired a Polish woman to teach gymnastics. He also allowed women and girls from a Polish gymnastics school to perform. *Our conservative German girls were quite surprised at the gymnastic performance!* Hosenfeld wrote. With the assistance of the Polish teacher, he was ultimately able to organize a rhythmic dance performance.

Hosenfeld systematically expanded the sports operations. There was intense activity at the sports center every day of the week, including Sundays. *I have created a central location for all the sports activities,* he wrote in a letter home. *Soon, we will be publishing a small newspaper that is meant as a bulletin for soldiers who are interested in sports.* In this letter, he imagined how Annemarie might be able to support him in his tasks through words and deeds. However, she was needed more at home. He considered his own work less important, even though the sports operations were again well underway. *I want to do my duty here, to be a comrade and role model for my people, and to awaken their spiritual energy, so that they are able to endure all that is expected of us warriors, and all that probably still awaits us,* Hosenfeld wrote.

Since there was little chance of a home leave, Hosenfeld considered bringing his wife to Warsaw for a visit. But his plan failed early on. Officers were strictly prohibited from inviting their wives to their place of work abroad. Every suggestion of doing so was immediately rejected. The prerequisite would have been an entry permit issued by the passport office in Kraków. To circumvent the restriction, Hosenfeld enrolled himself in a sports equipment training course starting on April 22 in Zakopane, a popular health resort town on the edge of the High Tatras mountain range in southern Poland. He told Annemarie an entry permit would likely be issued and gave her tips and recommendations for the long journey and the stay in Zakopane. *Of course, my superiors must not find out about this,* he wrote in one letter. *She need only bring a spirit of adventure and everything would be fine,* he said.

Hosenfeld had not thought the passport office would contact his superior, General Unruh. Hosenfeld narrowly escaped punishment, but had to listen to a rebuke. The general's aide advised him not to do anything foolish. The aide said, ". . . Forget about bringing your wife. The general is otherwise forced to lock you up for disobedience!"

Initially, Annemarie hesitated before agreeing to the adventure. But the chance to spend several days with her husband was just too appealing. She sorted out the train route and bought a new dress and matching hat. Her anticipation grew as the departure day drew closer. She felt extreme disappointment upon receiving the news their meeting had to be canceled. Annemarie felt emotionally and physically starved and could not live without him, she wrote in desperation. She had already begged him several times to find a way that would allow them to finally see each other again. *I so very much want to be a part of your life, but everything you do is foreign to me,* she wrote. *I have the great fear that over time we are ever more growing apart.*

Annemarie could not and would not accept the separation the war imposed, although over time she learned how to better deal with her pain. This time, she threw herself into garden work and dug up the soil, seeding and removing weeds until the tension and bitterness lessened and she rediscovered her equilibrium. In a letter, Annemarie wrote: *You see, Wilm, I try under all conditions to do my duty, to think of the things at hand, that helps immensely. . . .*

Wilm Hosenfeld was also very disappointed. He was again concerned his wife was unable to deal with her situation and was simply unhappy. The course in Zakopane, for which he had lost all interest, was scheduled to begin on April 22.

For reasons not given in their correspondence, Annemarie was suddenly granted permission to come. Perhaps Hosenfeld, as soon as he arrived in Zakopane, had contacted the town commissioner. In any case, the administrator issued the permit and Hosenfeld sent the happy news via telegraph to the district administration in Fulda and his wife. A few short hours later, Annemarie informed Wilm of her arrival time in Kraków. Hosenfeld picked her up on Friday, April 24. *She wants to fling her arms around my neck, but I have to fend her off because the reunion should not be too conspicuous,* he wrote in his journal. *We should not draw attention to me, since it is forbidden, after all.*

At the end of April they traveled together to Warsaw. In doing so, Hosenfeld increased his risk of being found out—which would lead to punishment since he had been explicitly warned against doing it. Annemarie even spent the night in the sports center. She was surprised at the scantness of his room: bare walls, sparsely furnished. She had imagined it to be very different—more comfortable and cozy. Nevertheless, she was finally able to see the sports facilities and surroundings with her own eyes, after he had written so often about them.

On May 1, Wilm and Annemarie Hosenfeld said goodbye to Helmut at the Warsaw station. Following his medical training in Kassel, he was on his way back to the front in eastern Ukraine and had stopped over in Warsaw. They gave him food and candy to take along on the journey.

A week later, Annemarie was on her way back to Germany. Detlev, Jorinde, and Uta met her at the train station in Fulda. *How nice it is to be home!* Annemarie wrote. *Everything is green and blossoming! The cherry trees are in full bloom, the flowers are in color in the meadow. Everything has grown in the garden. . . . my Wilm, I have it better here than you in your bleak casern* [military barrack]. Several weeks later, Hosenfeld discovered his superior did, in fact, know about his wife's visit to Warsaw. But Unruh assured a comrade he would not reveal the secret.

***

Another major sporting event kept Hosenfeld occupied in mid-May 1942. At the end of the month, teams from the Wehrmacht, police, and SS were to take part in a 37-mile competition outside Warsaw. This was Hosenfeld's idea, and he was also in charge of the preparation and administration of the event. Posters, winner's certificates, loudspeaker systems, route markings, security escorts—everything had to be planned in a series of meetings well before the relay teams could take to the starting line. A camera team from the Ministry of Propaganda recorded the competition for its weekly newsreel.

Hosenfeld enjoyed organizing such sporting events. He felt a sense of satisfaction when the events went off as planned. However, his work did not keep him from closely following the terrible happenings in Poland and beyond. Hundreds of innocent people had been shot in Łódź, he wrote in his journal, in retaliation for the killings of three

Pages from Wilm Hosenfeld's Warsaw journal, in which he recorded entries from January 1942 through August 1944.

police officers. Such retaliatory measures also occurred in Warsaw. The desired effect—spreading fear and terror throughout the general public—had not materialized; anger and increasing zealotry did instead.

When he wrote about partisan attacks, Hosenfeld used the term favored by the Nazi propaganda machine: "bandits." The attacks were usually airdrops from Red Army airplanes. At the same time, he wrote of his respect and admiration for these men. *What courage these men have*, he noted. *They must realize that they are doomed, but they continue to accept the risk. Every night they say new ones are arriving.* His wife was of another opinion. She could not admire the enemy in this sense. On the contrary, she said the efforts of German troops were partly in vain.

In her letter dated July 10, Annemarie described a gruesome punishment that had been carried out in a town near Thalau. In Ebersberg, Polish forced laborers were coerced to publicly hang a compatriot, who had fathered a child with a local German girl. The girl had been sentenced to two years in prison. Anna, Annemarie's domestic helper, had been near Ebersberg with the two youngest Hosenfeld children when she heard about the dreadful incident.

PART III:
COMPLICITY AND
RESCUE RESISTANCE

Bloodguilt

The violence carried out by the Germans did not end—and certainly not in Poland. Wilm Hosenfeld related in his writings how citizens of Zakopane had refused to give skis to the Wehrmacht. As a result, the Gestapo searched many houses, arrested 240 men, and sent them to the feared Auschwitz concentration camp. Hosenfeld described the conditions at Auschwitz in his Warsaw journal:

> . . . *Auschwitz, the deeply feared concentration camp in the east. The Gestapo torture people to death there. To speed up the process, the unlucky* [people] *are herded into a gas chamber where they are killed with gas. People are savagely beaten during interrogation. And there are special torture cells; for instance, one where a victim has hands and arms behind his back tied to a post, which is then raised up, so that the person is hanging there until he loses consciousness. Or he is stuffed into a crate where he can only crouch and left there until he loses consciousness. What other diabolical things have they devised? How many totally innocent people are held in their prisons?*

In retrospect, it is surprising to read the extent to which Hosenfeld recorded information about the extermination of Jews in his journal. His writings prove these horrific crimes were ultimately open secrets, and anyone who wanted to know could discover them. More remarkable is that the actions of so few Germans were guided by their religious beliefs or moral consciences. Wilm Hosenfeld was one of the exceptions.

The contrast between official statements propagated by the state-run press and the truth Hosenfeld encountered daily in Warsaw was ever more blatant. Reading the newspapers and hearing radio reports, one had the impression everything was in order, peace had been secured, and the war already won—and thus, the German nation could look to a future filled with hope. Hosenfeld, however, had not believed in such a scenario for a long time. On July 23, 1942, he wrote in his journal:

> *Terror reigns everywhere. The horror, the violence, arrests, abductions, executions are all a daily occurrence. The life of a person, never mind the personal freedom, plays no role whatsoever. But the yearning for freedom is inherent in every person and every nation and cannot be suppressed forever. History teaches that tyranny never lasts for long. Now we must add the bloodguilt for the killing of the Jewish population to our account.*

Little by little, Hosenfeld understood the full extent of this monstrous operation and was stunned time and again. In the same journal entry, he wrote:

> *Various credible sources report that the ghetto in Lublin has been cleared out, that the Jews were expelled and murdered on a mass scale, that they were driven into the woods, and some of them locked up in a camp. It is said of Litzmannstadt [Łódź] and Kutno that the Jews—men, women, and children—were poisoned in mobile gas carriages, the clothes taken off the dead, their bodies dumped in mass graves, and their clothes sent to textile factories for further use. Horrifying scenes were said to have taken place. Now the Warsaw Ghetto, with its 400,000 people, is in the process of being similarly emptied.*

Wilm Hosenfeld could not imagine Hitler himself had given the orders for these mass murders. He still had his doubts that any sane, humane German would lead such a bloody campaign. In the same journal entry, he further noted:

> *. . . But one cannot believe all that. I refuse to believe it, not only out of concern for the future of our people, who once had to pay homage*

> *to these monstrosities, but because I do not want to believe that Hitler*
> *wants that—that there are German people who give such orders. There*
> *is only one explanation: they are sick, abnormal, or insane.*

Only two days after this entry, Hosenfeld noted more unsettling news: 30,000 Jews from the Warsaw Ghetto had been taken somewhere in the east. The deportation of ghetto residents to the Treblinka extermination camp, northeast of the city, was now underway. Some sources that reached Hosenfeld made mention of "heating chambers"—along the lines of a crematorium—where people were burned alive. There was also talk of shooting executions and mass graves. He asked himself why the Jews did not fight back, but he knew the answer. *Many—most—of them are so weakened by hunger and suffering that they are unable to offer any resistance and apathetically surrender to their fate*, Hosenfeld wrote. *Others may find relief that their agony has an end.*

Ukrainian and Lithuanian police officers served to reinforce the German police force. They were given free reign of the valuables left behind, and in this manner, paid for their murderous services. In his journal, Hosenfeld wrote: *At headquarters, I met a businessman yesterday who called my attention to the fact that everything could be had very cheaply in the Ghetto now: watches, rings, gold, dollars, carpets, and whatnot. If it's true, what is being said in the city by reliable people, then it is no honor to be a German officer, then one can no longer take part.*

Even though historical research cannot substantiate every detail in the reports he received, Hosenfeld's decisive information about the extermination and destruction of millions of people, on an unprecedented scale, is in complete accord with what we now know. The program for the "final solution to the Jewish question" began prior to the Wannsee Conference meeting of Nazi officials in January 1942. When Hosenfeld wrote about the meeting, deportations and subsequent mass murders were already well underway—strictly coordinated and executed by various state authorities. The extermination sites were primarily located in Poland and within the Soviet Union's sphere of influence, in countries like Ukraine and Belarus. Reichsführer-SS Heinrich Himmler personally oversaw the construction and operation of extermination camps in the General Government.

Some things stirred up inside of Hosenfeld, things that would not let him rest. In addition to confiding his thoughts in his journal, Hosenfeld wrote to his wife about the horrible and incomprehensible things happening. In a letter dated July 23, he wrote:

> *I don't want to be here anymore. What is now again being done, how the Jews are being killed, in other cities they have already been murdered by the thousands. Now the Ghetto here, with its half a million Jews, is also to be emptied.* [Heinrich] *Himmler is supposed to have been here. Can a German still show himself anywhere in the world? Is this what our soldiers are dying for out there on the front? History has never experienced anything like this. Maybe the cavemen ate one another, but to simply slaughter a nation—men, women, and children—in the 20th century, especially us, who are leading the crusade against Bolshevism, that is such an abominable bloodguilt that one wants to disappear into the ground from shame. One must ask, are the people responsible for this still normal? Is it really so, that the devil has taken on human form? I don't doubt it.*

On July 24, Hosenfeld was informed he had been promoted to captain, retroactive to April 1. Under different circumstances he would have been happy at the news. However, by now his enthusiasm was tempered. His uniform felt more like a burden as he continued to hear about the Germans' crimes. *What you wrote about the murder of Jews in Warsaw shocked me*, Annemarie replied. *You see what can happen when a government of a few has the power over many.* She could understand the tragedy disgusted him, that the sorrow of poor people hurt him. *Is it not possible that you can get away from Warsaw? To Germany?* Annemarie wrote. She was heartbroken over her husband's belief that the Eastern campaign would not be over by the end of 1942. *How long is this life supposed to last?* she lamented. *If you were here with us now or near to us, you would be able to care for us.*

Captain Hosenfeld in Warsaw in 1942.

The number of people in Warsaw who reached out to Hosenfeld with their own concerns steadily grew. Krystyna Luckhaus, whom Annemarie had also met, asked him for help in having her husband classified as "u.k." (*unabkömmlich*), which meant he was "indispens-able" in his role as an engineer and could not be conscripted for military service. Hosenfeld, however, was unable to help his friend, and Eduard Luckhaus departed on a military train headed for the Eastern Front. (It is not known if Eduard survived the war.) In a letter to Annemarie, Wilm Hosenfeld wrote the following about Eduard's Polish wife, Krystyna:

> *She now still has the food ration card of her husband and is thankful that she receives something to eat. But whether or not she will be allowed to continue using the card is contingent upon her signing a declaration that she wants to become a German. But she will not do that. Such problems! Her husband is fighting on the side of the nation that has robbed her country of its existence and brought it unspeakable suffering.*

The Polish people were not only subject to the despotism of the SS and Gestapo; their supplies also dramatically dwindled. When it came to food, the Poles were clearly worse off than the ethnic Germans, or members of the German civilian administration or Wehrmacht. On top of that, the złoty had lost much of its value and people could barely afford to buy anything. The situation worsened so much that by mid-1942 Hosenfeld was concerned a famine might strike Warsaw. He wrote:

> *I played tennis for one hour. I did not have a partner, so I played with the Polish ball boy; he can play well. He is a poor devil. I still had soup left over from lunch. I gave it to him, along with bread and some artificial honey. He did not want money. His parents died in the war during the siege. He lives from day to day. The next time I will bring him old clothes. He works in the stadium for me, but he has nothing to wear.*

***

During the summer of 1942, Hosenfeld evaluated the military situation with increasing criticism. He compared the Wehrmacht's reports with information he received from his own sources, and concluded the troops had not been able to advance on the Eastern Front for a year. The German propaganda machine was downplaying and minimizing the second front, as if the Western Allies, led by England and the US, would not dare to attack Germany. On August 7, 1942, Hosenfeld wrote in his journal:

> *I think the only reason for the long wait is the fact that they are not yet sufficiently armed. They have time. What can we do to England? Our planes are too weak in the West and there is no way to reach America. They are calmly arming themselves, until the time that they are able to field an overwhelmingly superior force based upon their enormous supply of materials and available troops. Meanwhile, in the areas occupied by us, time is against us; hunger, deprivation, and German terror are inciting the locals against us. One day, when the*

second front has been opened, they will rise against their oppressors. The Russian[s] will then also become active again. All of these nations that were attacked and raped are fighting for their freedom, fighting with the certainty of their superiority.

As if he foresaw the Battle of Stalingrad, Hosenfeld wrote that the fight for life and death would start in 1943. On the same day he wrote this analysis in his journal, he told Annemarie he feared for her and the children—particularly Helmut—and for the future in general. His doubts as to the outcome of the war had actually increased. He could not understand the politics of terror in occupied territories, and in particular, the obliteration of the Polish Jews.

***

In the Warsaw Ghetto, Władysław Szpilman once again changed venues for his piano performances. He played in the *Szutka* (Art) Café on Leszno Street, usually in piano duets with Andrzej Goldfeder. The restaurant had a concert hall and was one of the most popular meeting places for Jews who still had money and connections. This is where Szpilman experienced the final highlights of his musical career in the ghetto, mainly playing waltzes to much applause. He earned good money to make ends meet for his family.

The pianist was aware this success could not continue for long. Danger lurked on every corner. People were starving in the ghetto and typhoid fever was rampant. When Szpilman walked home, he had to be careful not to trip over the dead bodies on the sidewalks. It was hard to tell if they had died of hunger or of typhoid. The bodies were usually wrapped in paper because their clothing had been removed. The clothes were still needed. When Szpilman arrived home, his mother examined his hat, suit, and coat with tweezers for lice, which she then killed in a bowl of ethyl alcohol.

Szpilman observed how everyday life grew harsher for people in the ghetto. Children begged for a piece of bread, a potato, or a small onion, but most pedestrians looked away, as they usually had nothing to give. In light of the universal suffering, Szpilman remarked, their hearts had turned to stone. Moreover, Szpilman wrote, there was a *chilling wind of fear* when the SS and Gestapo swept through the streets at night, pulling men from their homes and shooting them. The Germans mobilized reinforcements for their murderous activities. The Jewish police certainly did not treat the ghetto residents with any more consideration; rather, they emulated their German superiors. It was Szpilman's opinion that as soon as the officers put on their uniforms they were infected with the spirit of the Gestapo.

Szpilman's family watched a German patrol officer barge into an apartment where neighbors were eating their meager dinner. When an old man in a wheelchair could not obey the command of "stand up!", the police threw him and his wheelchair out of the third-floor window and onto the street. The old man died soon after.

The Lithuanian and Ukrainian auxiliary police were even more brutal. As did the Germans, they collected bribes for various concessions, only to then immediately shoot dead the person from whom they had taken the bribe. Szpilman later wrote: *They enjoyed killing: for sport, to make their job easier, for target practice, or simply for fun.*

The arbitrariness and terror of the guards was one thing. Then there was the paralyzing uncertainty about one's own destiny. New rumors constantly made their way into the ghetto—rumors about massacres, acts of extermination in the camps, and a planned resettlement of the Jews. "Resettlement" could have many meanings: labor camp, death in installments, or immediate extermination.

German authorities constantly enticed the Jews with promises they would not keep. For example, they held out the possibility of a right to stay in the ghetto for those with a work permit. As a result, many German companies sprang up in the ghetto that were willing to issue work permits in return for money or jewelry. Władysław Szpilman went from one such business to the next until he had permits for everyone in his family. Several weeks later, he was bitter when he discovered the papers were worthless and offered no protection for him or his family.

On July 19, Szpilman performed on his own at another café. Unbeknownst to him at the time, it was to be his last performance in the ghetto. *The Garden Café was filled to the last seat, but the mood was gloomy*, he wrote. Szpilman and his friend Andrzej Goldfeder had thoroughly planned a midday concert at *Szutka* Café for July 25, 1942, to celebrate the first anniversary of their initial joint performance. But it did not take place. The café was closed, as were other premises and businesses. Shopping was no longer possible.

The long-feared "resettlement" had commenced. Nighttime raids increased. One blow of the whistle, echoing against the walls of houses, and armed troops stormed into buildings where they led entire families away. Those who were spared for the time being remained in their homes, paralyzed by fear and shock.

Szpilman's parents and siblings resigned themselves to their fate and attempted, despite the terror, to maintain a normal domestic life. *Father played violin from morning until night, Henryk studied, Regina and Halina read, and Mother patched our clothes*, Szpilman wrote. He himself was near the point of surrender. As soon as he heard the sound of a vehicle, he panicked. The regular performances in the bars and cafés had given the artist something on to which he could hold. Now, he desperately searched for either a purpose or an exit.

The occupying forces lured Jews to the *Umschlagplatz* (the transfer point) with the promise of a loaf of bread and a few pounds of jam. Hoping to avoid certain starvation, many went to the large square where several streets and train lines converged. There, the Szpilman family found temporary work in a collection facility for furniture and clothes that had been confiscated from the Jews. Władysław Szpilman wrote: . . . *Sometimes, when I carried an armful of clothing away, the soft scent of a favorite perfume emerged very subtly like a memory, or colored monograms on a white surface were visible for just a second.*

At the *Umschlagplatz*, Szpilman watched as Janusz Korczak left the ghetto with the children of the Jewish orphanage after it was closed. The children were festively dressed and joyfully sang. Szpilman imagined Korczak had spoken to them of delightful things in order to spare them the horror of the passage from life to death.

More people gathered in the large square: old and young; children and adults; frail, emaciated people and those who still had their strength. Some still hoped for a life in some foreign place, perhaps in a labor camp or somewhere else. Others had no illusions anymore. The *Umschlagplatz* was the beginning of the end. Nobody returned.

A whistling freight train approached the square. It had cars for the transport of livestock and materials. The thick stench of chlorine in the cargo area was noticeable from a distance. With an effort, the throng of people moved toward the cars, among them Władysław Szpilman with his parents and siblings.

"Look at that! Look! Szpilman!"

Someone outside of the crowd recognized the pianist, probably a Jewish police officer. Szpilman was grabbed by the collar and pulled out of the police cordon. Within seconds, the musician was separated from his family.

Beside himself with anger, Szpilman pressed himself against the dense line of police officers. Under no circumstance did he want to live without his family. His efforts were in vain. The police stood back to back and did not let him pass. At the last moment, he saw his mother; his sisters, Regina and Halina; and his brother, Henryk, step into the train car. His father turned around once more, saw him, and appeared to want to go to him, but then stopped. *He was pale, his lips were trembling nervously*, Szpilman wrote. *He attempted to smile, helpless, sad,* [and] *raised his hand and waved farewell to me, as if I was heading toward life and he were greeting me from the opposite shore. . . .* Filled with despair, Władysław Szpilman called out several times, "Papa! Papa!", until his father also disappeared from sight.

2

The Fate of the Jews

On July 22, 1942, mass transports out of the Warsaw Ghetto began. The destination was Treblinka. At the same time, in Western Europe, trains filled with tens of thousands of Jews headed to extermination camps in the East. Jews from Holland passed through the Westerbork transit camp before they arrived at Auschwitz. Similarly, French Jews passed through the Drancy collection station near Paris on the way to Auschwitz. It was pretty much the same for Belgian and German Jews. Extermination by hydrogen cyanide poison gas or poisonous exhaust fumes from diesel generators, mass shootings, massacres—a never-before-seen killing machine neared its pinnacle during the summer and fall of 1942.

The fate of the Jews held Wilm Hosenfeld in its grip. Whether in letters to Annemarie or Helmut, or in his Warsaw journal, time and again the captain noted what he heard about the extermination camps. One of his informants was a Polish merchant from Poznań. The man sold fruits, vegetables, and other goods and regularly did business in the Warsaw Ghetto. Hosenfeld wrote: *He says that the things one sees there are unbearable. He dreads going there. He drives through the streets in a rickshaw. He sees someone from the Gestapo push a group of Jews—men, women, and children—into a building entrance before indiscriminately shooting* [them]. *Ten people are dead and wounded.*

There were no doctors, Hosenfeld noted; they had been seized or killed. *A woman tells my source that several members of the Gestapo barged into a Jewish maternity ward, took the infants, shoved them into a bag, and dumped the bag onto a hearse,* he wrote. *Neither the whimpering of the babies nor the heartbreaking screams of the mothers concerned these monsters.*

A Wehrmacht officer also told him about the clearing of the ghetto in Siedlce, a town approximately 45 miles east of Warsaw. The Germans chased Jews through the streets and publicly shot a number of them. *Women, writhing in their* [own] *blood, were left lying in the sun without help*, Hosenfeld wrote. *Children who had been hiding were thrown out of windows*. Near the Siedlce train station, people waited three days without water or food until they were packed into cattle cars. The officer who conveyed the events to Hosenfeld was disgusted and angry to such an extent *he completely forgot that we were in the midst of a larger group, among whom were also senior members of the Gestapo.*

Hosenfeld also received horrific details about the Jews' arrival at the Treblinka camp, which he noted in his journal. There were mass executions and killings by exhaust gasses from heavy diesel generators routed into closed rooms. Many people in the train cars were already dead upon arrival. The bodies were stacked next to the tracks; healthy men on the train were forced to dig pits, toss the bodies in, and cover the mass graves. Then those men were shot. Hosenfeld wrote: *These unfortunate people are brought from all parts of the country. A selection of them are killed immediately because there is not enough space for them all. When there are too many, they are taken away. A terrible stench of death hangs over the entire area.*

Another way details about these acts of madness reached the public was through Jews who had escaped. One man hiding in Warsaw had pulled a 20-złoty bill from a corpse, *so that the smell of the corpse would not be lost, and serve as a reminder to him to avenge his brothers.*

During a trip to the small town of Mińsk Mazowiecki, not far from Warsaw, Hosenfeld was having lunch with other officers. The conversation turned to political events, and the issue of the Jews and their expulsion from the ghettos. A first lieutenant defended the extermination of the Jews as necessary. Hosenfeld vehemently disagreed, while the other officers remained silent. Afterward, he wondered if it was wise to announce his views in the middle of the group. He could be accused of subversion of the Wehrmacht, which would result in a death sentence. *Unfortunately, we do not have the right to freely express our opinion*, Hosenfeld wrote.

On another occasion, Hosenfeld refrained from commenting, only to later reproach himself. He had been invited to dinner by his friends the Schoenes. SS Second Lieutenant Gerhard Stabenow and his girlfriend were also in attendance. Stabenow considered himself to be a mighty man, a kind of ruler of the ghetto, as Hosenfeld described. *He spoke of the Jews as if they were ants or weeds. He likened the "resettlement," or mass murders as it were, to the destruction of bugs.* Hosenfeld observed:

> *His lady is dressed in the finest clothes—those probably all come from there. No mention about the awfulness of war, of the victims, the hardship and suffering. . . . But does not one become complicit in all of it? Why am I eating at the abundantly laid-out table of the wealthy, when all around there is great poverty, and the soldiers go hungry? Why do we remain silent and do not protest? We are all too cowardly and comfortable, too fake and rotten, which is why we must all take part in the downfall.*

***

For the first time in a while, Soviet fighter planes attacked Warsaw on the night of August 21, 1942. The pilots targeted troop quarters, hospitals, repair shops, and other German military facilities. Bombs were also dropped near the sports school. Windows shattered and billows of smoke filled the building. Hosenfeld was jolted from his sleep. Flames flickered in the rubble. People were not injured at the sports center; however, the shock remained. Hosenfeld wrote about the terror in his journal:

> *You cower in a corner somewhere like a hunted animal, incapable of clear thought. The full madness of war seizes you and an impotent anger grips you thinking about those that are responsible for all of this. But the strongest sensation is the sorrow about the tragedy of so many innocents. There is a despondency that takes hold of you in*

*the face of the evil and the wickedness of people who use their mind
and spirit to kill one another.*

Hosenfeld understood—certainly not for the first time, but more
clearly than ever—that Nazi rule was based on a system of lies and a
distortion of facts. This network was like a curtain meant to hide the
monstrous crimes that took place behind it. He wrote:

*How we have been lied to, and how the entire public opinion is
related to that lie. No newspaper is free of dishonesty, whether it
speaks of military, political, economic, historical, social, cultural
things—everywhere truth is constrained, reality is distorted, twisted
and turned upside down. Can that end well, no, for the sake of the
freedom of human personality and the freedom of the human spirit
it must not be allowed to continue. The liars and distorters must die
and their tyranny stripped bare so that a free, honorable humanity
can take its place.*

Hosenfeld considered a speech given by Hans Frank, the
governor-general of occupied Poland, an example of this hypocrisy.
In his high position, Frank was chief among those responsible for SS
and Gestapo crimes in the General Government. Frank claimed in
his speech that even the foreign-ethnic populace—by this he meant
the Poles—profited from the new circumstances; the area had never
before been governed so clearly and cleanly. Hosenfeld laconically
responded: *You must be joking!*

***

The Combat Games of the Wehrmacht, a major sporting event
that had already been postponed once, kept Hosenfeld occupied for
most of August 1942. In the August 25th edition of the newspaper
he published, *Soldier and Sport*, he called for soldiers to be physically
fit and announced that over 1,200 competitors had signed up for the
big event.

The games lasted one week, from August 30 until September 5. Hosenfeld was happy things went well. Most of the competitors were former athletes who demonstrated impressive achievements. Both the opening and closing ceremonies were spectacular successes.

The only thing that displeased Hosenfeld was the obvious disinterest of older officers serving in Warsaw, who had no interest in communal activities. They were old, nervous, and discontent, and wanted to be left alone instead of taking part in public life—an attitude that was perhaps a form of silent protest. However, it was not Hosenfeld's style to stand on the sidelines and avoid participation. Instead, he was always on the go. In his journal, he wrote:

> As officers in the former proudest army, they no longer carry any relevance or respect within what is now merely an administrative service. They believe that their honor has been aggrieved in light of the outrages perpetrated by [Heinrich] Himmler's representatives upon the Poles, and recently upon the Jews. They must remain silent in the face of all of these atrocities, but also understand that they will also be held responsible for these things in a worst-case scenario and will have to fight alongside the soldiers.

Hosenfeld not only understood this responsibility, he also accepted it, and as a result, suffered on account of it. He was able to keep his distance from the crimes and help persecuted people thanks to his various roles in Warsaw. Admittedly, as he documented himself, on one occasion he participated in handing down a death sentence as a member of the Warsaw military court. A member of the group Organization Death was on trial on October 22, 1942, and in Hosenfeld's words, *a persistent, homicidal offender*, who, among other charges, was guilty of looting. Hosenfeld further observed: *When I voiced my decision for the death penalty, I felt as though I had committed a great crime. I only see the person in front of me, and a boundless compassion overcomes me. The court clerk noted the birthdate of the convicted. It was October 22, 1914. He was executed on his birthday.*

Wilm Hosenfeld's journal entry on October 23, 1942. The underlined text reads, "I only see the person in front of me and a boundless compassion overcomes me."

***

In September 1942, Wilm Hosenfeld took on an additional sphere of activity, one more in line with his disposition and skills than the sports operation (which he nonetheless carried out to the full satisfaction of his superiors). Since 1940, a vocational development program had existed at the Supreme High Command of the Wehrmacht in Berlin. Soldiers were able to further develop their professional skills, obtain missing school diplomas, and acquire additional education and qualifications. The program was meant to prepare soldiers for a return to civilian life.

Hosenfeld was the ideal choice to develop the vocational program, which was similar to the adult education classes he had successfully led during his time as a teacher. Hosenfeld planned courses, purchased educational materials, and engaged lecturers for the courses. He was able to quickly find vocational school teachers, engineers, and other specialists among relatives of Wehrmacht members. Hosenfeld chose to teach a history course, but did not have the necessary literature. All the history books available to him had been rewritten according to Nazi ideology. *When I come home, I will look for my old history books, those that have not been sanitized,* he wrote to Annemarie. *I do not agree with the current books—there is too much posturing for my taste.* He asked his wife to start looking for his books.

Right from the start, 550 students and 57 teachers signed up, including graduate engineers, agronomists, lecturers, construction engineers, and car mechanics. On October 19, four courses in automotive technology began. A captain from the Supreme High Command came to observe the launch and explain the goals of vocational development. The academic structure was described by a professor from Freiburg, and Hosenfeld outlined the practical side of the program. *I was free of inhibition and saw animated approval on the faces of the listeners,* he wrote. *I then conducted the discussion round and presented the guidelines of studies, which were accepted on the whole.*

The teaching had barely started, but Hosenfeld was already developing plans to offer soldiers the opportunity to take exams for a high school diploma or a master's certificate. His superior, Major General Fritz Rossum, was skeptical. But Hosenfeld was confident he would soon be able to convince Rossum of the importance of his ideas. After all, Hosenfeld was in his natural element: education.

The new task brought with it significant additional work. Hosenfeld put his great self-discipline to the test and managed everything, even having enough time for his letters and journal entries. He was, however, plagued by headaches, for which no cause could be found. Hosenfeld rarely had time to saddle a horse for a ride through the countryside. But on one such ride, he observed in his journal:

The farmers are plowing and seeding the potato fields, the smoke
of the potato fire reminds me of home. A white mist shrouds the
water, the creaking of the wheels, in between the voices of children.
Boys are roasting potatoes over a fire. I feel as though I should
be laughing and having fun with them. They are such fresh and
handsome boys, in meager clothes, barefoot with red, chilled skin.
The young girls also look smart and cheerful.

One girl asked him for bread. As usual, Hosenfeld had a loaf for
his horse in his pouch. He gave it to the girl, who ran off laughing
and shared the bread with the other children.

***

The "resettlement" of Jews from the Warsaw Ghetto continued
without pause during the summer of 1942. Young men were primarily spared selection; they were instead used as laborers. Władysław
Szpilman worked at construction sites under the supervision of Jewish
foremen and SS members, mostly assisting a bricklayer and his team.
The first order of business was to demolish the ghetto wall, after
which a castle would be built for a senior SS leader and barracks
erected for SS men.

One day, Szpilman met Jan Dworakowski, conductor of the
Warsaw National Philharmonic Orchestra, who warmly greeted
him and asked how he was doing. Szpilman revealed his family had
been taken away. The pianist held out hope they might still be alive.
Dworakowski, however, explained that he would never see his parents
and siblings again. At first, Szpilman did not know why the man
wanted to deprive him of his last glimmer of hope. Then Szpilman
understood: *At the decisive moment this assurance of certain death gave me the*
energy to save myself, he wrote.

Through a Jew who shopped for other workers in the city,
Szpilman reestablished contact with former friends to prepare for his
escape. He was, however, rebuffed on the first try. It was extremely

dangerous to hide a Jew, he was told. He should not even consider it, but the pianist kept trying, especially since the situation in the ghetto and the state of the war collectively held out the slight promise of better days. Talk of an armed insurrection against the Germans was making the rounds in the ghetto. Attacks on a café frequented by Germans, as well as the assassinations of informants among the Germans themselves, boosted the confidence of the approximately 60,000 Jews who remained in the Warsaw Ghetto.

They were happy about the Soviet air raids on Warsaw, although they could not outwardly show their joy. The Jews' will to survive was further bolstered by uplifting news: the Allies had landed in North Africa, the advance of the Wehrmacht on the Eastern Front had long since come to a halt, and a decisive battle at the Volga River drew near.

Jews being loaded onto trains leaving Warsaw for death camps in 1942 or 1943.

***

It is summer here, such a wonderful summer, Annemarie wrote to her husband. *I am sitting in the garden. The fragrance of the flowers and bushes with their intense colors are the vibrant melody of life.* When she watched her children, she was able to leave her worries behind and forget her concerns.

She wrote: *We have beautiful weather; the farmers are harvesting potatoes and plowing their fields. Potatoes are abundant, but everything is confiscated.* The food supply for people was deteriorating in Germany. Those who had their own gardens, like Annemarie, grew fruits and vegetables. She bottled and preserved pickles, plums, and mirabelles. Her domestic helper, Anna, and the children assisted her. Annemarie traded her leftover harvest for oats, flour, and milk. In one of her letters, she wrote: *My barter trade is in full bloom.* In the cellar, she stockpiled apples, pears, quinces, and potatoes (which were hard to come by) in preparation for the winter months. She also baked her own bread, for which she needed pure rye flour.

Sugar was in short supply. Honey was also in demand, and many things could be exchanged in return for it. In autumn 1942, the Hosenfeld family harvested around 1,100 pounds of honey. Trading could bring surprising returns or be used to gain favors like cutting firewood. The chickens and pigs needed feed in order to be fattened, but the stores had virtually none available, so it had to be procured by other means. Annemarie wrote her husband: *You know that hoarding and coping is not really my style, but I constantly have to provide for the food. I don't want my children to be malnourished the way my sister and I were during the* [First] *World War. Malnourishment is now also visible, especially with older people. . . .*

Many goods were only available with a ration card or by special request. Shoes for the girls, a bicycle for Detlev for his long distance to school—Annemarie was often out and about getting the necessary paperwork and managing day-to-day life with the three children who still lived at home. Her eldest daughter, Anemone, worked at a clinic in Schmalkalden, where she was training to be a nurse. Although Annemarie often complained about daily struggles, her letters are a reflection of everyday life during the war—which, because of the Allied air raids on Kassel and Frankfurt, drew ever closer. At the same time, her letters demonstrated she had everything under control.

It was a benefit that her relationship with the people in Thalau was improving, apart from occasional quarrels. Annemarie would visit the parents of a soldier who had been wounded or killed in battle, expressing her sympathy and consoling them. During such visits, she never mentioned her own agonizing fear about Helmut, whom she believed to be near Stalingrad.

The people saw she tilled the garden, fertilized the plots, and tirelessly took care of her home and yard, and for that they respected her. She wrote that she now had a different relationship with the village. She showed more interest in the people, and they hoped she would take on a more active role in the village. In a letter dated September 28 and 29, she wrote: *I have started all over again and am your simple, dear, humble wife, your Annemie, who neither belongs in Berlin* [n]*or Warsaw, but instead in Thalau and Worpswede! I am no lady and no farmer's wife.*

Two weeks prior, Annemarie had met her husband in Berlin. They took advantage of one of Hosenfeld's official trips to the capital to see each other again.

At the end of 1942, after the Warsaw vocational development program was up and running, Wilm Hosenfeld received two weeks of home leave. Much as they had done a year earlier, the couple wanted to use the time together to work through any existing misunderstandings and tensions. Annemarie wrote: *In the past, our relationship was so straightforward—the war has complicated it. I don't find my old Wilm anymore, and I have surely changed as well.* Such observations were snapshots, expressions of a constantly recurring fear their relationship could fail. She would have liked to see him jealous, as she often was. *The war is changing you,* Annemarie wrote to her husband. *I sensed these changes with every visit; this is what is causing the arguments.* She accused Wilm of facing every woman without being critical. *Every woman is a threat to you,* she wrote. *You can complain that I am petty, jealous, and narrow-minded, but that's the way it is.* Before long, though, she would again follow up criticism with a confession of her unconditional love. The most important factor for both of them was being together.

From fellow villagers, and during train rides in Fulda or Gersfeld, Annemarie heard about how the war mercilessly destroyed people.

She would often meet young soldiers on the trains who had lost limbs. In one letter, she vividly described an interaction with one soldier:

> *Not that long ago, I noticed someone with a serious, knowing face. He only had a tiny stump of a leg and was walking arduously on crutches along the platform. The crowd was pushing and shoving; I stayed next to him and made sure that nobody pushed him. I asked him, "Can you manage the steps?" Then he looked at me and said with an incomparable expression on his face, "I can do it." We must not become bitter or lose faith. Every new day is a struggle for me. Often, quite often, I am unhappy with myself. I miss you, my dear life's companion, you who motivate me and give me strength and love. The long nights that keep us awake with worry, they leave their marks on our faces.*

***

As her husband did, Annemarie followed the military situation on the Eastern Front with increasing concern. The Battle of Stalingrad had begun on July 17, 1942. The Germans hoped that after the fall of Stalingrad, Moscow would be next.

Helmut Hosenfeld was assigned to one of the Wehrmacht units marching on the city on the banks of the Volga River. In one of his letters, Helmut compared the Battle of Stalingrad to the fight for the French stronghold of Verdun during World War I; the losses during the battles were comparable. Wilm Hosenfeld agreed with Helmut. As long as Wilm received mail from the front, he felt somewhat reassured. With increasing reports the Red Army had encircled the German Sixth Army, the letters from Helmut ceased and Wilm was seized by fear.

Helmut later informed his family he had left the battle zone around Stalingrad on board a hospital plane at the end of January 1943. Whether he had been with the units who were encircled at Stalingrad or with those outside the area is unknown. Wilm Hosenfeld was greatly relieved to learn his son had escaped the battle. He immediately sent a telegram to Thalau to inform his wife.

Hosenfeld spent the Christmas holidays in Thalau. He returned to Warsaw just before the end of 1942. The Wehrmacht faced a devastating loss at Stalingrad. Hosenfeld understood what this meant. A lengthy entry in his journal recalled Hitler's pretentious announcements at the beginning of the year when the "greatest commander of all time" sent the Wehrmacht into a new offensive against the giant Soviet Union. Twelve months later, the Sixth Army was surrounded. The conquest of Moscow had not happened. The oilfields in the Caucasus region, which were an important means to resupply, remained under Soviet control. *The year 1943 will be bad for us,* Hosenfeld noted. *The Wehrmacht was unable to deal with the Bolsheviks. In addition to that, there is America with its huge supply of armaments and inexhaustible military force. I cannot even read the newspapers anymore. They are not allowed to tell the truth.*

3

The Banality of Evil

The Battle of Stalingrad weighed like a dark shadow on Germany at the start of 1943. In truth, the battle between the Red Army and the Wehrmacht had been decided for some time. The Sixth Army, led by General Friedrich Paulus, was encircled and for months could only be resupplied by air. The German reinforcements were significantly fewer than the overblown promises made by Air Marshal Hermann Göring. On their way back, the planes carried wounded troops. Hitler repeatedly refused Paulus's requests to retreat. The Nazi dictator simply abandoned the soldiers to their fate.

From the accounts of the Wehrmacht, it is impossible to get an accurate picture of the actual situation. That is probably their intention, Hosenfeld wrote in a letter home dated on January 1, seemingly desperate to find a glimmer of hope. Joseph Goebbels's grand statements in his New Year's Eve speech rang hollow and unconvincing. Instead of portraying

Wilm and Annemarie Hosenfeld sometime in 1942.

everything through rose-colored glasses, Hosenfeld observed, it would be better to admit the severity of the situation. *We have no other choice than to endure the suffering*, he wrote.

However, a small positive for Hosenfeld happened at this time. A two-week training course at the gas-defense school in Bydgoszcz (Bromberg) was planned for January. At the time, the town was part of the Danzig-West Prussia province. It had been the scene of numerous pogroms against Jews and Polish intellectuals, reprisals for the so-called "Bloody Sunday" of 1939 when ethnic Germans had been killed by Poles soon after the invasion of Poland.

Hosenfeld encouraged his wife to meet him in Bydgoszcz. She was to book a private room there and the two of them would be able to spend a few days together. Annemarie was still drawing energy from her husband's Christmas visit. On New Year's Day 1943, she let him know how much she had enjoyed the holidays with him and the children. Annemarie wrote: *During the past year, you have shed your reserve. You have allowed me to partake more in your life. You have made me happy and I know of your inner maturation during this past year.* The more Hosenfeld inwardly distanced himself from the Nazi regime, the more ashamed he felt about the crimes that were committed—and the closer it brought him and his pacifist wife together.

Annemarie did not have to be asked twice about the Bydgoszcz plan. However, traveling by train in the middle of winter could be tedious and—due to the constant threat of air raids—dangerous. Hosenfeld had been in Bydgoszcz since January 5, listening to lectures about gas-defense exercises. He was much more interested in history and literature, he wrote to Helmut, who was still on the Eastern Front. Hosenfeld assumed poison gas would still be used as a warfare agent.

Annemarie arrived in Bydgoszcz on January 14 and stayed almost a week until the conclusion of the gas-defense training course. Afterward, the couple journeyed to the village of Samter, northwest of Poznań, where the Cieciora family was administering the Karolin estate. Stanisław Cieciora was the prisoner whom Hosenfeld had released from the POW camp in Pabianice in 1939. The Hosenfelds were well received, and they stayed for two enjoyable days. They departed on January 22; Wilm returned to Warsaw, while Annemarie headed back to the children in Thalau.

Afterward, they glowingly spoke about their Polish friends, who provided them with abundant provisions for the return trips. *What warm-hearted and good people they are. I always ask myself, how are they able to spoil us like that*, Hosenfeld observed in a letter. About Zofia Cieciora, he wrote: *This plain, unpretentious, foreign woman, what a great soul and what inner decency she has. Do you know one among your acquaintances who can surpass her?* Annemarie was equally impressed by the Polish friends. *It was so completely perfect. Our trip to Karolin!* she proclaimed. *The evenings in the nightly Bromberg* [Bydgoszcz]*! I never want to forget that!*

Hosenfeld took along a package for Antoni Cieciora, the priest who had gone underground in Warsaw. Soon after, Hosenfeld met with Cieciora. The priest came to find him in his office at the sports school after Hosenfeld missed Cieciora twice and finally left his address behind. Hosenfeld ultimately hired Antoni Cieciora under the name "Cichocki" as a Polish teacher for the vocational development center. The course catalog listed Cieciora under that name. Under the patronage of Hosenfeld, a Catholic priest being hunted by the Gestapo helped German soldiers learn the Polish language.

Surprisingly, Helmut had now also returned to Thalau from the Eastern Front—unhurt and with the prospect of soon being able to continue his training to become a doctor. To Wilm Hosenfeld, it bordered on a miracle that his son escaped the battlefield unscathed.

***

On February 2, 1943, the newspaper informed Wilm Hosenfeld what he had long expected, but still could not believe: Friedrich Paulus, commander-in-chief of the Sixth Army, had capitulated on January 31 and was now, along with his soldiers, a captive of the Red Army. Paulus repeatedly asked Hitler for permission to retreat. Hitler refused and instead promoted Paulus to field marshal on January 30, noting that no German nor Prussian field marshal had ever before surrendered. In order to save the lives of his remaining troops, Paulus disobeyed commands and surrendered. How many German soldiers had already frozen or starved to death is unknown. Of the initial 200,000 soldiers, fewer than half survived. Of those, only 6,000 men returned home after the war. Hosenfeld wrote: *I don't think that we will recover from this blow. There are ominous reports coming from the remaining Eastern Front.*

It was clear to Hosenfeld the Allies were advancing on virtually all fronts: North Africa, the Middle East, and the Pacific, where the Japanese were on the defensive. He wrote in his journal on February 11: *Superior strength* [is] *everywhere.* The next day, he noted an appeal announced by the German governor of Warsaw, who had summoned Warsaw residents and their relatives with a German name to register for a German identification card. *One thinks that these men who are proclaiming such nonsense are idiots*, Hosenfeld wrote. *How they treated the Polish, and now they expect them to align themselves with us. They know perfectly well that they will only be conscripted into the German Wehrmacht.*

Due to the shortage of soldiers and workers, the police in Warsaw and other large cities were ordered to arrest people on the street. The detainees were then sent to Germany as forced laborers. Hosenfeld wrote in his journal of veritable manhunts. The Warsaw police indiscriminately arrested residents in churches and private residences. Hosenfeld observed:

> *In the areas of Lublin and Zamość, near Kraków, farmers are being expelled from their villages. Men and women are sent to camps, the old people shot, and the children* [are] *packed onto trains to be sent somewhere. They abduct 2- to 14-year-olds. Such a train recently passed through Warsaw. The wagons were opened at the Praga train station. A large number of them had starved and frozen to death. The civilians charged the wagons, wanting to save the children and take them to their homes. It was forbidden; the wagons were closed again and the train left again with the ill-fated children, without the dead having been removed. It is headed somewhere in Germany.*

The SS group leader Odilo Globocnik had been ordered by Heinrich Himmler to clear the Lublin district so German settlers could take up residence there. Globocnik carried out the resettlement in a most brutal manner. More than 100,000 farmers lost their homes and belongings. Many of them were murdered in the Auschwitz and Majdanek concentration camps or transported to Germany as forced laborers. However, the settlement project failed due to partisan resistance, which in turn led to retaliatory measures against the Polish civilian population.

***

Władysław Szpilman injured his ankle on a construction site in November 1942. He stumbled while bringing lime to the bricklayers and suffered a painful sprain. The foreman sent him to work in a warehouse where it was warmer than outside and he was better able to protect his hands. In January 1943, events confirmed what Jews in the ghetto had nearly lost faith in: the Sixth Army defeat at Stalingrad shattered the illusion of the Wehrmacht's invincibility. The tide was turning and the underground resistance in the Warsaw Ghetto felt a surge of momentum. Weapons and ammunition made their way into the hands of resistance fighters, smuggled in through the potato sacks delivered to the ghetto each day. Szpilman also received arms, and found himself in life-threatening situations when the SS decided to check contents of the sacks. Fortunately, the Germans did not insist on checking everything and instead performed random searches.

The frantic search for Poles strong enough to perform forced labor in Germany resulted in an almost absurd situation. Non-Jews fled into the ghetto because they felt they would be safer there from the threat of arrest. For several days, wearing an armband with a star was a safeguard, since the Germans were searching for "Polish Aryans."

This state did not last long. The Germans expanded their searches to include the ghetto. Szpilman witnessed a police officer shoot a boy around 10 years old, who, in his state of fear, had forgotten to remove his cap and greet the German. Without a word, the officer pulled out his revolver, placed it against the boy's temple, and pulled the trigger. The boy collapsed dead on the spot. The police officer calmly reholstered his weapon and continued on his way. Szpilman looked at the officer. *He did not even have a particularly brutal face and did not appear to be irritated*, Szpilman wrote. *He was a normal, calm man, who completed his numerous small duties during the day, which he would forget afterward, occupied with other, more important matters that awaited him.*

German prisoners being marched through Russia after the surrender at Stalingrad on January 31, 1943.

***

Wilm Hosenfeld never ceased asking himself how it was possible the Germans were capable of such outrageous actions. Being a deeply faithful Catholic, he sometimes struggled to understand why God allowed all of it to happen. He never had a good answer, instead finding solace in the concept of atonement. He believed the perpetrators had lost all sense of moral responsibility and were now completely godless. Still, Hosenfeld felt this answer was not enough to understand how his fellow compatriots had become cold-blooded murderers.

He was, however, aware of the consequences. In his journal entry for February 14, Hosenfeld recalled the murder of Jews and the slaughter of women and children that had been committed a year prior. It was clear to Hosenfeld that Germany would lose the war. He noted:

> . . . *Because with that the still justifiable fight for free access to food supplies and an expansion of ethnic territories had lost its meaning. It degenerated into excessive, inhuman, mass slaughter contrary to the ideals of a cultured nation, the likes of which can never be justified before the people of Germany and will be explicitly condemned by the German people. All of the agony of the arrested Poles, the executions of prisoners of war, the beastly treatment can also never be justified.*

Hosenfeld sometimes wondered what would happen after the war ended. He felt this war would push Germany over the edge. It could never again assert itself as a great nation. *Everything the Nazis do, what Hitler does, is bloody amateurish,* Hosenfeld observed. He wrote to Helmut that it would be the responsibility of the next generation, those whom the war spared, to make a fresh start. *Your ideals collapse like phantoms,* Hosenfeld stated. *You will need to build a completely new world; everything that lies behind you, you will need to renounce. You will not find this difficult to do because most of it was superficial, in appearance only and arrogance without an essential core.*

Hosenfeld reacted with derision and ridicule to the Reich Minister of Propaganda Joseph Goebbels's infamous "stay the course" speech delivered at the Berlin Sports Palace on February 18, 1943. Goebbels had posed the question, "Do you want total war? Do you want it, if needed, to be more total and more radical than we can today even imagine?" The answer was thunderous applause. Hosenfeld referred to it as a dog and pony show. *Had the mothers and fathers of the fallen been asked, had the people suffering from bombardment in the cities been asked, the answer would have surely been different,* Hosenfeld wrote. He recalled another question from the speech, something like, "Do you want those, who enrich themselves through the war, to lose their heads?" Hosenfeld considered how many Germans from the security service, the SS, and the civilian administration in Poland would then have to be decapitated.

Annemarie had also listened to the speech. *What will follow now is the complete downfall,* she wrote to her husband. *Will not one person stand up and cry out: "Stop the bloodshed, enough of this madness!"*

The defeat of the Wehrmacht at Stalingrad led to tumultuous actions within the German military forces in Warsaw and other parts of Poland. Hosenfeld lost some of his junior officers who were employed as lecturers and in other capacities. *I am on a very friendly basis with my people here,* he wrote. *Unfortunately, a change will also soon occur here; perhaps the sports center will be fully disbanded. There are big changes underway, movements of personnel and so on. That is tied to events on the front.*

In early February, Hosenfeld was working on a new course catalog. The departure of several members of his staff opened up the opportunity to employ additional Poles, especially those who were being pursued and in need of protection. The Poles were dependable, he wrote. When three of the junior officers with whom he had worked for almost two years departed, he felt a sting; it hurt him to let them go. Hosenfeld wrote: . . . *They are joining the field troops. One replacement has arrived, but there is not much that I can do with him. I have now hired two Poles; these are my main supporting staff.* His concern that the sports center would close and he would be deployed elsewhere did not materialize. Annemarie was relieved when her husband told her this.

Hosenfeld participated in a two-day conference for the heads of the sporting departments in the General Government, held in Kraków, beginning on March 20. There was free time to visit churches and historical monuments, including the memorial to the Polish general and national hero Tadeusz Kościuszko, who led the uprising against the partition of Poland in 1794. Hosenfeld wrote: *From every village in Poland a cartload of soil was brought to Kraków, where it was offloaded here, creating a virtual mountain. An exceptional idea, signifying the solidarity of the nation with its national hero.*

As always, Hosenfeld also keenly wrote about people whom he observed on the street: *The people are dejected and troubled. In contrast, the Germans are doing very well. I was surprised, how well they live here. From their perspective, the war can last a long time.*

Beginning in April 1943, Hosenfeld occasionally acted as the deputy for Lieutenant Colonel Felix-Ferdinand von Kamlah in the IC (military intelligence) staff division at headquarters. The division was responsible for counterintelligence, enemy reconnaissance, and the mental health care of the troops. The sports school was also under this section's control. Hosenfeld only hinted at this role in his letters, presumably because disclosing internal matters would have been too dangerous. This job would later seal his fate while in Soviet captivity. In a letter to Helmut, he wrote: *This* [counterintelligence] *is a very interesting job. You learn to look behind the setting. Warsaw has become* [an] *unsafe place. The most eerie things are happening every day.*

Seeing behind the curtain provided Hosenfeld with insight and information available to very few people. For example, he learned of the increasing partisan attacks and the damages incurred through aerial bombing raids.

All the same, the position allowed him to provide tangible assistance. Hosenfeld was increasingly being sought out by people who requested his help for themselves or their relatives, or who were in the clutches of the Gestapo. A Polish man named Novitzki asked Hosenfeld to help his brother who was incarcerated in Auschwitz. The brother was completely innocent. He had lived in the same house as a man accused of smuggling, and as a result, was arbitrarily arrested.

In order to submit a petition for clemency on behalf of the brother, Novitzki required a clearance certificate from the police. Hosenfeld visited SS Major Ernst Kah twice in an attempt to secure the prisoner's release. His notes appear to indicate he was ultimately successful. In one of his letters, Hosenfeld wrote: *How many have I already helped? I also brought the aunt of Olga* [a Polish worker at the sports school] *out of prison. My workers also constantly have concerns.*

***

In spring 1943, a crisis arose in Annemarie and Wilm Hosenfeld's relationship and extended into the summer months. It had been a long time in the making and was essentially a product of the war's circumstances. Since autumn 1942, there were signs Annemarie would have to do without her domestic helper, Anna. The employment office wanted to assign her elsewhere. Annemarie got along well with Anna, even though she did not always trust her. However, anytime she had to run errands, visit the doctor, or travel, Anna took good care of the children and the household.

Hosenfeld joined the search from Warsaw to help find a replacement for Anna. Zofia Cieciora—with whom the Hosenfelds were still in contact, and who on several occasions had sent packages with butter, sugar, and flour to Thalau—located a Polish girl who was prepared to go to Germany for a limited period. But this solution failed due to objections by the authorities.

Annemarie increasingly urged her husband to provide her with a Polish helper, as there were almost no available workers in Germany. Hosenfeld searched in his circle of Polish acquaintances and friends. His choice was a woman he had known for some time. She was 31 and had a five-year-old son whom she wanted to bring along to Thalau.

Annemarie had her doubts. A *spoiled city girl* would be of little help to her, she wrote. But she finally agreed—this solution was still better than none at all. Annemarie urgently needed help, otherwise she would not pester him with this unpleasant business, she conceded. In one letter, Annemarie wrote:

> *If you consider the woman to be hardworking and honest and think*
> *that she will be content with our circumstances here, then I don't see*
> *it as a risk if she comes. Whether she is German or Polish doesn't*
> *matter to me, because I have only met likable Poles up to now. You*
> *can assure the young woman that she will never encounter any hate*
> *or contempt from us.*

However, as the formalities dragged on, she again had misgivings. Hiring an educated woman with a small child as a domestic helper seemed risky to Annemarie. Nevertheless, she wanted to give it a try and prepared the room her previous help had used, setting up a child's bed for the boy. *The children are already looking forward to the small boy,* Annemarie wrote to Wilm. *Everything will be fine.*

The Polish woman arrived in mid-April. Annemarie met her at the Fulda train station. The woman appeared frightened and insecure. When Annemarie asked the woman for papers she would have to present to the employment agency, there was an awkward moment. Then, the woman spoke about her life. *Her relatives live near Litzmannstadt* [Łódź], Annemarie wrote of the woman. *She attended secondary school and studied law for one year. She became a sports teacher. She was social with the Luckhauses.* The details appeared familiar to Annemarie. She realized this was the woman Wilm had written about in his letters; he had known her for a long time.

Annemarie was initially irritated, but tried to make the best of the situation. This, however, was not easy. At the outset, the Polish woman created more work for Annemarie instead of relieving her burden. She was clumsy and untidy, but quite willing to work and not disagreeable, Annemarie noted. Conflicts between the women materialized; in fact, attempts to engage the Polish woman as a maidservant were predestined to fail. The domestic atmosphere was tense after Wilm Hosenfeld's next home leave. The Polish woman felt that reading a good book was more important than making the beds, dusting, cleaning the rooms, and completing the work at hand. Eventually, the woman even got sick. Despite their differences, there was no question in Annemarie's mind that she would care for the sick woman.

In contrast to the two women, the children got along very well. Uta, in particular, played with the boy for long periods of time. She had took the child into her heart and patiently taught him German words.

Annemarie eventually found a way to deal with the tricky situation. The temperatures were rising, and at midday, the two women sunbathed near a wind-sheltered spot. It had a calming effect.

The film *You Belong to Me* was being shown in Fulda and Annemarie wanted to see it. The Polish woman asked if she could come along. They missed the train home. Around midnight, they phoned friends in Fulda, asking if they could spend the night there. On May 16, Annemarie wrote to Wilm:

> *I didn't know if I should consider the situation funny or sad. We lay next to each other on the couch under a blanket in our short satin shirts. Life is strange. "I never would have dreamt that I would have to be together with you like this," I told her. She replied, "I have always wanted to come to you. I even dreamt of it." She told me about the dream. "No, I wanted to meet you in a different way," I said to her. "I wanted to scratch out your eyes . . ." We both laughed and fell asleep. . . .*

All in all, Annemarie weathered the crisis surprisingly well. She remained true to her convictions and defended the Polish woman and her son against criticism from her relatives. One visitor commented she could not understand how Annemarie could allow her children to play with a Polish child. Annemarie understood the Polish woman belonged to her husband's circle of Warsaw friends whom he had helped. She loved Wilm above all else and did not want to share him with anyone; Annemarie's letters reveal she was jealous and made substantial accusations against him. At the same time, she promised her husband she would never act in a vindictive, disingenuous, and ugly manner, and repeatedly underscored they had to stay together, especially because of the children. *I will never leave you*, she wrote. Over the years, though, Annemarie had learned to do without him.

She noted: . . . *Even you don't know me fully. Good and bad are flexible words. You can view every person from two sides. . . . It is my duty to stay at your side, during whatever hardship, and I am happy to do it, even though it is the most difficult thing I have ever been asked to do.*

— 4 —

The Warsaw Ghetto Uprising

Wilm Hosenfeld suffered from the difficulties with Annemarie in the spring of 1943. Their arguments came at a bad time for him: not only was he busy with his various tasks, but the mood in Warsaw had also turned. When he biked through the city, he felt the hostile gazes of the pedestrians. There were almost daily attacks on German occupiers. News of another German defeat or another Wehrmacht retreat were glad tidings for the Poles—the German chain of victories had ended.

In the Warsaw Ghetto, preparations for an armed uprising had been underway for weeks. The Jewish Combat Organization had formed in January. Rumors of the continued "resettlement" motivated young Jews in particular to fight against impending extermination. They would not be led to the slaughterhouse without a fight. The pianist Władysław Szpilman helped distribute weapons and ammunition in the ghetto.

By now, nearly 300,000 Jews had been deported from the Warsaw Ghetto. The roughly 60,000 who remained were mostly put to work as laborers on construction sites. Jews built administrative offices, barracks, and luxurious houses for senior ranks of the SS and Gestapo, who apparently expected to remain in Warsaw for some years.

When the "cleansing of the ghetto of non-working elements" rose to a new level between the end of January and beginning of February, many Jews faced a choice: underground armed resistance or flight. Residents barricaded themselves in when the first violent clashes erupted. Walking through the area, Szpilman saw the sidewalks covered with fragments of glass from broken windows. The gutters overflowed with feathers from torn pillows. Pillows were a popular place to hide money, jewelry, and other valuables—items for which the occupiers were looking. *Feathers everywhere*, Szpilman wrote. *Every gust of wind sent whole clouds upward, whirling them in the air as if heavy snow were falling, only in the opposite direction—from the earth to the sky.* Every few steps, the pianist had to walk around bodies of people who had been killed.

Some people used the charged atmosphere in the ghetto as a chance to flee. An opportunity to escape had opened up since the attention of the SS and Gestapo was now directed on the mounting insurrection. Szpilman contacted an artistic couple with whom he was friends and met them outside of the ghetto. He gave them compositions, a fountain pen, and his wristwatch, as he described, *everything that I wanted to take with* [me] *and had previously taken out of the ghetto and hidden in the warehouse.*

Jews being searched and interrogated during the Warsaw Ghetto Uprising in 1943.

The actor Andrzej Bogucki and singer Janina Godlewska-Bogucka, (both of whom were involved in the Polish underground resistance and fought in the Polish Home Army uprising in 1944) agreed to shelter

Szpilman in a painter's studio until another hiding place could be found. The three of them agreed to meet on February 13. Szpilman wanted to use a building inspection by an SS general as his chance to flee. When everyone's attention was on the inspector, Szpilman left. He wrote: *I put on my coat, took off the armband with* [its] *light blue star for the first time in three years, and slipped out through the gate with them.* The meeting with his friends succeeded. Szpilman slept on a cot in the studio. He had been forced to sleep on hard-planked beds until then. He was safe for the time being.

***

When the Warsaw Ghetto Uprising erupted with full force on April 19, 1943, Wilm Hosenfeld was still in Thalau. Shortly after his return to Warsaw, he went out to witness the dramatic events. It is not known if he knew about preparations for the insurrection. In the ghetto, *a real war was underway, with artillery and tanks; there are dead and wounded,* he wrote to his wife on May 5. Hosenfeld experienced the pinnacle of a military confrontation between two completely unequal adversaries. The Jewish resistance fighters faced a well-equipped army under the command of SS brigade leader Jürgen Stroop, who utilized all armaments at his disposal in Warsaw.

Hosenfeld vividly described the city's destruction in his writings:

> *Black clouds of smoke, coming from the ghetto, which had been burning for three weeks, drifted over the city. So much was destroyed, countless people killed. The police are still not finished. There is incessant shooting at night. Horrible scenes play out there. A new and permanent stain for those who are responsible for this, and an enormous disgrace on top of it.*

He continuously discovered new details about the uprising. A Jewish eyewitness who survived told him: "We were in a house in the ghetto. Seven days we held out in the basement. The house above us burned, the women ran out, us men also. Some were shot; we were brought to the transfer area and loaded into cattle wagons. My brother poisoned himself. Our women were taken to Treblinka and burned there. I ended up in a labor camp. We were abused and had to work hard."

In the first weeks after his escape, Władysław Szpilman changed his hiding place several times. Once they heard the pianist was alive, friends and acquaintances organized food and kept him informed about the progress of the battles in the ghetto. Reading underground newsletters encouraged Szpilman to not give up. In the ghetto, every house and street block was a battleground. The poorly equipped insurgents fought against a military force that employed artillery, tanks, and airplanes. And yet, the Jewish resistance asserted itself for weeks. Szpilman wrote: *If the Germans captured a house, the women and children remaining inside would go to the uppermost floor and throw themselves—including the children—onto the street below.* Similar to what Hosenfeld saw, Szpilman also observed a pillar of fire and smoke towering above the city at night, blotting out the stars in the sky.

There was no escape for the majority of Jewish resistance fighters. Overpowering SS and police units fought their way through, street by street, blowing up houses, setting fire to buildings, and shooting at anything that moved. They did this until the ghetto was a wasteland of ruins. Hosenfeld struggled to put into words what he felt when the insurrection was defeated:

> *Now the last of the remaining Jewish residents of the ghetto have been liquidated. An SS assault leader boasted how they had blasted the Jews scrambling from the burning houses. The entire ghetto is a burning ruin. This is how we want to win the war. These beasts. With this horrifying mass murder of Jews we have lost the war. An indelible shame, we have brought a curse that can never be extinguished upon ourselves. We deserve no mercy, we are all complicit. I am ashamed to go into the city; every Jew has the right to spit in front of us. Every day German soldiers are being shot; it will get still worse, and we have no right to complain about it. We don't deserve anything else.*

Jews being marched out of the ghetto during the Warsaw Ghetto Uprising in 1943.

The brutal suppression of the Warsaw Ghetto Uprising turned out to be a sign of weakness. It took fully armed German forces four weeks to defeat the sparsely armed underground fighters. The Wehrmacht finally resorted to flame throwers, heavy artillery, and tanks. The Poles' disgust of their occupiers grew. Several days after the resistance ended, Hosenfeld observed the way Jews were being treated as a big mistake. He wrote:

> *Everywhere they were stamped as second-class people. He is the servant, the inferior being. This is shouted into their ears and brought to their attention by any means possible. Before this, the Polish people were cowering and submitting to their fate, but today they carry their burden with pride because they are full of hope that we will lose the war. They have taught us what it means to despise and no longer seek our fellowship.*

✳✳✳

This did not impact the friendly relationships Hosenfeld had established in Poland. People knew the crimes committed by his compatriots against the Poles—be they Jews or Catholics—greatly pained him. The more Polish people he hired, the more often he was invited to their homes to visit with their families. Hosenfeld made progress in learning Polish; he attended the language course taught by Antoni Cieciora, or "Tolka," as he sometimes called him. *How happy I am when I can converse with the Poles, I mean, when I understand them and they understand me*, Hosenfeld wrote.

Because of the general shortage of workers, he employed a Pole of Russian descent as his personal valet. The man knew some German, and Hosenfeld could also practice his Polish language skills with him. *My old Suchalski*, as Hosenfeld called him, *has experienced all of Russia from Lake Baikal to the Caucasus, Baku, and Crimea*. The man brought order to his immediate surroundings; he started the oven in the morning and served him breakfast. *My previous valet did not take care of me as well as he does*, Hosenfeld wrote.

Hosenfeld took part whenever Pastor Cieciora read a mass. This was a dual violation because Cieciora was still wanted by the Gestapo. Hosenfeld avoided religious services in Warsaw conducted by German priests; he felt more comfortable in the company of the Poles. *How soothing this devout assembly of the faithful is*, Hosenfeld wrote. *Everything occurs so unconstrained and naturally*. Cieciora accompanied Hosenfeld on his trips outside of Warsaw and to Kraków. At first, he hesitated to publicly show himself. But he soon came to feel safe in the company of a German officer. Conversely, the priest offered a certain safeguard for Hosenfeld in dangerous situations because he was able to quickly communicate and explain the situation.

Zofia Cieciora once again invited the Hosenfelds to the Karolin estate at the end of May 1943. Hosenfeld asked his wife to accept the invitation. He wanted to talk things over with her; it had not been possible during his previous home leave. *I would be extremely happy*, he wrote. *I have never looked forward to it more than I do now! Come!* He managed to convince Annemarie to come. He met her and their daughter Jorinde at the station in Samter on May 29 and accompanied them to the Karolin estate. The day after, the Ciecioras and their guests went on an excursion to a nearby estate. On June 2, it was again time to part ways.

However, the time together did not end on a harmonious note. During their farewells, Annemarie thought about the situation in Thalau and was once again frightened. As soon as she arrived home she regretted having reproached him yet again. Annemarie wrote: *Don't be angry with me! . . . It is difficult to understand one another after all that has happened. But I assure you that the days in Karolin showed me how loving you are and how lucky I am to be loved by you.* She promised to forget everything and become more aware of her own shortcomings. No person could escape their own skin. She asked her husband to be patient while she figured out how to cope.

In her letter dated June 9, Annemarie underscored that even after almost four years of separation and occasional rifts, she still found herself drawn to him. *I do not know of a stronger desire than to be with you and to share a simple, work-filled life with you,* she wrote. *Everything I do, in the house and garden, in the village or out and about, I experience it all with you and let you take part in it. I miss your advice, your help—your love—daily and by the hour.*

In his letters, Wilm Hosenfeld did everything he could to resolidify the relationship. The children remained the common thread; their welfare was his main concern. He again regretted he could not see them grow up and was unable to be an influence on their development. Uta was six and would soon start school. Jorinde transferred to the secondary school in Fulda. Impressions made during childhood were lasting and crucial in shaping the future. In one letter, Hosenfeld wrote:

> *Dear Annemie — I believe that you would now be very pleased with me, if you could see my daily life. I have much work to do, my tasks are very diverse, and from early until late in the day I am mentally and physically busy. I feel healthy and happy with what I am doing. With everything that I do, the bittersweet feeling that I cannot have you here with me and that I miss you accompanies me.*

5

Help for People in Distress

During the summer months of 1943, Wilm Hosenfeld again increasingly directed his focus toward the military situations on the various fronts. For him, the question was no longer whether Germany would lose the war, but when. His opinion about the specific time wavered. Sometimes he felt the fighting could soon end; other times he was no longer certain.

His analysis and observation gained in sharpness and clarity. At the beginning of July, Hosenfeld recognized there was virtually no more mention being made about the operations of German submarines; the number of Allied ships they sank had also significantly declined. In conversations with Waffen-SS officers, he was informed the subs had retreated for tactical reasons and were preparing a counterattack. In his journal, Hosenfeld described this assumption as naïveté. In fact, the English had developed a very effective submarine defense strategy that made it difficult for German boats to attack convoys. What he and the German high command did not know was the British had successfully broken the Wehrmacht's Enigma codes at the end of 1942, thereby ending the string of successes of German submarines against Allied ships.

Hosenfeld noted a distinct shift of power had taken place on the Eastern Front. *The initiative now rests with the enemy,* he wrote. *He dictates the course of the war. We have moved from blitzkrieg to sitting and waiting for the enemy to act. But a war has never been won from a defensive position. We also do not have to wait for the enemy to be worn down, but instead, our enemy can wait for this to occur.* Hitler had ordered soldiers to march into the

Russian wasteland, and now they felt abandoned, lied to, and betrayed. This was the main reason for the setbacks on the Eastern Front, and it would eventually lead to a collapse. Plus, of course, there were problems getting supplies.

On July 10, Allied troops under the command of US General Dwight D. Eisenhower landed in Sicily. Within a few weeks, they forced German units to abandon the island. The military reports at first indicated the Wehrmacht would push the attackers into the ocean. Hosenfeld did not believe it. *On the opposition, the English and Americans are fighting with great superiority in equipment and armament and are united, while the relationship between German and Italian troops is not good and the Italian civilian population is clearly hostile to the German troops*, Hosenfeld noted.

The Allied landing in Sicily triggered an exchange of power in Italy on July 25. The Italian dictator Benito Mussolini was forced to resign and was subsequently arrested. The Italian king appointed Marshal Pietro Badoglio to head the government. *Fascism is experiencing its first failure*, Hosenfeld wrote. Six weeks later, German paratroopers freed Mussolini from prison. Hosenfeld distrusted Badoglio's announcement that the war would continue. What Mussolini had failed to achieve over the years would not be attainable for the military dictatorship under worse conditions. Besides, Hosenfeld wrote, *the yearning for peace is as strong in Italy as it is in Germany.*

Hosenfeld was proven right sooner than he thought. Marshal Badoglio negotiated a ceasefire with the Allies on September 3, but made this news public five days later, perhaps out of fear of Italy's ally, Germany. The Nazis had already suspected the "betrayal," and thus occupied central and northern Italy. (Mussolini was appointed head of this territory.) Hosenfeld used the term "betrayal" when he wrote to his wife on November 9. *In Warsaw, news of the betrayal of the Italians has brought about great joy to the Poles*, Hosenfeld observed. *To mark the occasion, they have been getting drunk. Our neighbor is so happy that he closed his store and is sitting in the adjacent bar. He is treating everyone and kisses everyone who comes through the door.*

Hosenfeld was not in a mood to celebrate, even if he had predicted the development in southern Europe. Instead, he offered a sober and self-critical reckoning: he asked how it was possible National Socialism had become so powerful. Whereas most Germans were willing and able to admit their own complicity many years later—if at all—Hosenfeld underwent his own self-scrutiny in the middle of the war. In a journal entry dated July 6, he reflected:

> We like to put the blame on others instead of looking for it in ourselves. . . . At the time that the Nazis came to power, we did nothing to prevent it. We have betrayed our own ideals, the ideal of personal freedom, of democratic freedom, and of religious freedom. The worker went along, the church observed. The citizen was too cowardly, as were the top spiritual leaders. We allowed the unions to be smashed, that religious denominations were oppressed, there was no freedom of opinion in the press or broadcasting. In the end, we allowed ourselves to be driven to war.

What conclusions did Hosenfeld draw from this awakening? First, he did what he had done since the start of the war in Poland: he helped people in distress, which he viewed in accordance with his religious beliefs and which the Auschwitz survivor Arno Lustiger called "rescue resistance."

Without regard for risk, Hosenfeld expanded his assistance once he understood the extent of the crimes committed in the name of Germany. In his writings, he considered how the Nazi regime could be stopped, and arrived at an idea other officers had embraced. *It appears to me that the only hope for a reasonably favorable cessation of the war is in having the generals of the Wehrmacht take over the command and end the war*, he wrote. He believed Germany was still fairly strong at the time. *We might still be able to manage a fight against Russia if we mobilize all of our forces in the East.*

Several (34 in total) assassination attempts on Hitler by senior military members had already failed. For example, a time bomb smuggled onto Hitler's plane by Colonel Henning von Tresckow on March 13, 1943, had not exploded due to a defective detonator. Hosenfeld was not aware of these attempts. Had he been asked, would he have participated? At one point in his journal, Hosenfeld wrote: *An overthrow can also not be expected to come from the army. They are allowing themselves to be willfully driven to their deaths.*

Hosenfeld assured his wife he was keeping an eye on the general situation and the coming political events. It could not be ruled out he might also be sent to the front. Several of his comrades had already gone, but he no longer seriously expected to be deployed there—he was still needed in Warsaw.

Wilm Hosenfeld.

***

The sports activities kept Hosenfeld busy again during the summer of 1943. He organized the athletic festival of the Hitler Youth. This was mostly a compulsory event for young recruits and members of the League of German Girls, which featured marches and parades. Joyless faces looked back at Hosenfeld, and he regretted that Polish youths were not allowed to take part in sports activities. He considered this to be an admission of weakness, a fear of the self-asserting will of the Polish people.

Another Wehrmacht Sports Week was scheduled for the end of August. This event required extensive preparation. In between planning, Hosenfeld looked after a camera team from the Ministry of Propaganda, which had commissioned a film about the recreational activities of soldiers for its weekly newsreel. In front of the cameras, sergeants chased recruits across the field and harshly insulted them. It was meant to present an appearance of rigorous training and rigid discipline.

Hosenfeld was given an additional task in August. He was to organize an event for students serving in the military in the form of a one-week intensive refresher course. He brought professors from various German universities to Warsaw. Hosenfeld described his responsibilities to his wife: *I am responsible for the courses, must look after the professors, create a lesson plan, provide food and shelter for the participants, hold the opening address, welcome the professors, also carry out the closing ceremony in the name of the commander, procure theater tickets, and who knows what else.*

The first course covered economic science and technology. During the opening presentation, Hosenfeld again experienced a university-like atmosphere. The students, including some who had already completed their studies and started their professional lives, welcomed him with the stamping of feet and drumming of hands. In addition to the regular sports courses, vocational training, and exams for a general high school diploma and a master's certificate, the sports school now also offered tertiary education courses—another highlight for Hosenfeld's educational efforts.

The thank-you letters Hosenfeld received after the conclusion of the course indicate the students appreciated the seminar. One sergeant wrote he would never forget the days he spent in Warsaw. After the monotony of army life, the quest for knowledge and mental agility had been reawakened. *If I am capable of doing so, I will make every effort to belong to the "sourdough" that you, captain, spoke of in your closing remarks!*

the sergeant wrote. A rifleman who had also participated was not quite sure why he felt compelled to write to Hosenfeld: *Perhaps what makes me so thankful is the feeling that for the first time in quite a while a human being was speaking with me.*

Such lines never led Hosenfeld, the progressive teacher, to become arrogant. He sensed how lonesome these young people were and how it benefited them to find a considerate and understanding officer. Some of the young participants assured him that his statements had meant more to them than some of the professors' lectures.

Annemarie could only marvel at her husband's many activities. She wanted to know about everything related to his work. She received copies of his lectures, reviewed them, and provided her critical feedback. Her situation at home had not changed in the meantime. Annemarie was still trying to make the best of the complicated situation with the Polish domestic helper. Land was leased to plant potatoes. A new pig had to be procured to fatten and slaughter. Annemarie required an official permit for the purchase. She negotiated a price with a farmer and found sufficient feed for the pig.

The dark-haired pig was, interestingly enough, called Adolf and soon developed quite a reputation in the village. It plundered the children's schoolbags and constantly escaped and barged into neighboring farms. Uta had to go with a bucket of food to entice the animal to come back home—which did not always work.

Other unforeseeable things occurred. One evening, Annemarie forgot to switch off the light in the pantry—a violation of a national blackout directive. Some unknown people then shattered the kitchen windows, terrifying everyone in the house.

Detlev Hosenfeld was conscripted as a helper for the air force in Kassel. Annemarie was unsettled by the mere thought of her boy in a uniform. When he brought a suitcase down from the attic, tears came to her eyes. She now followed reports about Allied air raids on German cities even more intently. When bombs fell on Kassel, her fear increased.

Hitler with Nazi officers inspecting damage from Allied air raids.

***

Wilm Hosenfeld also felt helpless despair as large German cities were reduced to rubble. Hamburg, Cologne, Munich—the German air force was no match for the Allied bomber groups. Something else that heavily weighed on Hosenfeld was the security situation in Warsaw, which had dramatically deteriorated in fall 1943. *Life here is becoming increasingly unbearable. Bold and cold-blooded organized gangs are attacking police cars, shooting dead hated Germans, invading homes and offices, and kill*[ing] *those Germans whose behavior against the Polish has made them unpopular,* he wrote on October 20, 1943.

Two days earlier, 20 Poles who had randomly been arrested and held hostage in Warsaw were publicly shot and killed. This execution, the kind that occurred almost daily, was meant to act as a deterrent, but achieved the opposite result. The residents viewed the murdered Poles as martyrs. Meanwhile, attacks on Germans increased. *On that same day and for days following, the residents of Warsaw held processions at the place of the execution. The square was filled with flowers*, Hosenfeld wrote. Before their executions, some of the hostages appealed to the gathered masses for continued resistance, stating there should be no mourning since they were dying for a free Poland. One of them even sang the Polish national anthem before the deadly shots were fired.

One day at lunchtime, Hosenfeld passed by a crowd of people standing around an advertising column. The occupying forces had released a notification with the names of over 100 men who were recently shot as hostages. Everyone looking for the names of relatives and acquaintances scowled at Hosenfeld. He quickly continued on his way. Several weeks later, he came across a list of names of 270 Poles who had been publicly executed as an act of retaliation. The majority of Polish residents denounced the attacks, but they were powerless to stop them. *I actually believe that the secret state police welcomes an excuse to eradicate the Polish population*, Hosenfeld wrote. *It has been their policy from the start of the war to destroy the Polish intelligentsia.* According to Nazi documents, between mid-September and mid-October, the Warsaw headquarters registered 46 injured German soldiers and police officers due to raids and attacks. There is no mention made of the number of Polish hostages executed during this same period.

***

Hosenfeld traveled to Thalau at the end of October for two weeks of home leave. During his stay, there was much work to be done in the house, yard, and garden. Annemarie appreciated having her husband home to help. (The Polish woman and her son had left at the beginning of the month.) But this third home leave of 1943 also meant Wilm would not celebrate the Christmas holidays with his family. He had to remain in Warsaw.

The letters Annemarie sent to her husband in November and December were always about the children, her daily concerns, and especially the war, an end to which was her fondest wish. *How are things in Warsaw?* she wrote in one letter. *Do you have much work? When do the new courses start? The news from the front is depressing, in addition to the attacks in Germany, in Ludwigshafen, Berlin. Where will these poor people stay during this cold?*

At the end of November, she wrote:

> *The enemy bombers are buzzing above us without a pause. We are still safe here, but our dear loved ones elsewhere! I have received no news from Helmut since he was last here. I made a package for Detlev today; a comrade of his will take it along from Fulda. The air raids on Frankfurt and Stuttgart were terrible, and much worse still in Bremen. The darkness of November. The wind howls around the house and the rain lashes against the windows. Advent season!*

The weather was equally stormy in Warsaw. On November 27, Hosenfeld was once again en route with a delegation from the Ministry of Propaganda. This time, a plane took him to Minsk, Belarus. From there, he was to lead a team of filmmakers to the Eastern Front, where the reporters were supposed to interview Polish defectors in a prison. Due to inclement weather, the plane made an unscheduled landing at a military field near Baranavichy, Belarus. It was Hosenfeld's first-ever flight and he was airsick. He was happy to have solid ground under his feet upon his return to Warsaw.

In December, Hosenfeld was notified that Karl Fischer, one of his former students whose parents he met during his latest home leave, had died. The young soldier had both legs amputated after a battle on the Eastern Front. Already weak from blood loss upon reaching a hospital in Lviv, Ukraine, blood poisoning and diphtheria proved too much for his body to handle. *And so the calamity passes from house to house and town to town,* Annemarie wrote, following a memorial service for the fallen soldier. The entire village felt the pain. The number of "mothers of heroes" in Thalau was increasing. Annemarie wrote: *It is difficult to understand God's love.*

Hosenfeld wrote to his wife about another event that exemplified the full horrors of the war. An officer—like Hosenfeld, a teacher by profession—who taught at the sports school in Warsaw, was summoned to Berlin by a telegram that mentioned "airplane damage." The officer arrived just in time to see the bodies of his three children, his wife, and her parents being pulled out of the basement of their collapsed house. About the incident, Hosenfeld wrote: *He said he could not touch them; he had only stared at the workers and the bodies. When he saw the hands of the 10-year-old boy and the 12-year-old girl, he recognized that they had scratched off their fingertips on the walls in agony. Something had broken within him at that point.*

Hosenfeld had not known how to console his comrade. Instead, he remained silent. With tears filling his eyes, the man softly squeezed Hosenfeld's hand and told him that he had planned to celebrate Christmas with his family. Hosenfeld further related the man's words: *I never would have imagined that it was possible to be left with nothing. Sometimes, it's as though I'm standing at the top of the Strasbourg Cathedral, where I grew up, and step across the parapet onto thin air. I sometimes feel how I tumble to the ground, and I see my shattered body lying down there.*

While Annemarie still hoped for a miracle that would bring him home at the last moment for the Christmas holidays, Wilm resigned himself to remaining in Warsaw. On the day before Christmas Eve, he celebrated with his Polish workers—there were 30 of them by then. They prepared a dinner and cleared a classroom to make space for all of them. Antoni Cieciora, Hosenfeld's right-hand man in many situations, introduced him to Polish Christmas traditions, insofar as these could be realized in a time of acute food shortage. Hosenfeld vividly described the setting in his writings:

> *We began with borscht, which is a tasty beetroot soup with white bread. Thereafter, Herr Cieciora first spoke in Polish, before address-*

ing the good wishes in German. Everyone had a wafer before them; not round in form, but square. As this was my house, I had the largest. Now, one after the other came to me. I broke off a piece of each wafer held out to me, while they all each took a piece of mine, which we all ate. At the same time, everyone wished each other all the best.

After the meal, Hosenfeld made a speech in Polish. He had procured candy from a confectionery factory in Warsaw and gave each employee a bag of candy. Finally, after thanking him for hiring them, the workers cheered for Hosenfeld.

Father Antoni Cieciora or "Tolka."

On Christmas Eve, Hosenfeld's thoughts were with his family in Thalau. Pictures of his wife and five children stood on a nightstand. Two candles burned next to them. *I am lying on the bed and am not lonely,* he wrote. *All of you are standing before me. I see you, how you are singing your songs and how you are happy and how you are sad.*

Among Hosenfeld's staff was a German who had arrived in Warsaw shortly before Christmas. He was supposed to replace a private who had returned to his family in Germany. Karl Hörle came from Hanau and was a communist. Hosenfeld was curious as to why the man had walking difficulties. Hörle responded he was not allowed to speak about it. Eventually, though, Hörle opened up and told Hosenfeld he had been tortured by the Gestapo in a concentration camp. Hosenfeld described the man's situation:

> *He showed me his feet. They were covered with scars and black and blue contusions. He had been subject to "bastinado," the beating punishment. They hit the bare feet with sticks until the flesh hangs in strips. He has no more teeth; they were knocked out during the interrogation. As he was lying on the floor, a member of the SS had kicked him in the face, shattering his lower jaw. He now has a heart condition from the horrible torments he suffered during one and a half years in the concentration camp.*

In his journal entry dated December 28, Hosenfeld noted he had heard much about the inhumanity of the SS, but always thought it could not be true. Now, for the first time, a person stood across from him who could irrefutably prove it all. Hosenfeld recorded everything Hörle told him and all he had previously heard about the SS and Gestapo torture methods, so as to keep a record of it. In one entry, he wrote:

> *The victims had their teeth smashed out, their fingernails torn off, holes bored into their kneecaps with a drill. [They] were hung up with their arms crossed behind their back[s], so that the shoulder joints dislocate. [They also] wrapped wire around someone's genitals and pulled him, before hanging him from it. He died of that. Many suffered an agonizing death. Now I can imagine how the unlucky Jews and Poles were made to suffer, if their own ethnic compatriots were treated in such a way.*

Among other examples, this written record also proves that Nazi crimes were known in detail. Hosenfeld feared the "thugs" at the top of the regime wanted to drag the entire nation toward ruin. He saw a connection between the murders committed in Germany and those carried out in the East and where he was stationed:

> *The atrocities here in the East, in Poland, in Yugoslavia and Russia, are merely a straightforward continuation of what had initially happened to political enemies in Germany. And we fools believed that they could lead us to a better future. Every person must be ashamed today at ever having—even in the slightest—professed faith in this system. How we have been deceived and made to look like fools.*

***

For Hosenfeld, 1944 began as depressingly as the previous year had ended. *At night when I cannot sleep, the concerns about Germany's future and fears about our own fate come crawling to me, frightening me*, he confessed. There were no longer any indications things would improve. The previous year had brought heavy casualties on the Eastern Front. The Wehrmacht had retreated approximately 800 miles. Hundreds of Allied bombers flew over Germany almost daily with the aim of destroying industrial plants. Before long, no German business would remain intact.

At the beginning of the year, German newspapers were critical of the American advance into southern Italy, claiming the Allied troops had seized treasured works of art. To Hosenfeld, this appeared to be the height of hypocrisy, considering the Germans had carried out large-scale raids to plunder the cultural artifacts of Poland and Russia.

Hosenfeld was admitted to a hospital during the first week in January, suffering from intense pain and breathing difficulties. The doctor diagnosed influenza and inflammation of the lungs, and he was bedridden for a week. He was allowed to go home for two weeks of sick leave at the end of the month. In contrast to previous visits, Hosenfeld did not rush into working at home, instead taking things slow. He made time for long talks with his wife and the children. Detlev, who had received a few days' leave from his job as an air force helper, recalled, "I still remember Father speaking about the concentration camps, the extermination of Jews, and the gas chambers; also about the teams that had to remove the dead bodies and who were then shot, so they could not be able to report about the mass murders." The visit was the last time Detlev saw his father.

Hosenfeld had only just returned to Warsaw when another round of uncertainty set in. The sergeant who picked him up at the train station told him that he was to immediately undergo a medical examination. The criteria for classifying soldiers as "fit for military action" had been loosened in order to fill the massive gaps in the rows of German troops. The doctor initially classified Hosenfeld as "conditionally fit for military action," but soon afterward removed the word "conditionally."

Captain Hosenfeld thus expected he could be sent to the front or another country occupied by Germany. His Polish staff members were dismayed. If Hosenfeld were no longer there to look after them, most would be in grave danger. He was calm at first, but then also began to despair. *What is left to still fight for? All of the senselessness of this life came down upon me like lead,* Hosenfeld wrote. He felt like a chess piece that was moved back and forth on a board, and became depressed.

Hosenfeld's superiors tried to keep him in Warsaw, but their efforts seemed to make no difference. All indications were that he would soon depart for a new task. He tried to calm Annemarie by telling her it was surely no longer in the cards he would be sent to the front. Hosenfeld invited his comrades to a going-away party on March 12. He had known some of them for a long time and built friendly relationships. He did not want to simply disappear from their lives. The farewell celebration took place, but his call up did not occur. Suddenly, it was uncertain if Hosenfeld would leave at all.

At any rate, his daily routine continued. The teaching activities needed to regain momentum since participation had declined as a result of nighttime curfews. Hosenfeld decided to move courses into hospitals and military facilities on the edge of the city so soldiers would not have to travel so far. *I occasionally need to stop off at the hospitals, and*

I always make sure to visit the injured. My eyes fill with tears; the sight of these wounded and maimed soldiers moves me every time. There was one lying there with his hands shot off, the stumps stood upright on the pillows. He even tried to make a salute, he wrote.

The continued training of soldiers was important to Hosenfeld, even though his uncertain future distracted him from fully concentrating on the matter. The response from the troops to the new course selection was mixed. Most of the soldiers welcomed the opportunity to continue their education. Others wanted to instead idle away their time. Hosenfeld thankfully noted on March 23: *Presently, three of my students are taking the examinations for a high school certificate.*

Wilm Hosenfeld in 1944.

***

Meanwhile, Władysław Szpilman's struggle for survival continued unabated. At times, he was able to spend a few weeks in a hideout friends had prepared for him, feeling relatively safe. Other times, he would stay only a few days because neighbors spotted him and he had to again flee to avoid being turned in. The SS, the Gestapo, and an army of informants created a climate of fear and intimidation.

The situation was only made worse by the setbacks and defeats the Wehrmacht experienced on the various fronts. Helping a prominent Jewish fugitive in such a situation represented a special risk. Shelter was not the only problem; the pianist also had to be supplied with food. Anyone who interacted in any way with Szpilman put their own life in grave danger. Nonetheless, the network functioned, albeit with disruptions.

One day, Szpilman observed a group of SS men enter the building where he was hiding. They began to search individual apartments. It was already too late to flee. He barricaded the door and knotted a rope with which he would hang himself if need be. Szpilman did not want the Germans to capture him alive. But they did not find him. They were searching for someone else. However, the building remained surrounded so he was unable to receive food deliveries. Szpilman made his reserves last as long as possible until these were also gone and he had only water to drink.

Szpilman prepared himself for starvation until one day a man knocked on his door and finally brought him something to eat. Szalas was the man's surname. Szpilman later found out the man had collected money for him throughout Warsaw on behalf of an underground organization. *Because people were not stingy when the rescue of a person was at stake, a considerable amount of money was collected,* Szpilman wrote. *He assured my friends that he visited me almost daily and that I had all that I needed.* In reality, Szalas only appeared every now and then and almost let Szpilman die of hunger. Szpilman fell ill with jaundice and suffered from gall-bladder inflammation; thus, he also required medication. *If the Gestapo had come now, I would not have been capable of hanging myself,* Szpilman wrote. For the most part, he was in a semi-conscious state. As soon as he awoke, he was plagued by hunger pangs.

Once Szpilman's friends found out about Szalas's deceit, the untiring efforts of a Polish woman with whom he was friends slowly brought Szpilman back from the brink. *Thank God that I was not dependent upon the "care" of Szalas at this time,* he wrote. *Instead, I was taken care of by the best, most self-sacrificing of the women, Frau Helena.* With her help, he gradually regained his health during the early part of 1944.

***

In a long letter to his wife, Wilm Hosenfeld considered what would happen after the war. He had previously written similar thoughts to Helmut. Hosenfeld had no ambition for himself other than to return to his career as a teacher. It would be a rather humble new start, both he and Annemarie understood this. They owned no valuables and no home of their own. The family just barely made ends meet. *Peace will be very hard, it cannot be otherwise,* Hosenfeld wrote. *All of us must help to rebuild the destroyed cities and provide a roof over the heads of the homeless and feed them.*

Hosenfeld thought less of himself, and instead, more about the large social problems the war had caused. He was convinced the victors would not allow themselves to be ruled by hate and revenge in their dealings with the Germans; they would not enslave people. The yearning for peace and the will for reparation had been awakened in all nations. *A truly great democratic era will be ushered in,* Hosenfeld observed. But what would be the consequences for the extermination of the Jews, the exodus and expulsion and forced labor, and the destruction of cities? On March 25, he wrote to Annemarie:

> *For as long as the earth has existed, never have such masses been in movement as in this war. Starting with the fleeing and returning inhabitants of the border areas in Poland, the resettled ethnic Germans, the refugees in France, now in Italy, in Russia. Two, three times the people were forced to move. The Russian civilian population has endured unspeakable things. Then, the extermination of several million Jews, the destruction of German cities, and the scattering of its residents. In addition, there are millions of people of foreign ethnicity who were brought to Germany as forced laborers. And above all of that, the millions-strong armed forces of the hostile nations stand across from one another prepared to destroy each other.*

At the end of March, the Polish workers at the sports school expected Hosenfeld to leave them. Granted, it was still not clear if or when he would be reassigned. The employees, however, wanted to show their appreciation for Hosenfeld's willingness to help and what his friendly character meant to them. They prepared a type of certificate, written by hand in Polish and German, with 27 signatures. The first signature was "Cichocki A," the code name for the Polish priest Antoni Cieciora. A finely drawn branch with leaves and blossoms decorated the envelope. The signatories' letter was addressed to *Panu Kapitanowi Hosenfeldowi* (Mr. Captain Hosenfeld). It read:

> *Dear Captain! During the time that we had the honor of being allowed to work together with you, we have come to know and appreciate you as a caring father and exemplary boss. If we could, we would want to always work together with you.*
>
> *Today we have come together, not to say goodbye to, but to honor you with the offer of a small gift. May this gift serve as a lasting remembrance and always remind you of the Polish workers of the sports school.*
>
> *May the [Black] Madonna of Częstochowa bring continual happiness and blessing upon you and your family.*
>
> *Warsaw, March 29, 1944*

Hosenfeld would have been hard-pressed to imagine a more striking acknowledgment of his actions. Amid a sea of persecution and violence he had succeeded in creating an island of humanity. What his coworkers actually wanted to express—and what they would much later testify to when efforts to secure Hosenfeld's release from Soviet imprisonment were underway—was something they could not write about in the spring of 1944 without endangering themselves and their rescuer.

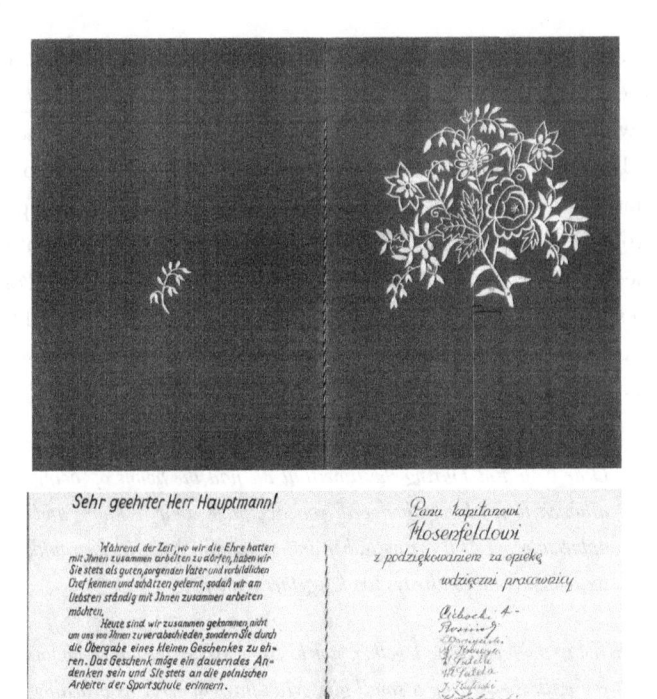

The thank-you card given to Wilm Hosenfeld by his employees at the Warsaw sports complex on March 29, 1944.

Hosenfeld sent the document to Thalau so it would not be lost. He also sent other documents home. Hosenfeld anticipated impending hardship more clearly than ever before. Annemarie immediately reacted when the post arrived in Thalau: *Today your certificate arrived, the thankfulness of your Polish workers. How touching their devotion is. I am very happy for you. They will surely be sad when they lose you.*

She included a poem by Manfred Hausmann with her letter dated April 4. Annemarie had recently met the poet in Worpswede. A visit to the artists' colony, and seeing her father and friends again, had been good for her. It offered a pleasant change from the daily monotony in Thalau. *Worpswede is a different world, and the homesickness for this world has never left me*, she wrote. Annemarie would have liked to visit Bremen, but it was too risky due to the frequent air raids. On the return trip, she waited for hours on her connecting train in the extensively destroyed Hannover station.

Annemarie informed her husband about the groups of refugees she had encountered during her trips to Fulda and the neighboring villages. People left the large cities by the thousands, heading for the country, including Thalau in the Rhön Mountains. Annemarie observed:

> *Refugees from Frankfurt, Nürnberg* [Nuremberg], *Kassel, a woman with four children, one in a carriage, the other three walking alongside with packages and backpacks. The father with two suitcases, one giant backpack leading the way. Ladies dressed in black with packages, suitcases, some wearing incredible combinations of clothes. Before you would have wanted to laugh. Who laughs today!*

While the propaganda of the doomed Nazi regime proclaimed optimism and a willingness to make sacrifices, Hosenfeld perceived the mood of the Germans in Warsaw quite differently. *The Germans are demoralized, jaded, and almost indifferent to the war*, he wrote. Everyone was preoccupied with their own personal problems.

As there had been one year prior, another two-week gas-defense training course was scheduled for April in Bydgoszcz. Hosenfeld convinced his wife to meet him there again, although travel had become even more dangerous. The Allied bombers increasingly attacked trains. Anemone had successfully passed her nursing exam, but had yet to find a job. Therefore, she returned home and took care of her young siblings and the household, allowing Annemarie to spend two weeks away. Annemarie arrived in Bydgoszcz on April 17. She had a room in the Hotel *Danziger Hof* where her husband was staying.

On their return trip, the couple stopped in Danzig and Gdingen, which the Germans renamed Gotenhafen and expanded into a naval base for large warships during the occupation. The Hosenfelds viewed one of the ships, a heavy cruiser. Hosenfeld was excited about the technological marvel. He and his wife made a further stopover in Samter to visit their Polish friends, the Ciecioras.

Back in Warsaw, Hosenfeld found his workplace unchanged. On May 8, he wrote to Thalau: *I am approaching my work with a renewed sense of courage. I thoroughly enjoy it after the relaxation and the nice and peaceful time we spent together.* He planned his next visit to Thalau for the middle of May. Hosenfeld wanted to spend Pentecost with his family.

6

Final Home Leave

Wilm Hosenfeld spent only three days, from May 27 to 30, 1944, with his family in Thalau. Except for Detlev, who was still carrying out his duties as an air force helper, all the children were home for Pentecost. Helmut returned to Frankfurt after a short visit. None of them could have suspected this would be Wilm Hosenfeld's final home leave or that they would never see him again. Following the visit, Annemarie wrote: *My dear Wilm! Oh, how nice it was last week. I keep recalling the memories of the short, but blessed days; they give me strength each day for the hard work and difficulties of my daily routine.*

Wilm Hosenfeld with Jorinde (*standing*) and Anemone (*sitting*) during his final home leave.

Her husband had similar feelings:

> *My dear Annemarie, my dear three girls. . . . My thoughts are always with you in remembrance of the lovely days. Today it seems like a dream to me. Every day was unique. On the first day we worked in the garden, the second day was characterized by the enemy planes, on the third day we did sports. . . . On my way back, as the train pulled into the Eisenach station, the sirens were howling. The other passengers told me about the frequent attacks on moving trains and a nervous tension spread to the people, but I had the feeling that nothing would happen. . . . At the train stations, always the same scenes, parents saying goodbye, women and children. I can still see you standing at the Schmalnau station, how you were waving to the departing train. . . . Yes, it was wonderful being with you!*

***

On June 6, 1944, an enormous military force of American, British, and Canadian troops landed on the beaches of Normandy on the French Atlantic coast. The mission, Operation Overlord—commonly known as D-Day—was carried out by land and air. The Allies' battle to break through the German Siegfried Line in Western Europe was the second front for which Soviet leader Joseph Stalin had repeatedly called, so the Red Army could continue its forward offensive in the East before delivering the final blow against Germany. *This is the end*, Hosenfeld commented. It was, in fact, the beginning of the end. But Hitler had no intention to capitulate.

Hosenfeld was aware the Western Allies had considerable military superiority on the sea and in the air. But he did not want to believe Germany no longer had any air defenses. Following the Allies' successful landing at Normandy, a new Soviet offensive was expected. Thus, for the time being, he put aside any hope of visiting his family. All the same, Annemarie ardently hoped he would be able to come home soon—the visit over Pentecost, after all, had been short.

Outwardly, life in Warsaw continued as usual. Hosenfeld even took time to visit a German bookseller he had known for a long time. The man liked to bring him to a back room where he kept banned or ostracized books.

Hosenfeld was thankful for every day he could still enjoy in peace and quiet, he wrote to his wife on June 15. He expected an imminent transfer, where to remained unknown. In the middle of a letter to Annemarie, one of Wilm's sentences read like a last wish: *Raise the children as God-fearing. You are surprised that I write such a thing. But I am serious, and I know otherwise we build upon sand.*

Antoni Cieciora, whom Hosenfeld now referred to in his letters as *my acquaintance* for reasons of safety, invited him to a service commemorating his 10-year anniversary as a priest. The Eucharist celebration took place under conspiratorial circumstances in a Warsaw church. Cieciora confirmed after the war that Hosenfeld—in full uniform—assisted as an acolyte. The German soldier knelt before a Polish priest wanted by the Gestapo and whom he employed under an alias at his sports school.

One day, when Hosenfeld entered a Polish church where a children's mass was being conducted, he became the focus of attention. Some of the youths recognized him from the sports fields and warmly greeted him. *They are very happy to see me and want to demonstrate their friendship*, Hosenfeld wrote. *One of them came from the other end of the church and stood near me, smiling at me.*

The piety of the Polish people impressed him. *The devout assembly of people of faith is very soothing*, Hosenfeld wrote. Everything happened informally and as a matter of course. His personal interpretation of being a Christian was not limited to forms and rituals. When Father Cieciora told Hosenfeld the Germans had removed a sacred heart of Jesus statue in Poznań, he told Annemarie that while tangible things can be destroyed, those that cannot be seen are beyond grasp. *Modern heathenism can probably forget about them and even try to eliminate them*, he wrote. *They will destroy something to demonstrate their power somewhere at some time. The supernatural is the true reality.*

In one of his last letters from Warsaw, Hosenfeld addressed rumors being circulated by Joseph Goebbels that Germany would soon possess a secret weapon of immense destructive power that would lead to a turning point in the war. Hosenfeld wrote: *Nobody believes that. He* [Goebbels] *surely does not. Our friends* [referring to the Allies] *possess such air superiority that they are in a position to bring about a decision in their favor merely through their air force.*

***

On June 29, 1944, two young officers from a military police detachment sought out Hosenfeld during a lunch break to speak with him about his next assignment. The reason for their visit was the renewed command, personally ordered by Hitler, to locate personnel reserves who could fill gaps on the fronts. About the men, Hosenfeld wrote: *Both of them* [were] *decorated with medals, officers from the front, dashing young men, self-important on account of their authority.* He brought them onto a porch and was subjected to rigorous questioning about his functions. Hosenfeld showed them the current course catalog and voluminous reports he had compiled over time, and confidently paged through the long list of his responsibilities and activities.

The two military police officials, who had no idea as to the duties of a sports officer and surely viewed Hosenfeld as a candidate for the front, were astonished and accepted defeat. *Their drawn pencils disappeared, and the large, empty printed forms stayed blank,* he wrote. *Later on, I still brought them to the swimming pool, showed them the sports fields and the boathouse. They were quite interested and registered themselves for sailing during their next free time.*

This was an easy victory, but Hosenfeld derived no satisfaction from it. Everything that would happen around him in the following days and weeks foreshadowed nothing good. The Warsaw civilian administration ordered the closing of German schools. Children were forced to leave Warsaw, and their parents and relatives joined them. In a matter of days, an exodus of people developed, initially in an orderly fashion. Hosenfeld wrote to his wife on July 2 that she could not imagine what was happening in Warsaw:

> *The evacuation started yesterday. First women and children, of course only the German civilian residents. The trucks were on all streets, furniture vans were in the German neighborhoods. People are only permitted to bring the most essential items. The things that they acquired here during the war must stay behind. Mostly, it was confiscated property. The trucks are fully packed with crates and sacks, bedding and household dishes, and on top of everything perch the refugees.*

The female support staff of the Wehrmacht, who had worked at headquarters, also left. The exodus was a clear indicator of how the occupying force envisioned upcoming developments would play out. Huge stockpiles of provisions and various goods that filled warehouses were either transported or destroyed; some were blown up and others were simply set on fire, Hosenfeld reported. He also made his own preparations. The things he did not absolutely need in Warsaw were sent by express delivery to Germany. *I have, of course, packed all of my things*, Hosenfeld wrote. *But if we are able to take much with us is another question.* At times, he apparently still expected to return to Germany before the situation further deteriorated in Warsaw. But he could not be certain.

Personnel was moved back and forth between the administrative headquarters and city headquarters. It seemed as though one office did not know what the other was doing. The coordination between the Wehrmacht (running German military operations) and the civilian administration (running Poland) was also not working, which increased the overall level of uncertainty. On July 26, Hosenfeld wrote in his journal:

> *I have not received any orders yet. Occasionally, I have to take care of this and that. Today I had to prepare a train for 400 civilian workers who are supposed to dig antitank ditches in Góra Kalwaria.*

The employment agency issued the order, but nobody showed up. The Poles are no longer following the German commands. It is high time that the civilian administration departs and the Wehrmacht assumes command.

***

It was expected the Red Army would use Góra Kalwaria, about 15 miles southeast of Warsaw, as a staging area for their attack on the capital. The Wehrmacht's idea was to stop the Soviet advance there, but Warsaw residents refused to follow German commands. Summons and appeals were ignored.

There was another sign of the worsening situation: trains heading west, which had previously been filled to the last seat with people going home on leave, were now empty. Instead, many soldiers had to break off their home leaves in order to reinforce troops on the front. Warsaw was designated a "fortified area" in preparation for expected battles. According to a direct order from Hitler, cities near the front were to be militarily fortified, potentially allowing them to be surrounded by enemy troops. Doing so would thus commit and allocate Axis troops to the siege.

There is a nervous tension affecting everyone, a restlessness, and also a gallows humor, Hosenfeld wrote. He expected the worst, even more so since the Army Group Centre (two German army groups) collapsed under the pressure of the Red Army's summer offensive. With that, another dam designed to hold back Soviet troops advancing toward Warsaw had given way. In a letter home, Hosenfeld wrote: *You write that you are often downhearted and sad. Who is not at present? There are very few people who do not have to carry their burden. When I think of all of you at home, it is as though I am on the lookout for a calm and happy island.*

The situation became even more ominous toward the end of July. Detachments of the Red Army were within 30 miles of Warsaw. It would not be long before they reached the Vistula River. On July 30, Hosenfeld wrote in his journal:

There was a full alert last night. All soldiers and officers were deployed for securing the area. Nobody was permitted to sleep in his bed. Everyone had to stay at an alarm post or in his duty room in preparation for battle. During the night, and still now, the thunder of the cannons at the front around Warsaw can be clearly heard. I expect the Russians to surround the city from the southwest and east. They have not yet crossed the Vistula [River], *but they will attempt it today. I was today ordered to the Warsaw Wehrmacht headquarters. With that, I am in the same boat as all the other German soldiers who are stationed here. Hardly anyone will escape if a withdrawal does not occur very soon.*

The Wehrmacht initially tried—and temporarily managed—to stop the advance of Soviet troops by engaging them in a tank battle east of Warsaw. The Soviets suffered heavy casualties. The Wehrmacht could not, however, prevent the Soviets from solidifying their stance at the Vistula River, where they had built two bridgeheads and positioned their troops for a frontal assault. This dashed any hopes held by soldiers and officers in Warsaw that an exodus from the city and a withdrawal toward the west might still be possible.

***

Władysław Szpilman found out from his protector, Helena Lewicka, about the Allies' landing at Normandy and their advance through France. The positive news strengthened his will to survive. *The nicest shock news reports were now increasing with lightning speed: the taking of France, the capitulation of Italy, the Red Army on the border of Poland, the liberation of Lublin,* Szpilman wrote. He also heard about preparations for another imminent uprising in Warsaw, the purchase of submachine guns, and the reinforcement of the underground army. Shortly before the fighting began, Lewicka visited Szpilman one more time in his hiding place to say goodbye. She wept and asked, "Will we ever see one another again, Władek?"

The Polish *Armia Krajowa* (Polish Home Army), in conjunction with the exiled Polish government in London, decided the time had come to liberate Warsaw—before the arrival of the Red Army. Alternatively, if liberation could not be achieved, they would work in unison with the Red Army to defeat the occupying forces. The armed resistance, known as the Warsaw Uprising, began on August 1, 1944. Other underground groups joined the *Armia Krajowa*. The approximately 30,000 fighters managed to initially capture important parts of the city.

During this time, Hosenfeld again assumed the duties of an IC (counterintelligence) officer at city headquarters. He was responsible for obtaining information about the enemy and ascertaining the situation at the front. This duty also included the interrogation of captured underground fighters. Hosenfeld reported his findings to Lieutenant General Rainer Stahel several times a day.

Hosenfeld expected the Soviets to aid the Polish insurgents. But, in spite of requests by the British and Americans, the Red Army refused to help. British and Polish pilots in the British Royal Air Force flew 1,400 miles to drop supplies for the Polish fighters in Warsaw. However, the Soviets did not allow Allied pilots to use their airfields, and a number of pilots lost their lives. Joseph Stalin wanted German troops worn down before launching an attack.

In a letter dated August 4, Hosenfeld informed his wife about the Warsaw Uprising and endeavored to shine a positive light on his duties. It was an interesting new responsibility he enjoyed, but with which he still had to familiarize himself, he wrote. He was doing very well. However, he added: *I am suffering under the effect of this horrible destruction and the many victims on both sides. Until now I have not had to see the horrors of this war. That is why these current experiences are shocking me. I hope that all will still end well and that there is still a way out of this unholy mess.*

Hosenfeld was impressed by the bravery and fighting spirit of the underground army. *Even the use of tanks and heavy aerial bombardment did not appear to make much of an impression* [against the insurgents], he wrote. *Streets are systematically burned down, the civilian population is fleeing somewhere, insurgents occupy the ruins and keep shooting. Whoever is seen on the street is shot.*

Hosenfeld wrote this passage on Sunday, August 6. He took for granted the mail would be delivered to his family. Almost every evening, a convoy, accompanied by tanks, drove to the western suburbs of Warsaw where letters and packages were transferred onto trains. Deliveries in the opposite direction did not work as well. Most of the letters Annemarie sent to her husband in the second half of 1944 did not survive. Perhaps Hosenfeld took them along with him to Russian captivity. On July 13, she anxiously inquired: *How are you doing? Have my letters reached you? I imagine that because of the bombing of Berlin and Leipzig the mail service has been interrupted.* The waiting made her nervous; it was almost unbearable. She ended her letter with a question: *Do you have courage and hope?*

In a letter dated July 16—the last surviving letter Annemarie sent to Wilm in Warsaw—she told him the mail was being delivered only once a week in Thalau. Munich, where Annemarie's sister, Gertrud, lived with her husband, had been heavily bombed. In the letter, Annemarie lamented:

> *It greatly saddens me that there is no chance that we can see each other again in the foreseeable future. There is so much I want to talk to you about and above all else, I need you so much, your love and your comfort. Do you also need me?*
>
> *We hear much about what is currently happening, particularly on the fronts. Should I be happy and relieved, or will the burden of fear and concern become even more unbearable? Probably both are true. What will happen when the Russians come to Warsaw?*
>
> *My dear husband, please send me news as often as it is possible. I have become nervous during the past weeks, it may be related to the strain of too much work.*

Annemarie also reported in the letter about a birthday she had celebrated that day, the honey extraction, and the removal of weeds in the garden. She did not forget to mention the flowerbed with the

Soldiers in the Polish Home Army taking cover during the Warsaw Uprising.

red poppies in full bloom; her husband loved the soft leaves and vibrant color.

Considering all that Wilm Hosenfeld wrote about while in Warsaw, it appears he saw himself as an eyewitness and a chronicler of events meant to later find their way into history books. The entire world looked to Warsaw, the capital city on the Vistula River, which had risen for the second time against a brutal occupying regime. With bravery borne out of desperation, the Poles were trying to win back their freedom.

In order to do whatever was necessary to suppress the uprising, SS Reichsführer Heinrich Himmler sent assault troops to Warsaw. *With every passing day, the city is further reduced to rubble*, Hosenfeld wrote. *Heartbreaking scenes play out in the burning streets. The residents are in their basements and are driven out into the streets—men, women, and children. Yesterday only the men were killed. The day before women and children were also murdered.*

Hosenfeld quoted a first lieutenant of the police forces as saying Himmler had ordered all men to be killed. In fact, tens of thousands of civilians were murdered by units under the command of SS Senior Group Leader Erich von dem Bach-Zelewski during fights in August and September. Himmler had received the order from Hitler that Warsaw was to be "razed to the ground" and the residents "indiscriminately slaughtered."

For the Polish people, Hosenfeld was convinced every day they were able to hang on was a victory. He fully expected the Soviet army to attack; it had assembled a strong force the Wehrmacht would not be able to stop. The only thing that remained uncertain was the time of the attack. After the capture of Warsaw, the Red Army would not stop until it reached the German border. Hosenfeld confided to his journal: *I have accepted the fact that I will not be able to leave Warsaw. The best-case scenario would be Russian captivity.* He was surprised many officers still did not understand their hopeless situation and continued to overestimate the strength of the Wehrmacht.

Hosenfeld gave a letter addressed to his wife to a German officer from Stade in Lower Saxony who was supposed to leave Warsaw, along with his watch and a small set of silver cutlery. He had held on to these valuable items because he considered it too risky to send them by mail. He made no mention to Annemarie about the severity of the situation, not wanting to worry her even more.

***

Meanwhile, a mass exodus was underway in Warsaw. Hosenfeld watched from his office as the entire city was being cleared. With that, Warsaw, and even the war, was lost. In his journal, Hosenfeld wrote:

> *We acted as though we were the rulers and would never leave. Now, when we are forced to admit that all is lost, we destroy all of the work done by the civilian administration, who saw this is a cultural responsibility and was proud to prove to the world its necessity. This is the bankruptcy of our Eastern policy, and with the destruction of Warsaw, this policy has received its final memorial.*

The insurgents did not possess heavy weapons. And the Red Army did nothing to assist the underground fighters. Instead, they hindered the Allied air support. *The Russians would have disdainfully abandoned the Polish*, Hosenfeld wrote to his wife.

He also reported Father Cieciora had come to see him. Cieciora found safety in a camp and asked for written confirmation he had worked for the Germans. At the end of August, Father Cieciora came to him again. This time, he was desperate and begged Hosenfeld to save him. Wilm Hosenfeld wrote:

> *But how? I did my best. Will he make it? I could not take him in with me. He just came from building a barricade. The Poles have to dig trenches in the streets while everything burns around them. Cieciora lived in a part of the city that had been recaptured by the Germans. He could not go back there. I was very sorry, but what could I do?*

Hosenfeld was completely cut off from his other workers. He spent many hours in the office at city headquarters with other German officers. He rarely went outside anymore and complained of headaches. *All around us is an army camp of tanks, soldiers, vehicles, and so on*, he wrote. So far, the military headquarters had not been directly attacked. In a letter home, Hosenfeld wrote: *You are all of course very worried about me. I don't want to lie to you and tell you that everything is looking rosy, but I believe that we will be able to leave in time.*

7

I Try to Save Everyone
Who Can be Saved

How small all concerns and troubles were before when viewed from the chaos of a large city in the throes of death. I would like to pull myself away from all of these thoughts and remember nice and happy times, but I cannot. I can't even find the composure to pray. You must do it for me. How I am waiting for news from you!

When Wilm Hosenfeld wrote these words to his wife and children on August 12, 1944, the battle between the Polish Home Army and the Wehrmacht had not yet been decided. But the defeat of the Polish Home Army was foreseeable, especially since the Red Army, which had advanced to the Vistula River, remained idle. The fighting was concentrated around the old city of Warsaw, where over 30,000 residents were caught between the fronts and held out in basements and partially destroyed buildings. There was also intense fighting in the city center.

Hosenfeld was still working at the city military headquarters. Despite his enormous workload, he continued to write what happened around him or what was on his mind. Perhaps he sensed he did not have much time left to maintain a connection with his family and to keep a written record of the dramatic events around him.

As a staff officer of headquarters, Hosenfeld served as the right-hand man to General Rainer Stahel, who had been transferred from Lithuania to Warsaw in July. The general had broken through the Soviet encirclement at Vilnius, Lithuania, and fought his way over toward the west.

Stahel repeatedly placed Hosenfeld on risky assignments. Hosenfeld and two Polish clergy drove through the city beyond the river to the district of Praga. On the way, the priests were to view the extent of the destruction and prompt residents of Praga, which was still intact, to vacate that part of the city. General Stahel had told them that impending battles made the clearing of Praga imperative and necessary.

On August 20, again on the orders of his superior, Hosenfeld brought auxiliary bishop Antoni Władysław Szlagowski, the acting head of the archdiocese of Warsaw, to safe surroundings. The trip first took them to Sochaczew, about 35 miles west of Warsaw. Szlagowski took a hotel room there. The next morning, Hosenfeld accompanied the bishop to a nurse's residence where a temporary emergency residence was set up for him. *The last part of the journey, about 1 kilometer* [a little over half a mile], *passed through a partisan area, and the venerable old man* [age 80 at the time] *had to get into an armored car*, Hosenfeld wrote. *He was afraid that something would happen. But everything was fine.* General Stahel gave Hosenfeld some medicine to take along for a nun. The woman had been seriously injured when she was caught in the crossfire between German soldiers and partisans in an attempt to recover an injured German soldier. Another nun had been killed during the incident.

The headquarters of SS General Erich von dem Bach-Zelewski was also located in Sochaczew. Bach-Zelewski had the sole responsibility of suppressing the Warsaw Uprising. At any rate, Stahel was happy with Hosenfeld and praised him during an official meeting.

In the opinion of the historian Thomas Vogel, the special mission Stahel assigned to Hosenfeld may have been related to the Germans' attempts to use important Polish figures for ceasefire negotiations with the insurgents.

The fighting came closer to the city military headquarters. Hosenfeld not only heard the sound of machine guns and the impact of the artillery, but he could also see it. On August 23, he witnessed the baroque Holy Cross Church on Kraków Street reduced to rubble. *From my window I watched how the large and magnificent church was set on fire and destroyed,* Hosenfeld wrote. *One tower after another collapsed into the sea of flames. Now only the ruins stand amidst the smoke.*

There were no further German connections to the sports school and its facilities on Łazienkowska Street. Insurgents occupied the building. The SS troops were ruthless in their response to the underground army. They exacted cruel revenge on the civilian population, carrying out mass executions and rapes. Particularly conspicuous during the carnage was SS standarte leader Oskar Dirlewanger, *a fat, uncouth man with a horrible face, his sleeves rolled up high like a butcher.* The so-called Dirlewanger Unit had, according to the historian Włodzimierz Borodziej, previously left a wide trail of blood during their time on the Eastern Front. "It consisted of German criminals—poachers, career lawbreakers, [and] members of the SS with suspended criminal sentences," Borodziej noted.

***

The interrogation of prisoners was one of Hosenfeld's main responsibilities during the Warsaw Uprising. Captured members of the *Armia Krajowa* usually paid immediately with their lives. They were only—temporarily—spared if there was a chance they might provide information about the size and tactics of the underground army.

Hosenfeld's writings indicate he repeatedly found himself in a moral conflict during the interrogations. Oftentimes, very young Poles, whose courage and idealism impressed him, stood before him. He wrote about the interrogation of a 19 year old:

> *He made his statements unselfconsciously. I believe that he was somewhat proud of his attractive uniform. Because he was wearing items of German clothing, which they had taken from a German warehouse. He was wearing German lace-up boots, a white snow sweater, and over that a German camouflage suit, padded pants, and [a] shirt. He proudly wore a Polish eagle on the German cap.*

Young women, who acted as couriers and provided the insurgents with basic provisions, were also interrogated. They did not beg for their lives, but rather, responded self-assuredly to Hosenfeld's questions. Hosenfeld wrote of the women:

> *They no longer expected anything from life. No mercy from the Germans and no help from the Russians and the Allies. But still the leaders of the insurrection hold on to the hope that the Soviets will arrive soon. Some of the prisoners were wounded. I insisted that they receive treatment. With all of this immeasurable suffering it's no matter to help someone now and then. But the people are so happy when they feel there's just a little kindness.*

The longer the insurrection continued, the more prisoners there were to be interrogated. Hosenfeld turned into their advocate and attorney. He appealed to Stahel to treat the fighters as regular POWs, which would afford them more safety. At first, Stahel categorically denied this and referred to the orders of SS Reichsführer Heinrich Himmler, whereby members of the Polish Home Army were classified as "bandits and rebels" who were to be ruthlessly annihilated.

Hosenfeld opposed this position, and the general ordered him to consult two military legal experts for "instruction." The men confirmed Stahel's position and were of the opinion the executions were not Captain Hosenfeld's concern—it was a decision for his superior. Hosenfeld again approached the general, who evasively replied that the security service or police would carry out the executions. Nevertheless, Hosenfeld's persistence must have left an impression. After his second attempt to convince the general to treat the fighters as POWs, Stahel agreed. Injured fighters thereafter received medical attention, and other detainees were housed in a reception camp. Hosenfeld prevailed, and in the process, saved the lives of around 30 more Poles.

In one letter home, Hosenfeld vividly described a day of interrogations:

Today another activist and a 16-year-old girl. But we could get no information from either. Maybe I can save the girl. A female student was brought in yesterday. She also blundered into the resistance movement through a foolish circumstance. Then a Polish senior watch master of the police. 56 years old. These people are acting out of pure patriotism, but we cannot spare them. I try to save everyone who can be saved. I will try to get the policeman through as well. I am not the right person to lead such investigations, certainly not in the heartless way that is most often used here. And yet, I am thankful that I have to do this because then I am able to still make some things right.

In another letter, he described to his wife new cases he was working on. He wrote: *There were three young girls again, students, who were caught as they were getting fliers and card materials from the courier service. What should I now do with them? If the severe rules are applied, they will be shot. If it's possible, I will get them out.* What Hosenfeld achieved in these individual cases is not found in his writings. It would have been reckless to include such details in a letter.

The personal items of executed partisans also ended up on his desk. Virtually every wallet contained a picture of Mary, the mother of Jesus, or a medallion. *That touches me extraordinarily*, Hosenfeld wrote. *One would think that even the Mother of God could not help him, but who knows if perhaps she actually did.* He secured the belongings of an English pilot whose plane was shot down while providing assistance to the insurgents. Hosenfeld found a rosary among the pilot's things, which again led him to reflect on events in the same way the religious mementos of Polish freedom fighters did.

When he found himself a captive after the war, Hosenfeld was interrogated by Soviet security agents in Minsk, Belarus. At that time, he detailed the treatment of underground fighters. According to Hosenfeld's protocol, injured prisoners were bandaged at the infirmary before being taken to Saint Roch Hospital. Altogether, he interrogated around 20 or 30 civilians who were suspected of belonging to the Polish Home Army. Three men had been handed over to the SD for further interrogation with the explicit order to bring them to the reception center in Pruszków, a city southwest of Warsaw. *The remaining civilians were brought to the Pruszków reception center personally by me*, Hosenfeld wrote. *Mistreatment or executions did not occur.*

***

On August 24, 1944, official business took Hosenfeld to Żyrardów, a town about 40 miles west of Warsaw where the general headquarters of the Ninth Army was located. He was relieved to escape the ruins that surrounded him in Warsaw, if only for a few hours. Farmers worked in the fields, children happily played with one another—everything appeared peaceful in the countryside. But Hosenfeld knew appearances could be deceptive—there were no families nor villages where a carefree existence was possible.

Hosenfeld was again on the road, carrying out the orders of General Stahel. He was delivering documents. When he returned to command headquarters, Hosenfeld was informed the general had traveled to Bucharest on orders from Hitler. Romania was about to switch allegiance and declare war on Germany. It was later disclosed that Stahel soon after became a Soviet POW. (Stahel died of a heart attack in 1955 as he received the news of his release.)

Stahel's successor was Lieutenant General Hans Schirmer. Hosenfeld wrote to his wife about Schirmer: *This is a completely different person. He is a superior whose only demand to his subordinates is military service. He has no personal relationships with people. That was a strength and a certain magic of the other.* Hosenfeld also described Schirmer as big, bulky, and ruthless, a man who expected everyone to speak with a precise military vocabulary. *Yes, yes, now I am almost 50 years old, but I have to work hard and be alert like a schoolboy*, Hosenfeld remarked. *Why do I write to you about this, my dear Annemie? I have to speak with someone about this.*

Hosenfeld was isolated from all his friends and acquaintances in Warsaw. There were no more invitations, no open discussions, no social evenings. Warsaw was in a state of war more cruel and brutal than when the Germans first attacked five years prior. The Wehrmacht experienced setbacks on virtually all fronts: in the Balkans and in southeast Europe, on the Eastern and Western Fronts. American and British troops marched into Paris on August 25. That day, Hosenfeld wrote: *Of course, this greatly boosts our Polish freedom fighters. Now they will be even less likely to back down. The civilian population is forced to endure terrible things. For the most part, the civilians do not agree with the uprising, but they are terrorized and cannot escape.*

A further change went into effect at the end of August. The command headquarters was relocated to the western edge of Warsaw, to an old fort about three miles from the city center: Fort Wola. As a result, Hosenfeld was no longer confronted with actual fighting. However, he still had business in the city and therefore traveled between the city center and Fort Wola. *I have just now again returned from the city and cannot get the wretched images and nightmare scenes out of my head,* he wrote to his son Helmut. *Even more appalling than all the suffering is the brutality and animalistic nature of some of our deployed troops.*

The underground fighters were forced to give way to German artillery in the old city of Warsaw in early September. Some fighters escaped through the canals of the city's sewage system. The remaining trapped residents—over 30,000 people at that time—surrendered. *You cannot imagine what wretchedness came out of there,* Hosenfeld wrote. *Many were bundled into train wagons; some headed to Germany, where they would be used as forced laborers, the others headed toward the concentration and extermination camps.*

On September 10, intermediaries of the insurgents began negotiating their capitulation with the Germans. Almost simultaneously, the Red Army stirred for the first time and attacked German positions in the Praga section of the city. Thereupon, the Polish Home Army, hoping for a broad offensive, pulled out of negotiations and continued fighting, mostly in the city center where it had been entrenched since the start of the uprising. Hosenfeld wrote:

I think that we are nearing the end. The Polish have no heavy weapons, which is why they are at the mercy of the Stukas [German dive bombers]. *The city is almost entirely in ruins. But still the basements are full of people and the insurgents are bravely defending themselves. Even the women, particularly young girls, join in, mostly as paramedics.*

***

Hosenfeld continued to be well informed about the progress of the fighting. After sending his journal—hidden in a bundle of clothes—to Thalau, he recorded his insights in letters to his family. For example, Hosenfeld described the destruction of a 16-story high-rise in the center of Warsaw that had been a stronghold of the Polish Home Army for weeks, before it eventually collapsed under the hail of German artillery shells.

He could imagine the effect the letters had on his wife. Hosenfeld sought to find a balance between writing about things he absolutely wanted to communicate, while not constantly frightening her. On September 13, he wrote: *Why are you so concerned? Don't have such dark thoughts because of me. We are not directly involved in the fighting.* He sent several explanatory notes in reference to his Warsaw journal, which had arrived in Thalau. His intention was to calm Annemarie's worries. In one letter, he wrote:

As concerning [as] *the chronicles in my journal* [are], *this is to be understood as being the result of the mental and physical depression I was experiencing due to my expectation of upcoming critical events. I was exhausted physically during the early days of the Warsaw Uprising and had a very gloomy outlook. I was also impacted by other things that I do not want to get into here. I suffered because I could not comprehend how innocent people who were carrying out their duty to their fatherland could be treated in such a way, or that the majority of our people could have no feelings for the fate and suffering of other people. Details to follow. All of this weighed me down and*

distressed me in the same way that it did when I had these feelings
for the first time in October 1939. I always had the feeling that this
cannot end well, that it would bring down the wrath of God upon us.

The situation had in fact frighteningly intensified. Danger now
approached from two sides: the insurgents and the Red Army, which
only waited for the order to launch a full assault. Perhaps out of
concern for his family, but also maybe because of the mail censors,
Hosenfeld did not want to explicitly state this. Certainly, his numerous
earlier writings would have landed him in front of a military tribunal
had they been found by counterintelligence or the Gestapo.

Hosenfeld was aware that the more the German occupiers found
themselves on the defensive, the more they mercilessly pursued those
who stepped out of line. Hosenfeld refused from the start to be part of
the system that employed persecution and murder, as he noted in one
letter. He found solace knowing that even now, a few months before the
end of the battle for Warsaw, Annemarie stood by his side. Alluding
to crises and conflicts they had long since overcome, he assured her:

> *You write of your unique bond to me, alas, how could it be otherwise.*
> *For me you have been for a long time the only woman with whom I can*
> *share everything. You do not need to search for another support. How*
> *could we hurt each other again? It cannot be ruled out that we may*
> *at a later time quarrel over something. We are too temperamental and*
> *different in our world-views, despite the many years of our marriage.*

One day, in a Warsaw suburb, Hosenfeld and another officer came
across a field of overripe tomatoes. They were unharvested because the
owners had been expelled or were missing. The men eagerly collected
tomatoes for themselves and their comrades. Hosenfeld described the
day's events to his wife, as his thoughts carried him to Thalau:

> *Now the work in the garden is almost finished and fall begins with*
> *its fog and rain and cold and storms. How cozy it was there, sitting*

in the room or the warm kitchen after having completed the work in the garden. The scent of the apples comes up from the basement when the front door is opened, and you can eat the sweet, large pears until the belly is full.

How idyllic and far removed from the reality of Poland in the autumn of 1944.

Hosenfeld also wrote about the interrogation of two Russian soldiers in a letter dated September 15. They had crossed the Vistula River in an amphibious vehicle from the Praga side of Warsaw, which was now controlled by the Red Army. The men were arrested upon reaching the opposite shore. One of the prisoners immediately wanted to know if they were going to be shot, to which Hosenfeld emphatically said no.

The 18-year-old Red Army soldier candidly responded to Captain Hosenfeld's questions. His comrade had been shot through the lung and was taken to a hospital, leaving him in no condition to be interrogated. Hosenfeld forwarded the soldier's statements to army headquarters without delay. He was interested to hear about the food provided to Soviet troops, their fighting morale, and replenishments of supplies like fuel. He took the prisoners to the Ninth Army general headquarters in Żyrardów, where they were to undergo further interrogation.

Hosenfeld also discovered and handed over about 45 pounds of molten silver in their bags, which had come from the home of a wealthy Polish family. The SS collected gold and silver by the ton, taken from Jews and other victims.

On his trip back to Warsaw, Hosenfeld stopped off at a village market that was enjoying brisk business. *I bought several kilos of pears,* Hosenfeld wrote. *It did appear somewhat bizarre to me. A few dozen kilometers* [about 15 miles] *away, Poles and Germans were killing each other and here I am the only German being served with extreme politeness and friendliness.* Hosenfeld again expressed his understanding for the Polish people and their armed resistance against the German occupation: *The uprising certainly has its justification, even if we want to deny it, but it is one-sided and especially a nationalistic nation should understand that a nation must fight for its freedom.*

***

When the Warsaw Uprising started in August 1944, Władysław Szpilman was still in his hiding place on the Avenue of Independence. A friend of Helena Lewicka was now responsible for providing him with food; she also lived in the multistory house. Within a few days, the entire street was engulfed in fighting. Szpilman observed from a window how SS units employed heavy artillery against the insurgents, while captured fighters were led away. Before long, his building also came under fire. When it finally began to burn, he had no choice but to leave his hiding place. A charred body blocked the stairwell. *You could hear the crackling of burning rafters, the rumble of collapsing ceilings, the screaming of people and shots being fired*, Szpilman wrote.

There were more corpses lying amid the rubble in the streets. Szpilman took cover at fences and walls to avoid being caught in the hail of bullets, or he played dead when SS members came near. He was plagued by hunger and thirst. Szpilman found salty water in the ruins of a hospital and a crust of moldy bread somewhere else, which he hungrily devoured.

Szpilman witnessed the weakening of the Polish Home Army resistance against the occupiers. On some days, Allied planes dropped replenishments for the insurgents. His joy about the uprising gave way to a renewed desperation. Szpilman sensed the struggle for survival—his own and that of all Poles—was a long way from being won, and that maybe the worst was still to come. Szpilman carried a razor blade with him at all times. He did not want to be taken alive by the Germans—he would slash his wrists before that happened.

***

On September 19, 1944, the Wehrmacht moved its command headquarters even further west. The German forces relocated to a Polish estate with an adjacent park near the town of Macierzysz. This allowed the Wehrmacht to follow the battle for Warsaw from a distance. The chaos that had prevailed in the city center ceased and gave way to a peculiar calm. Hosenfeld started thinking about horseback riding again; he wanted a horse to explore the beautiful autumn landscape. Once again, he had more free time and inspiration, as evidenced by the length of his multi-page letters. The collection of information about the progress of the battles did not cease altogether, but rather continued at a more leisurely pace.

Hosenfeld discovered some Polish military units fighting under the command of the Red Army. Their mutual aim was to expel the Germans. He called them Sovietpoles. They ached to assist the insurgents in Warsaw; however, they were forced to follow Soviet commands. In his letter dated September 23, Hosenfeld wrote: *Until now, the Russians, or rather the Sovietpoles, have not crossed the Vistula* [River]. *The 1,000 men who attempted to cross were captured or shot or drowned. They have not been able to link up with the insurgents in the city.*

The fate of the Polish Home Army was sealed. The insurgents delayed the capitulation negotiations to the second half of September. The occasional replenishment supply drops by the Western Allies kept alive the hope the situation might improve. Eventually, though, the fighters understood the Red Army hampered the aerial assistance and had no intention to launch a full offensive at that time. Thus, the capitulation agreement was signed on October 2. Under the terms of the treaty, the 15,000 Polish *Armia Krajowa* fighters, including 2,000 women, were afforded the status of combatants, meaning they would be treated as regular POWs. The Wehrmacht transported the women to the Oberlangen camp in western Lower Saxony, near the Dutch border, where Polish and Canadian troops freed them in April 1945.

Hosenfeld watched the prisoners leaving the capital on October 5. In a letter, he described the scene:

> *I was in the city today. On the way I encountered endless convoys of captured insurgents. We were endlessly amazed at their proud bearing.*

They were nicely dressed, freshly shaven, almost well-groomed. All were young people, only the officers were around my age, but there were not many. And this army existed for five years of German rule, and we had almost no idea about them. Ten-year-old boys proudly wore their caps; they had served as lookouts and they were honored to march into captivity with the men. Behind each section of around 60 men followed the young girls and women. They sang patriotic songs and you could not tell by looking at them that they had endured terrible things.

Hosenfeld planned to visit the reception camp, located near a former fort, where the Poles were to be housed before being transported onward. He recalled Pabianice, where he had oftentimes listened in on the prayers and songs of Polish prisoners. Hosenfeld wanted to experience this passion firsthand once more. He noticed the insurgents were no longer referred to as bandits, but were correctly identified as POWs. The fighters were disappointed by the lack of English aerial support. But their disillusionment about the Red Army was even greater; they believed the Soviets had abandoned them. There was great mistrust between the Poles and Russians. Polish Home Army officers fully expected to be sent to Siberia once the Red Army took control.

A postwar memorial in Warsaw honoring Polish resistance fighters.

***

At the Polish estate, Hosenfeld was again contacted by Poles for help. Word had quickly spread that this German officer was sympathetic to the suffering of the civilian population. The first requests were for permits to reunite families who had been separated by the war. Hosenfeld managed to safely bring the Polish estate owner's wife and child out of the destroyed city, where the pair had been hiding in basements for weeks.

Hosenfeld made a list of cases where it was possible to search for relatives or to contact them. A Polish farmer located his elderly mother in a reception center. A man who had not heard from his wife and two small children for two months also sought Hosenfeld's help. When they disappeared, they had been on the way to a neighboring village with a horse and cart to sell vegetables at a market. It was discovered the woman had been taken to a hospital in the region of Silesia where she now worked as a maid.

In another case, a young woman with a Polish father and Irish mother wanted to return to Warsaw to find her mother-in-law, and if possible, recover some works of art from the basement of their destroyed home. Hosenfeld was able to help her. An ethnic German who had been separated from his wife and children during the fighting was determined to search for them near the front. Hosenfeld advised him it was too dangerous. Hosenfeld described the man's situation in a letter home: *He said, "For two months, my only thought was to see my wife and children again. I can't now just go somewhere else without having done everything possible to find them." Carrying a heavy load, he went out into the rain to begin his search, having received the pass from me.*

The number of people who asked for help continued to grow. Soon, however, Hosenfeld's hands were tied. The Wehrmacht prohibited civilians from returning to the capital. There was still ongoing destruction. Buildings and structures were being leveled and over 300,000 people were forced to leave the city. On October 8, Hosenfeld regretfully wrote:

Every day the people come to me and want passes so that they can enter the city to get household goods or clothes or the like from their burned homes. Today a woman came; she was barefoot. She had nothing to wear other than a thin summer dress. I cannot help her, though. Civilians are not permitted into Warsaw. I have to turn away hundreds.

***

Be it in Germany or Poland, in France or Holland, everywhere people had to endure a horrible fate. Hosenfeld believed that the hate between nations decreased with the duration of the war. The volleys of bullets fired by Germany or even its enemies were tools in the hands of the blind. But, Hosenfeld thought, a new age of peace would arise. He wrote: *Our generation will have to bear the cost of this war. And yet we must not simply submit to our suffering, but we must allow God's will to be carried out through our active participation and cathartic love for our fellow human beings.*

Hosenfeld spent his evenings together with comrades in the parlor of the estate house or went back to his large room, which also served as the operations room. During the day, a young soldier attended to paperwork there, organizing incoming messages and registering the current state of fighting on maps. Although the Red Army would sporadically attack German troops north of Warsaw, it otherwise remained on standby. Everyone attentively followed news on the radio. Hardly anyone—least of all Hosenfeld—still believed the information from the Supreme High Command of the Wehrmacht. He wrote: *The Wehrmacht bulletin always ends with the successes, when in truth, things keep getting worse. But they don't want to see it and the people are not to notice. How much longer is this deception meant to continue?*

In his letter of October 19, Hosenfeld intended to write to his wife about how much he liked his room. The tiled stove gave off a pleasant warmth. A picture of the Black Madonna hung on the wall. An officer had brought it from town for him and he liked it very much. But he was unable to present a tranquil image of his surroundings.

Constant uncertainty and worry about the future weighed on his mind, Hosenfeld wrote.

Three days later, his new superior, General Hellmuth Eisenstuck, who had taken over command headquarters, asked Hosenfeld to accompany him to Warsaw. The trip did not lighten his mood. He visited the sports school, the stadium, and the remaining facilities. About the trip, he wrote: *I was also upstairs in my room, but everything was so destroyed that I shuddered. I only removed the sign from the door and then quickly left again. The piano and the reed organ still stood in the large salon, the rain dripped from the ceiling. The windows were barricaded with books, school benches, and mattresses.*

The nearby church lay in ruins. The theater, which Hosenfeld visited afterward, was no less a scene of devastation: curtains, costumes, sheet music—everything was spread around the ruins. It was the same with the once grand national library.

The estate contained its own park, where Hosenfeld spent time whenever possible. Behind a row of trees, he discovered a cemetery with fresh graves. Soldiers who had fallen in the Warsaw fighting were buried there. Sometimes there was no time to immediately bury the dead. One day, Hosenfeld slowed his pace as he approached the cemetery. He could already see it from the distance:

> *A body is lying there, the arms folded back, his head leaning on the tree. He appears to be big. The tarpaulin covering him is not sufficient. I stand before the dead body and cannot walk on. [What] if that were my son? I bend down and pull the cloth aside and look into a young, beautiful face, the eyes are slightly open, as are the lips. I can see no wound. The hair is tousled. I take his cold hand, then I straighten his hair and stroke his cheek. I look at him for a long time and think about the fact that I am the last person who will see this boy for the final time. I am his father, mother, brother, and sister.*

Hosenfeld asked the responsible officer for the name of the fallen soldier. It was senior rifleman Josef Zieringer, a 19 year old from Bavaria. The young man had been killed on October 14, in a battle with the Soviets at the Narew River, a tributary of the Vistula. Hosenfeld procured the address of the soldier's parents. On October 25, he wrote them a detailed letter: *I do not know your son. I only encountered him this one time. I am the last person who has looked upon your dear child through eyes of love and I may be allowed to believe that he has directed me to send this last greeting to you. You see, that is why I write to you. I am not able to console you, only God can do that.*

The tenderness toward a dead soldier whom he did not know, and the profound compassion for the soldier's parents, who received a final certainty as to the fate of their son through him—hardly any other letter can better exemplify Hosenfeld's empathy, his gift to see things from another person's perspective, and his ability to feel compassion for them. The parents later thanked Hosenfeld for the note.

***

On October 28, the command headquarters was once again relocated, away from the western edge of the city and back into the largely destroyed center of Warsaw. It appeared the Wehrmacht was preparing for a decisive battle against the Red Army. Warsaw had been declared a "fortress," meaning it was to be surrounded by a ring of defensive positions so it could withstand a lengthy siege. Hosenfeld's superior, General Hellmuth Eisenstuck, was given the title of "Fortress Commander." With that, the brief period of relative calm came to a close. A renewed hectic pace set in. Together with Eisenstuck, Hosenfeld visited numerous command posts and investigated the situation on the ground. One day later, Hosenfeld wrote to his wife: *We relocated to the east, back into the city and have moved into the command post here. Now you will be frightened again, but that is not necessary. There are thick basement walls here, and I have one or two large rooms. No shots have been fired in our area so far.*

The same afternoon, Hosenfeld led a group of journalists from several different European countries *through the sad ruins* of Warsaw.

He did not participate in the following reception hosted by Governor Ludwig Fischer. Not only did he have a lot of work to do, but he was also no longer interested in meetings with senior Nazi officials who had caused so much harm.

In early November, Hosenfeld was assigned a task for which he had long wished—though in this final phase of the war it would be a rather temporary stopgap. He was appointed company commander of the *Landeschützen* Battalion 996. He had been part of the regiment before being assigned to run the sports school and other tasks. Through his work on different staffs, he had, for the most part, lost connection with the soldiers, Hosenfeld wrote. Only now did he notice how much the people needed a superior who was concerned for them. The battalion, comprised mostly of older soldiers and those unfit to serve on the front, was tasked with preventing residents from entering the city and providing guard and control functions. The battalion was likely sent to the front for reinforcement a few days later, again leaving Hosenfeld without the post.

***

Hosenfeld was strangely attracted to the ruined landscape around him. During his walks through the streets he came upon the ruins of a church. Amid candlesticks, paintings, and vestments he found a Gothic-style golden monstrance almost three feet tall. Initially, he did not recognize its special value. Up close, he was fascinated by the liturgical vessel, which is used during Catholic services to hold the consecrated host. Hosenfeld also discovered a second, smaller monstrance. He reached out to Bishop Szlagowski, who arranged for the monstrance and other sacred objects to be picked up.

The intense exchange of letters between Wilm and Annemarie Hosenfeld continued during October and November. The news from Warsaw must have caused further concern in Thalau. Although Annemarie's letters during this time have been lost, her husband's responses indicate her concerns. Hosenfeld gently attempted to prepare her for the misfortune he anticipated. *We must also endure the coming grief,* he wrote on October 27. On November 8, Hosenfeld wrote:

> *You believe that I have again erred about my prediction of the war's end. It may be that the timeframe was too early, but it will not take much longer. You will see. Everything is coming to a head slowly, but it is unstoppable. Whether or not it will still take several weeks or months cannot be certain, in light of the giant dimension of the war. The only thing that is certain is that we are taking giant strides toward the end.*

Since his future military purpose was still unclear, Hosenfeld took it upon himself to keep the soldiers physically fit. As a former sports officer, he had enough experience to pull his mostly older comrades out of their rooms for a round of early morning exercise. Most of them felt quite foolish, but they joined in and before too long even started to enjoy themselves. The training took place in Fort Wola, where Hosenfeld had previously been housed. He would ride his bicycle out of town early in the morning to the former casemates in the west of the city, which were now part of the fortification ring around Warsaw. Physical activity was one component of the training; the other was health care. A young doctor held a lecture on this topic. *How cold and unemotional such a man speaks,* Hosenfeld wrote of the doctor. *The 180 soldiers stood in the narrow, dark casemate. Only the first few rows could be seen; the others were a mass of people filling up the gloomy room. The soldiers are such patient sheep. They allow everything to be done to them and loyally play along.*

Ever since the failed assassination attempt on Hitler on July 20, 1944, it was mandatory to greet others with a "Heil Hitler!" It was no longer permitted to open a greeting with "Good morning" or "Good day." Hosenfeld witnessed the battalion commander demand the prescribed method of salutation be observed. The commander announced that *only Jews and other rabble said "Good day," but not German men*, Hosenfeld wrote. It is unknown if Hosenfeld followed the command. Considering the precarious military situation, he may have considered the new greeting absurd and laughable.

Other things occupied his time, as he wrote about on November 11. *It is such a strange time,* Hosenfeld observed. *It appears as if there is a standstill on the fronts. I only read the Wehrmacht bulletin. I don't hear any radio* [reports] *and get to see no newspapers. It doesn't interest me. And yet, I sense that large things are being prepared everywhere, pushing for a decision.*

In mid-November, Hosenfeld received confirmation that Detlev was now also being called to serve in the Wehrmacht. *What do they want the small boy for in a war?* he wrote. Hosenfeld found comfort in the belief Detlev would most likely have to first endure a lengthy training period, by which time the war might be over. If not, then his son would also have to set out on this difficult journey. He was in a somber mood when the news reached him. There was no electricity in his basement room and the candle supply was limited. Moreover, at night when he could not sleep, Hosenfeld was haunted by the fatalities of those close to him. *Is it the dark, long nights, or is it my loneliness that called them?* he lamented. Nonetheless, Hosenfeld found something comforting in his dialogue with the dead: he thought of his parents and close friends. *I feel myself locked into this communion, even though I am still living,* he wrote. *All things small and perishable pass away.*

It remained unclear how the military planned to use Hosenfeld. Starting on November 23, he filled in for the regiment's aide-de-camp for 10 days. The aide-de-camp stood at the right hand of the commander for questions about tactics and training and also acted as the supervisor for headquarters staff. Hosenfeld had previously filled this job in 1941, albeit under different circumstances. The war in and around Warsaw had almost come to a standstill, but no one expected the Red Army to simply pack up and withdraw from the Vistula River. Patience was called for, which grew increasingly difficult for Hosenfeld and his comrades as the days passed.

On November 22, he wrote to Annemarie that he yearned to receive a letter from her. Answering correspondence was always easier than reaching for pen and paper oneself, he wrote. But the mail took much longer than usual to reach him. Hosenfeld had nothing new to report concerning the military situation. *The waiting is just unbearable, and the longer it takes, the more hopeless our situation becomes*, he wrote. *But you don't believe in my prophecies.*

As he did in almost every letter, Hosenfeld again assured Annemarie that he was doing fine. He felt healthy and able-bodied and began each day with physical activity. He wrote: *At the end of my run, we go to church. It is an old Gothic church, very large and wide. At first it was eerie going in. Everywhere there are still old clothes, beds, pieces of uniforms, stretchers stand there, bullets, weapons. Everything is disheveled. Then I am standing in the large, dark room and say my morning prayer.* He ended his letter with a plea: *Be brave, my dear Annemarie, and wait for me; I will come to you one day and kiss you. Your Wilm.*

A Most Unusual Rescue Mission

In the fall of 1944, Warsaw was nothing but ruins as far as the eye could see. Palaces, churches, centuries-old cultural monuments, museums, and libraries—large parts of the city were reduced to rubble. The commandos of the Wehrmacht and SS had gone all out. The residents were first evicted. Then the city was fire-bombed; explosive charges and flamethrowers virtually leveled Warsaw.

Formerly called "the Paris of the East" because of its urban elegance, Warsaw was dead. No other large European city experienced the extent of destruction and killing in World War II as Warsaw. More than 800,000 Warsaw residents died during the German occupation, 500,000 of whom were Jews.

Amid the mountains of rubble, individual buildings still stood. Or there were lone chimneys, coated with soot from the inferno, black stains in a landscape of ruin. Underneath the rubble, corpses decomposed. Some residents waited too long or had not wanted to leave their belongings behind and thus became victims of the firestorm. Many of the deceased fighters in the Warsaw Uprising were also somewhere in the wreckage. The stench of dead bodies rose out of basements.

The Polish Home Army's struggle against the German occupiers ended in October 1944. The brave men and women had hoped in vain that the Red Army would come to their aid. But the Soviet dictator Joseph Stalin had other plans. He wanted the Polish *Armia Krajowa* to weaken the German enemy so the well-rested Red Army would be able to go into a full offensive against the Wehrmacht—as it had done two years earlier at Stalingrad. Warsaw was the last big hurdle on the way to Berlin.

***

Following the suppression of the Warsaw Uprising, a ghostly silence settled on the ruined city for several weeks. Occasional artillery fire sounded in the distance. It was now strictly forbidden to enter the ruined city. Some residents nonetheless returned during the day to search for food and valuables.

Very few inhabitants remained in the city. Most of them were people on the run like Władysław Szpilman. By fall 1944, he already had a long odyssey behind him. It bordered on a miracle that Szpilman was still alive. The pianist had experienced the full extent of the crisis that beset his hometown since the Wehrmacht's invasion of Poland in fall 1939: the creation of the Warsaw Ghetto, the uprising of his Jewish compatriots in 1943, the deportation of his parents and three siblings to the Treblinka extermination camp, fleeing from one hiding place to another, summary executions, and the murderous nature of the Germans, Ukrainians, and Lithuanians, who took sadistic pleasure in grabbing children by the legs and whipping their heads forcefully against a wall.

When the Warsaw Uprising was squashed by German artillery and tanks—the final victory of the occupation force before the Red Army drove the Wehrmacht out of the city—Szpilman found refuge in the attic of a residential building. He was mentally and physically drained. The search for food and water became increasingly problematic as German and Ukrainian patrols searched houses, looking for anything they could turn into money.

Szpilman was rarely able to leave his hiding place. Hunger tormented him. In the prior weeks and months, he had only managed to stay alive with the utmost effort. During the day, he stayed in his hideout. At night, if it was safe, Szpilman searched the basements for something to eat. He seldom brought anything back. His food supply often lasted only one or two days.

Szpilman's rigid discipline had somehow led to a structured daily routine. He mentally recalled all of the compositions he had ever played. Later, this proved to be an advantage as he did not require sheet music to play many pieces. He also attempted to recall the contents of books he had read and tried to learn English words.

In the fall of 1944, however, Szpilman was no longer able to do these things. He was deeply shocked when he saw his reflection in a window one day: his hair was shaggy and tangled, his beard straggly and full of dirt, his skin almost black, his forehead covered with scabs. Szpilman sacrificed some of his precious water so he could at least clean his face. The questions of how much longer he could endure living as a fugitive among the ruins, and when the Red Army would finally end the German reign of terror, constantly tormented him.

One day, Szpilman found some canned food in the pantry of an apartment he was searching. He was so engrossed with the discovery that he did not notice a German officer step into the adjacent kitchen. Suddenly, the German officer stood before him—a tall, elegant man with his arms crossed over this chest.

"What are you doing here?" the officer asked.

When Szpilman did not look up, the officer repeated his question and added, "Don't you know that the staff of the Warsaw Fortress Command will be moving into this building any time now?"

Szpilman was so bewildered he did not know what to say. *Where could he go?* The mere thought of another flight robbed him of his strength.

"Do with me what you will. I am not moving from here," he finally answered in resignation.

The officer—Wilm Hosenfeld—assured him that he intended no harm. Instead, he struck up a conversation and inquired as to the profession of the Pole.

"Pianist," Szpilman answered.

Hosenfeld pointed to an adjacent room. When Szpilman saw the piano, he knew what awaited him.

"Play something," the officer requested, continuing to treat the fugitive with respect and politeness.

Szpilman hesitated to comply with Hosenfeld's request to sit at the piano. Having always to be on guard, he realized his playing might give him away. The window glass had been shattered so any sound would immediately be heard outside. But Hosenfeld had a solution.

"Go ahead and play!" he said. "If someone comes, hide in the pantry and I will say that it was me who played to test the instrument."

Szpilman, who wrote of this fateful encounter in his memoir *Death of a City* (published in 1946 in Warsaw), approached the piano with trembling hands. He had not practiced for God knew how long. His fingers resisted. Szpilman's fingernails had not been trimmed *since the fire in the house where I had been hiding*, he wrote. Moisture affected the piano's mechanics so the keys could only be moved with difficulty. He finally played Frédéric Chopin's Nocturne in C-sharp Minor. Szpilman wrote: *The glassy, tinkling sound of the untuned strings rang through the empty flat* [apartment] *and the stairway, floated through the ruins of the villa on the other side of the street, and returned as a muted, melancholy echo.*

This was an extraordinary encounter between two very different people before the end of World War II. One, a German officer—a teacher by profession—and the other, a Polish Jew—a pianist. A single fateful encounter in a building in the center of a destroyed Warsaw. The mutual appraisal and assessment, and initial distrust, gradually made way for incredulous astonishment. It all seemed so unreal, and yet, it was very real.

As the final tone faded, both men remained silent and looked at each other. Then, Hosenfeld broke the thoughtful silence and said he would safely take Szpilman to a village outside of Warsaw. It was too dangerous to stay. The pianist, who looked like a ragged beggar after months on the run, shook his head. Hosenfeld suspected what might stand in the way of an escape. It was neither his appearance nor the destroyed city.

A postwar picture of the building where Szpilman and Hosenfeld met.

"You are a Jew?" Hosenfeld asked.

Szpilman nodded.

In his book, Szpilman described how Hosenfeld reflected on what he could do for him, a Jewish refugee, in this hopeless situation. He then asked to see Szpilman's hiding place in the attic. He thoroughly examined the space and discovered it had a sort of dropped ceiling that could only be reached with a ladder. Hosenfeld felt Szpilman would be safe there; he would only have to pull up the ladder. He also wanted to know if Szpilman had enough to eat. When the pianist answered no, Hosenfeld said he would bring him food.

Before Hosenfeld left the attic, the pianist ventured to ask, "Are you a German?"

After all he had experienced, Szpilman could not imagine there were any Germans who felt and acted humanely. Germans had leveled Warsaw. Germans had murdered Szpilman's parents and siblings. Germans were also trying to destroy his life. Now, a person wearing a Wehrmacht uniform stood before him and wanted to find a safe hiding space for him and bring food. The officer immediately understood what the question implied. Szpilman described in his book how Hosenfeld almost lost his composure at the question.

Hosenfeld shouted out in anger, "Yes! I am a German! And after all that has happened, I am ashamed to say it. . . ."

Hosenfeld returned three days later with bread and jam. He appeared to be in a hurry. A guard had seen him enter the building so he could not stay long. Szpilman inquired about the advance of, Soviet troops and wanted to know where the Red Army was. The answer filled him with hope.

"Already in Warsaw, on the opposite bank of the Vistula [River]—in Praga!" Hosenfeld replied. "Hold on! Only a few more weeks. The entire war will be over by spring."

On numerous occasions during the past months, Szpilman wanted to end his own life. Now he had a reason to be hopeful. The newspapers in which Hosenfeld wrapped the bread confirmed what he said: the Wehrmacht experienced one defeat after another and retreated on all fronts.

However, danger lurked nearby for the pianist—in fact, in a side wing of the building where Szpilman hid. He watched from upstairs how German soldiers of the command headquarters entered and exited the building. At night, the sound of the guards' footsteps on patrol in front of the building haunted him. The danger of being discovered was greater than ever.

The last encounter between Władysław Szpilman and Wilm Hosenfeld was on December 12, 1944. This time, the captain brought more food than usual, especially bread. He also gave Szpilman a warm blanket and a military coat. Winter had arrived. It was icy cold under the roof. Hosenfeld said he and his people were leaving Warsaw. He emphatically told Szpilman to not give up; the Red Army offensive would begin soon. The battles he associated with the major offensive triggered renewed fears for Szpilman. *How would he survive?* he thought.

Hosenfeld reassured him, "Since you and I managed to survive this hell for five years, it is obviously God's will that we will persevere. You must believe that."

Before the officer left, Szpilman wanted to give him a sign of his thankfulness to take along. Since he had no possessions of his own, he decided to tell the man his name since Hosenfeld had never asked for it. Hosenfeld had also not given his own name, probably as a precaution for both of them.

Szpilman said, "You are a long way from home. I—in case I stay alive—will most likely immediately start to work here again, for the same Polish Radio as before the war. In case something happens to you or you are in need of help, remember, "Szpilman—Polish Radio! Szpilman."

Szpilman recalled Hosenfeld's reaction in his book: *He smiled, half dismissive, half bashful, but I felt that I pleased him with my naïveté willingness to help.*

Władysław Szpilman.

***

Wilm Hosenfeld made no mention in letters or journals of his encounters with Szpilman. Hosenfeld was equally cautious about not mentioning other Poles whom he had saved from life-threatening situations.

Another instance that came to light after the war involved Mr. Koschel, the brother-in-law of Antoni Cieciora. Along with other hostages, Koschel was being taken away on a truck to be executed. As the truck drove through the city center, Koschel recognized Hosenfeld from a previous meeting and frantically waved to him. Hosenfeld stopped the vehicle under the pretext he immediately needed a worker. He looked over the men and chose Koschel, thus saving his life.

Including the insurgent fighters Hosenfeld was able to spare from execution, all available information indicates he saved the lives of over 60 people. It is understandable that he did not write about these perilous activities. He not only protected himself, but also Poles who were in lethal danger from the Germans.

The rescue of Szpilman, however, represented a special risk. He had hidden a Polish Jew in a building that was in the process of being occupied by the Fortress Command of the Wehrmacht. Had the German authorities discovered this, it is likely both men would have faced a firing squad. It was the most audacious of all his rescue operations—and the most dangerous. And yet, from their very first encounter, Hosenfeld was determined to help Szpilman.

**

Shortly after his last meeting with Szpilman, Wilm Hosenfeld was assigned to a new unit. He also moved into new quarters in a multi-story building the Wehrmacht had occupied since the Warsaw Uprising. He was in charge of a unit comprised of about 200 men. Their area of responsibility encompassed several city districts and included guarding the Polish Radio building and various warehouses. Some of the troops also upgraded the fortifications around the Polish capital.

The men were spread across many locations, and Hosenfeld had some difficulty with his unit's morale. Two soldiers, for example, simply stayed in their rooms during a nighttime training exercise. At another guard post, a physical altercation ensued after copious amounts of alcohol were consumed. The men almost did not care anymore. They wanted to survive the war and get home as soon as possible. Hosenfeld understood that some of his men occasionally went too far. After all, his company was an *indiscriminate collection* of men whose previous units had wanted to get rid of them. About the men, Hosenfeld wrote: *I had thought that punishment would not be necessary, but for purposes of overall discipline, you cannot do without it.*

Emergency telegrams from Germany kept arriving. Relatives of Hosenfeld's men had been bombed out of their homes or died during air raids. In most cases, Hosenfeld immediately sent the soldiers home so they could take care of their families.

As company leader, Hosenfeld tried to create a calm atmosphere reflective of the upcoming Christmas holidays. A common room was set up for celebration. He had a pump organ brought over from the former sports school. There was already a piano. Somewhat chaotic scheduling resulted in the Advent celebration coinciding with a lecture on the use of rocket-propelled grenades. In between, the soldiers sang popular songs and Christmas songs. *The magic of Christmastime already surrounds us*, he wrote to Annemarie. Hosenfeld saw himself as the "father" of his company. Once more he experienced the camaraderie for which he always wished—albeit under entirely different circumstances and certainly not in the face of a catastrophic military defeat.

On December 26, he described in a letter home how he had spent Christmas Eve in the company of around 100 men. *There were two large fir trees set up in the big gym, nicely decorated. The soldiers had brought a large amount of Christmas decorations. There was a special dinner with Glühwein* [spiced, warm red wine], Hosenfeld wrote. Christmas in the middle of a ruined city. In the spur of the moment, Hosenfeld delivered a speech. As he went to light a candle for Jesus, some of the soldiers asked him what it meant. They only knew the "Yule celebration," propagated by the Nazis to replace the Christian celebration.

Annemarie and the children had hoped up to the last minute Wilm would be able to spend Christmas at home. But to no avail.

Seventeen-year-old Detlev was also not home. He had been called up a few days earlier to join a tank reconnaissance unit in Meiningen, Germany. On Christmas Eve, 23-year-old Helmut Hosenfeld, who had completed his medical studies in Jena, Germany, performed the role his father normally carried out—and which he repeated in the following years—he read from the Gospels. Afterward, everyone sang traditional Christmas songs, and Uta, the youngest daughter, recited a Christmas poem.

In a letter dated December 28, Annemarie wrote to Detlev and described the horrible damage caused by Allied air raids on Fulda, Schmalnau, and the surrounding areas. More than 700 people died. She wrote: *We were all terribly afraid in the basement. . . . I held Uta in my arms. . . . Things are said to look appalling in Fulda. The Mehlers' factory, the rubber plant, and Bellinger were directly hit, as were the train station and the freight depot. Various bunkers have collapsed and many people died. . . .*

By the end of November, there were air raids that shattered windows in Thalau, causing frightened residents to flee to their basements. Hosenfeld considered how his family could be protected. In one letter, he wrote: *I think the best protection would be a trench close to the church, directly against the wall, or even in the corner between the church and the sacristy. The planes will probably not bomb the church.*

People lived in fear as 1944 drew to a close. The new year brought with it new dread. Hosenfeld read about the bombings on Fulda and the surrounding areas in the January 4th edition of the Wehrmacht bulletin. He wrote: *I am greatly concerned about all of you. . . . How did you celebrate Christmas? How are you doing?* He received a short letter from Uta, which provided him some solace. *Father should not be sad that he was unable to spend Christmas with us; I will pray for you,* she wrote.

Hosenfeld wrote a short note to his family on January 12, 1945, consisting of only a few lines. He talked about mundane things like combs he had purchased and wanted to send home. At the end of the letter, he gave his usual assurance: *I am doing well.* That same day, the long-awaited major Soviet offensive began across the entire Eastern

Front, from the Baltics to the Carpathians. The "Warsaw Fortress" withstood the onslaught of the Red Army for four days.

One of Hosenfeld's last letters from Warsaw, dated January 16, was to Detlev: *You will have learned from the Wehrmacht bulletin that the Russians have attacked Warsaw. They are marching on us from the south, to the west of the Vistula* [River]. *They will probably take us from the rear.*

On the evening of January 16, German troops abandoned their posts, violating Hitler's orders. Hitler wanted the fortress to be held under all circumstances. But any resistance would have only meant bloodshed. The Wehrmacht units hastily departed the Polish capital, heading west. But the Soviet tanks were faster. The company led by Hosenfeld was surrounded near the town of Błonie, about 20 miles west of Warsaw. The escape route to the west was permanently barred. There were several deaths during the short fight. Hosenfeld and most of his comrades surrendered to the enemy on January 17. The specific details of his arrest are not known.

The last long letter Wilm Hosenfeld wrote to his wife before his capture was dated January 17, 1945. In it, he wrote about a Protestant priest with a foot injury who had managed to hold a service for the Protestant soldiers in his unit. He and a Catholic priest had also discussed Psalm 90 of the Old Testament, about the impermanence of human life. Hosenfeld arranged for his company to spend an evening together discussing religious topics. In the process, his thoughts were not only with his soldiers, but also with his family. Hosenfeld wrote: *I can only implore God's gracious protection to keep you safe. You and the dear children are in my thoughts as I go to sleep and with every new day. Wishing you all the best from the bottom of my heart, Your Wilm.*

***

Władysław Szpilman survived. Although it was a few weeks after his liberation, the military coat Hosenfeld had given him almost cost him his life. Szpilman's compatriots took him for a German soldier as he stepped onto the street wearing the Wehrmacht coat. They wanted to shoot him on the spot. At the last moment, he was able to make them understand he was not a German. Many people still recalled his name, but most thought he had died. There was all the more delight at the unexpected news. Polish Radio went back on the air in 1945. The pianist opened the broadcast with Chopin's Nocturne in C-sharp Minor in remembrance of the German officer who had saved his life, and whose name he did not know.

At the end of January 1945, the Polish violinist Zygmunt Lednicki returned to Warsaw. He had been living in the outskirts of the city during the fighting and wanted to walk to the Polish Radio studios where he had performed before the war. On the way, he passed a German POW detention center guarded by Russian soldiers. The prisoners sat on the ground. Seeing them, the thought suddenly came to Lednicki to complain about the barbaric treatment he received at the hands of the Germans. They may have considered themselves to be a cultured people, but they had taken his most prized possession—his violin.

Lednicki had just reached the barbed wire when one of the prisoners arose, approached him, and asked, "Do you perhaps know *Herr* Szpilman?"

The violinist replied that he did.

Then the German told him, almost whispering, ". . . I helped Szpilman when he was hiding in the attic of the Fortress Command in Warsaw. Tell him that I am here. He should save me. I beg of you. . . ."

Just as he was about to give his name, a guard interrupted the conversation and instructed the Pole to be on his way. Lednicki walked a few paces and turned around. He very much wanted to know the name of the German because the man had turned around once more and called out something to him, but the violinist did not understand him. By then, Hosenfeld had already disappeared from view.

Władysław Szpilman described the unusual encounter at the camp fence—which might have helped to rescue Hosenfeld—in the epilogue of a newer edition of his memoir. Lednicki told Szpilman about it when they saw each other for the first time again at the Polish Radio studios. The pianist immediately recalled his savior; however, he did not know his name. Szpilman looked for the camp, but was unable to locate the German prisoner, although he did everything in his power to find him. About Wilm Hosenfeld, Szpilman wrote: *The detention center had been relocated in the meantime, where to is a military secret. But maybe that German—the only human being I met who wore a German uniform—was happily back in his homeland.*

PART IV:
PRISONER OF THE
SOVIET UNION

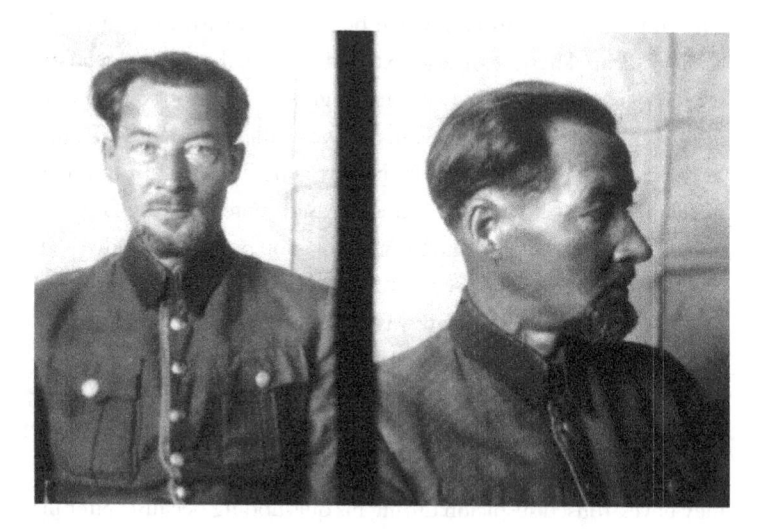

The Fate of All of You Is My Constant Concern

Wilm Hosenfeld spent about two weeks at a temporary camp before he was transported to Belarus. His captivity lasted for seven years. The stations of his ordeal, which began in Warsaw and ended in Stalingrad, are known to a large extent. However, the sources detailing what happened during this time are fragmented. His postcard letters mostly survived. But these contain relatively little information of value because he was allowed to write in only general terms. Testimonies of fellow prisoners who were later released, statements by German doctors who treated him, and the interrogation protocols handwritten by Hosenfeld himself allow several conclusions to be drawn.

The first stop after Warsaw was the Belarusian city of Brest, where he was held from February until May 1945. There, Hosenfeld was questioned by Soviet officers about his official functions in Warsaw, wrote Thomas Vogel in *Wilm Hosenfeld, "Ich versuche jeden zu retten"* (*Wilm Hosenfeld, "I Try to Save Everyone"*). Vogel suspected Hosenfeld may have aroused suspicion during his questioning because, after his transfer to a special camp for German officers in Minsk, Belarus, he was placed in pretrial detention.

A number of subsequent interrogations began on June 13 in Minsk. According to interrogation protocols, these questionings were carried out by Soviet officers of the People's Commissariat for Internal Affairs (NKVD). The protocols were for the first time analyzed and commented upon in Vogel's book.

The first interrogation concerned Hosenfeld's family, profession, military service, and the various functions and tasks he carried out during the German occupation of Warsaw. There was particular interest in his posts as sports officer and gas defense officer, and his responsibility for the vocational training of soldiers and officers. The Soviet officers' interrogations on July 23 and October 22, 1945, were in regard to his activities in the IC (counterintelligence) division of the Wehrmacht command headquarters. Hosenfeld listed six tasks related to his job:

> 1. *Management of the situation map for the overall situation on the Russian front in the area of the Ninth Army.*
> 2. *Management of the situation map of Warsaw on the situation of the Warsaw Uprising.*
> 3. *Daily orientation of the commander.*
> 4. *Compilation of messages from the subordinate units and notification to the army.*
> 5. *Interrogation of the delivered civilian prisoners.*
> 6. *Management of the relationship with the SS and police leader and with the security service.*

The officers wanted to know from where the news about the state of the insurgents came. Hosenfeld replied the information was provided by his own unit, the SS, the police, the security service, and from interrogations of captured insurgents and Polish civilians. From the start, he attempted to provide forthright and honest answers. Hosenfeld also made no attempt to gloss over the crimes committed by the Germans in Poland. In hindsight, this was a mistake. He could have concealed his IC work and may eventually have been released. At the same time, Hosenfeld wanted to explicitly name the war criminals. The majority of the German nation, he emphasized, was innocent of these crimes and had not known about them. Hosenfeld wrote:

> *Whenever it was within my power, I helped every Polish person with whom I came into contact. Many witnesses will still be alive*

who can confirm this. Even before the uprising, I had demonstrated a humane attitude toward the Polish population. There are many people I can list by name who will testify to that. For example, I saved the lives of many Jews by keeping the Gestapo from getting to them, and did this under threat to my own life.

Hosenfeld suggested an attempt be made to locate the witnesses he named. He hoped a public appeal through the Polish press and radio would turn up people like auxiliary Bishop Antoni Szlagowski, Leon Warm-Warczynski, Władysław Szpilman, Antoni Cieciora, and his 30 employees from the Wehrmacht sports stadium; this would allow the veracity of his claims to be verified. Given the opportunity, he said, he could also obtain the names and addresses of Poles who could bear testimony that he was disgusted by the war crimes committed by his compatriots. Hosenfeld felt an obligation to the German people, and especially to those German soldiers who had not participated in the crimes. He wrote passionately:

It was only a small group of terrorists and followers who committed these crimes in their own name, not in the name of the German nation. The Russian and the Polish people, and especially the Jews, as well [as] all of humanity, have a right to find out who committed the war crimes so that a fair judgment can be brought against those who are truly responsible.

Hosenfeld was questioned in detail about the roles of the Wehrmacht, SS, and police during the Warsaw Uprising. He informed his captors about his efforts to convince General Stahel to classify the Polish *Armia Krajowa* fighters as members of the traditional military. *Not recognizing the army of the Polish uprising as a wartime force in terms of international law is the gravest offense committed by General Stahel,* Hosenfeld wrote. *Instead, he referred to them as bandits and rebels who were to be indiscriminately destroyed.* He refused to acknowledge the general's argument that a Polish state no longer existed, thereby nullifying the application of international law. Hosenfeld wrote: *I replied that Poles had a government in London who, despite the German occupation, considered itself as a sovereign country and that every nation had the right to fight for its freedom.* Hosenfeld had indeed succeeded in convincing his superior, but only upon approaching him a second time. He informed Stahel that Polish officers put great emphasis on treating captured Wehrmacht members well, whereas members of the SS, police force, and security service were shot.

During the interrogations, Hosenfeld was permitted to state his position on the events, but the Soviet military was not interested in investigating his role. Based on their previous experiences with the Wehrmacht, they probably considered it unthinkable a German officer would save Polish lives for purely humanitarian reasons. Thus, they did not believe they were detaining a harmless and compassionate sports officer. Because of his work in the IC division, they suspected Hosenfeld of being an anti-Soviet agent.

At any rate, considerations on the rule of law or even issues of fairness played no role. The investigators followed specific orders from higher up; their mission in the immediate aftermath of the war was to identify and punish as many German war criminals as possible. A lone German captain who had contravened his own troops and saved Polish citizens from capture and death did not fit into the overall scheme of things; nobody was interested. Stalin, and many other communists, despised the Poles and viewed them as inferior. The slaughter of over 4,000 Polish officers in Katyn, Russia, near Smolensk, soon after the Red Army marched into eastern Poland in September 1939, served as a dreadful example of this anti-Polish stance. Hosenfeld's assumption he could impress his interrogators with honesty and openness was wrong. On October 22, 1945, he signed the third interrogation protocol, wherein he affirmed having made his statements with *free will and without coercion.*

The pretrial detention, during which time Hosenfeld was held in solitary confinement in a separate section of the prison, lasted until

December. According to Detlev, it was likely his father was repeatedly tortured during his imprisonment. The lengthy solitary confinement surely affected Hosenfeld's health.

Klaus Wagner, a former commander of an assault-gun brigade and 24 years younger than Hosenfeld, was a fellow Soviet prisoner. Following his own release in January 1949, he sent the following account to Annemarie:

> *Your husband was then finally released from the pretrial detention that had lasted half a year. He walked in the evening to regain his health. At that time, there were over 2,000 of us officers in Minsk and in the former RAD [Reichsarbeitsdienst;* Reich Labor Service] *barracks, sleeping on wooden beds. We were moved into the so-called OK-camp* [recreation camp], *where again there was an unpleasant intimate relationship with millions of bugs and fleas.*

Indeed, this was a difficult phase, particularly as Hosenfeld was unable to send news to his family. An immense mental pressure weighed on him.

Thousands of the nearly three million German POWs held in Soviet captivity.

Following the solitary confinement, Hosenfeld returned to the general camp for German officers, where he could freely move about. He developed close friendships with a number of his comrades there, including Wagner. In his letter to Annemarie, Wagner also wrote: . . . *He told me at that time the Russians did not believe that he had been a sports officer, but instead believed that he had been in contact with Russian agents who had been working for the Germans. But he was under the impression the Russians had finally realized the senselessness of this theory.*

***

Hosenfeld was finally permitted to write again. He had to use pre-printed POW postcards from the Red Cross. The contents, scope, and frequency of Hosenfeld's postcards were subject to strict guidelines and control, although these were often arbitrarily applied. His postal address was CCCP Moscow, Red Cross, PO Box 56.

On December 25, he sent Christmas greetings to his family from Minsk. He wanted to reassure them because he knew how worried they were about him. *I am in the best of health,* Hosenfeld wrote. *Today I feel the most heartfelt bond with you.* He was allowed to receive unlimited amounts of mail, and he very much looked forward to hearing from his family. *I have the hope and the firm feeling that you are all alive and have overcome the difficult time,* Hosenfeld penned in the same letter. *I live in the belief that we will be reunited soon. I greet you with all my heart, you, dearest Annemarie, Helmut, Moni* [Anemone], *Detlev, Jorinde, Uta, your Wilm, your father.*

Hosenfeld sent his next postcard on January 1, 1946. It contained greetings for the new year and anxious questions about the children. *Are the dear boys at home, or do you know where they are?* Hosenfeld wrote. *If I only knew! The fate of all of you is my constant concern.* These brief lines were followed by five months of silence, during which time Annemarie received no further correspondence from her husband. The reason for this is not known. According to Klaus Wagner, they were transferred at the end of May to a POW camp in the Belarusian city of Babruysk, southeast of Minsk, where the release of officers was supposedly intended.

While in Babruysk, Hosenfeld acknowledged the receipt of a note from his wife dated April 22, which he had gotten about five weeks later. He finally had certainty his family survived the war unscathed. Helmut received an orderly discharge from the military, passed his state examination, completed his doctoral thesis, and worked as an assistant physician at the Heilig-Geist Hospital in Fulda. Detlev deserted his military unit in Sondershausen and walked home to Thalau on foot. *You are all alive and together in Thalau,* Hosenfeld elatedly wrote. *That the two boys came home so soon and happily survived the war is wonderful. I was most concerned about the two of them. Now I can confidently await the end of my imprisonment in God's name, as much as it pains me to be separated from all of you.*

He again assured them he was doing well. He was in good health and spent a lot of time in the sun and doing gymnastics. Because Hosenfeld was a handyman and enjoyed working, he volunteered for wood processing, which took him outside the camp and provided some variety. The work included pulling tree trunks out of rivers and cutting wood in a workshop. Although he was only supposed to send one postcard per month, Hosenfeld managed to send several during June and July. Perhaps it had something to do with the camp management assigning him to sort the mail.

In July, Annemarie received a number of postcards from her husband. She was overjoyed. *We vowed to ourselves during the difficult times that no sacrifice would be too great for you. How we have been rewarded. Your speedy return would mean the end of our trials,* Annemarie wrote.

Annemarie waited a long time before she first received details about her husband's fate. Chaplain Josef Gith informed her that in January 1945 he and Wilm Hosenfeld were taken into Soviet captivity. Gith was released in 1948. While imprisoned, Gith spent most of his time with Hosenfeld and was thus able to provide details about him later.

***

Since the end of the war, things had taken a turn for the worse for Annemarie. She had to fight to provide for herself and the children. The school had a new teacher. Thus, she was expected to vacate the house. Annemarie appealed to the superintendent who decided on her behalf. In the summer of 1946, she finally had assurance that a part of the house and garden would continue to be hers to use. *We enjoy the protection of the school board and military regime*, Annemarie wrote. *I accepted their help one time and now nobody dares to touch us anymore.*

Annemarie had no income. Only in 1949 did she begin to receive a modest pension. *We live on the earnings Anemone receives as an employee of the military regime*, Annemarie wrote to her husband. Helmut worked as an assistant physician in a small hospital. He lived in Fulda and visited Thalau every Sunday to help support his mother and siblings.

Annemarie received additional notes from the Babruysk prison camp in early August 1946. Because the cards were numbered, she could tell if all arrived. Every time a card came, Annemarie's joy was great, especially since her husband wrote of only pleasant things. Copies of several postwar letters she sent to her husband—at least those written on a typewriter—still exist. Some handwritten drafts are also extant. On August 6, Annemarie wrote:

> *We have been made homeless, destitute, our rights have been taken away and we are defenseless. We proudly endured it all. I put our fate into the hands of God, and this has given me solace. What strength, what comfort, and what deep joy your dear words give me.*
>
> *When I became yours many years ago, I carried my love like a burning light in my hands. Today I have myself become the flame that shines, warms, and consumes itself for you. How happy and relieved I am at the good news from you. You have many more calories to eat than we do.*

Wilm Hosenfeld, of course, tried to paint a reasonably bearable picture of camp life, not only because of the censorship that forbade critical remarks or mention of certain off-limit topics, but above all else, because of Annemarie, whose life was already very difficult. He did not intend to add to her burden. But the reality of camp life was different. Hosenfeld did things in the hope he would avoid the notorious camp psychosis and not fall into utter despair. Alongside physical exercise, he also wanted to remain mentally nimble and fit. Hosenfeld read any German literature he could find and returned to his previous habit of writing about the day's events. He penned poems, lyrics, and chronicles—none of which survived.

Hosenfeld had a small circle of comrades with whom he learned Russian, including Josef Gith and Klaus Wagner. Hosenfeld discussed his years in Warsaw with Wagner, including the uprising in fall 1944 and the Eastern Campaign. He distanced himself from most of the other officers, not agreeing with their opinions on the reasons for the war and the defeat.

Many of Hosenfeld's comrades did not understand his deep religious faith. He had always been a devoted Christian and it was faith that helped him through the hard times. He kept his missal and rosary close to him. In one letter to Annemarie, Klaus Wagner wrote:

> *His strong religious beliefs would have provided him support during the difficult years and all the hardships he had to endure. His love for you, dear madam, and for his children, gives him strength of will and perseverance, despite many small instances of malice carried out by certain elements who also called themselves German. Such an upright man as is your husband will not permit his character and willpower to be broken by such elements, and he will return home as the person who followed the call of his fatherland in 1939.*

In mid-July 1946, Hosenfeld managed to hide a two-square-inch secret message in the shoe of a prisoner who was released. The message stated:

D[ear] Annemie: Please write to the following
people in Poland. They owe me a debt of
gratitude and can be of help to me;
give them my address.

1. *Josef Pacanowski, in Petrikau*
2. *Achim Prut, Pabianice near Łódź*
   (an old friend)
3. *Father Antoni Cieciora*
   <u>*Samter*</u>
4. *Władysław Szpilman, Pianist*
   at the Warsaw Polish Radio,
   Warsaw

I cannot contact these people from here.

Wilm Hosenfeld smuggled this two-inch note out of his camp in the shoe of a released prisoner in July 1946.

On February 26, 1944, Hosenfeld had written about Josef Pacanowski in his journal; a Viktor Pacanowski is also mentioned—perhaps a brother. During his Russian interrogations, Hosenfeld mentioned *Josef Pacanowski and his family* as witnesses. Thus, it is conceivable Hosenfeld protected several Pacanowski family members.

Annemarie immediately recognized two of the names listed on the message: Achim (Joachim) Prut and Antoni Cieciora. She contacted the priest in Poznań to ask for his help. On July 22, 1946, Cieciora sent Annemarie two papers, one in German and one in Polish. The content goes beyond what Cieciora and the other Polish employees of the sports school were able to express at Hosenfeld's farewell ceremony two years earlier. In the first note, Cieciora wrote:

> *I, Father Antoni Cieciora, resident of Poznań, Mariackstr. 15, declare the following:*
>
> *1. I [have] known Captain Wilm Hosenfeld since 1942.*
> *2. At the request of my family, Captain Hosenfeld sought me out in Warsaw. As the head of the Wehrmacht sports school and Wehrmacht sports stadium, he hired me as a clerical worker for his office. Because I was in hiding from the Gestapo, he provided me with the necessary identity document and employee card, which saved me from death two times. He was aware that I performed the Holy Mass two times each day.*
> *3. Captain Hosenfeld treated all Polish workers courteously and tried to help them all. That is why the Poles put so much trust in him. He referred to himself in Polish as "father of the Polish workers"* . . .
> *4. Captain Hosenfeld was a practicing Catholic. The Polish workers often saw him going to confession and holy communion, even in a Polish church, which was forbidden.* . . .

In the second paper, Cieciora emphasized that Hosenfeld sharply punished soldiers under his command for any assault on Poles. He also conducted himself mildly toward Poles. Wilm Hosenfeld was not a follower of Hitler nor a fascist. Everyone who worked in the stadium could testify to that, Cieciora wrote, *over 30 of them, including two Jews under assumed names.*

It is not known if these significant documents were included in Wilm Hosenfeld's prisoner file. Annemarie forwarded the papers by mail to Babruysk. Valuable time passed before her husband received the documents. In October and November, he was still impatiently waiting for Cieciora's statements; he inquired about them in several letters.

Hosenfeld would have forwarded the documents to the camp supervisors without hesitation. But he received no response. Another attempt ended similarly. Hosenfeld appealed to the Polish state leadership to be extradited to Poland so he could prove his innocence there. The camp administration supposedly forwarded the request. There was, however, no response.

On July 17, Hosenfeld directly addressed his children in a long letter:

> . . . *Treat your mother well and be good to one another. Don't make things unnecessarily difficult for her by being disobedient, selfish, or intolerant. Help each other as much as possible and obey your dear mother. You, my dear Helmut, Moni [Anemone], and Detlev, discuss all things together with her before you make any important decision. Whatever she tells you also means that I am telling you this. Counsel your younger siblings, don't argue in front of mother. Spare her all heartache and also smaller troubles.*

He added: *I, your father, am unable to demonstrate my love for you; this is like a punishment for me.*

Hosenfeld's thoughts were always with his family; he often worried about his children. Perhaps his admonition to them was unnecessary because the children grew into a tight-knit group that rallied around their mother. Jorinde Krejci, the second-youngest daughter, remembered, "Father taught us a responsibility toward people, and that probably also [had] a big impact on me. Taking on responsibility for the family, for the person that is standing next to you, whom you are growing up together with, whom you are dealing with. He always set this example." Annemarie was always waiting, saying, as Jorinde recalled, "Father just has to come home. There is no other way. Father dominated our lives—from Warsaw, also from prisoner-of-war captivity when the postcards arrived. We prayed for him daily. When the electricity went out, we sat in the kitchen, [and] prayed [with] a rosary for the return of father. We had to constantly make sacrifices, as if to practically pay for the return of father from God."

Now a doctor and medical journalist, Jorinde emphasized the large influence her oldest brother had on her and her siblings in the postwar years. Helmut assumed the paternal role. "When Helmut came home after the war, he was actually the 'father' who took care of everything," she said. "My brother made great sacrifices for the family. He thought that by doing this he could in some way force God to send father home to us. That is how I interpret it today. Mother also always demanded, 'You must be good! You must study well for school! Or father will not come home.' This ruled our lives. I always felt the pressure to do everything so that father would return."

For his 19th birthday, on July 17, 1946, Detlev Hosenfeld received a long letter from his father. Wilm Hosenfeld vividly portrayed his captivity in the distant Belarus:

> *There are still thousands of miles of land and the barbed wire of the Russian prison camp that is holding me and isolating me from the outside world. I am sitting on a bench by the wall of one of the barracks, a few steps from me the barbed-wire fence stands three yards along to my left and two hundred yards to my right. A sentry watches from a guardhouse. On the street behind the fence, an endless column of vehicles is just now moving along; they have horses formerly belonging to the Wehrmacht. My view goes above the large willow trees and comes to rest on the houses in the town of Bobrujsk [Babruysk]. But above all else, I see the blue sky, the radiant sun and the big clouds, and over all this endless land to the*

west I mentally see my home, I see it palpably as my eyes see the actual landscape around me here, I see you, my dear ones, and you, my birthday boy, as if you were all standing before me.

Hosenfeld asked his son what he had in mind in terms of a profession since he was going to graduate from secondary school in the spring of 1947. He recommended Detlev consider being a doctor or a theologian. He had last seen Detlev during his home leave in February 1944; Detlev was not home during his father's last visit at Pentecost in May that year. In the letter, Hosenfeld also wrote:

When I saw you in Kassel the last time, I was so sad on my way back. We had spent so much time in Kassel at the train station and I knew that you were not far away, but we were not together; I could have accompanied you to your unit. It has made me sad thinking about this over the years, and the thought that our farewells back then may have been our last has often caused me great pain.

***

During the second half of July 1946, Hosenfeld alternated between hope and trepidation. A repatriation transport to return prisoners to Germany had been organized. He believed himself to be one of the lucky ones who would finally be allowed to leave the camp, but that hope was shattered. On July 27, Hosenfeld wrote: *You can imagine how that tore me apart inside. I was so despondent for days that I almost could not even pray. I was so foolhardy that I doubted in God's grace and mercy. But now I have found my peace again and carry my fate with willing submissiveness to God's guidance.*

The same mail with Hosenfeld's letter included a scarf for Annemarie. He had worn it often and it was dirty, but he did not want to wash it. *My love for you is without end*, Hosenfeld wrote. *These words almost seem inadequate for what I feel for you.* On August 28, Annemarie confirmed she had received the scarf. *I carry it near my heart; at night it lies against my cheek*, she wrote. *This way you are always with me.*

When she knew with certainty her husband would not be released at that time, she was very disappointed. A fellow prisoner who returned home had greatly raised her hopes that Wilm, too, would soon return home. *Yesterday I was so sad that I cried almost the entire day*, Annemarie lamented.

In order to somewhat cheer him up—and probably also herself as well—Annemarie added that Jorinde diligently helped with the housework. She was the best student in her class and was moving up to the next grade level. *Maybe you will be a little happy when I tell you that my essay "Childhood Remembrances of Paula Modersohn" will appear in the newspaper published by Hausmann*, Annemarie noted.

At the beginning of November, she wrote that, like in the days of old, the local Thalau fair was being celebrated again with dancing, a carnival tent, and stands. She and the children, however, were not planning to participate. *Detlev is busy studying for his final examination, Helmut is helping him*, Annemarie wrote.

2

Rescue Attempts

Soon after the end of the war, Annemarie Hosenfeld endeavored to have her husband released from captivity. She turned to Karl Hörle in Hanau with a plea to campaign on Wilm's behalf. Hörle, a communist and former unionist, had been sent to a concentration camp where he was severely beaten. He was released in 1943 and sent to Warsaw where he worked for Hosenfeld in the office of the sports school. In a November 9, 1945, letter, Hörle wrote an exceptional character reference on behalf of Wilm Hosenfeld. He confirmed he had often warned Hosenfeld to be careful about his critical remarks regarding the Nazis, particularly the SS, as an informant might betray him. Hörle said that Hosenfeld risked being arrested on account of his harsh criticism, and his anti-fascist conduct as a person, soldier, and colleague had been exemplary.

Hörle also said he was convinced Hosenfeld would direct his full energy toward democratically educating youth in the new Germany. This comment was probably aimed at Annemarie's concern her husband would not be hired again as a teacher due to his membership in the Nazi Party and the SA.

As 1946 came to a close, there were no signs Hosenfeld could expect to be released from captivity anytime soon. In a letter dated November 19, he acknowledged his receipt of a photo of his wife. In an unusual telegram-like style of writing, Hosenfeld described details of his captivity. He mentioned occasionally being sent to Babruysk, the winter having already started, and having warm clothes and sufficient food. *Living together with comrades* [is] *often not easy, human weaknesses intensify in captivity*, Hosenfeld wrote. [I] *have good friends, but am lonely. You are my support and comfort and the safety in God. Working and living with teams. Good relationship. Better than the officers in craftsmanship. I mostly saw wood, sometimes* [I] *work as a carpenter.*

One week later, on November 26, he wished his family a blessed and joyful Christmas. He would be with them next year, he assured them. *I will not give up*, he wrote. *My dear, you also must be brave and endure. We still have much to live for.* On the last day of 1946, he wrote a letter from the infirmary, where he was being treated for bronchitis. He again expressed his yearning to reunite with his family. Since Annemarie wanted to know how he looked, if he had lost weight and so on, he replied his weight remained fairly normal. Yes, he had wrinkles in his face, but as he said, they represented life's wisdom. On top of that, he did not require glasses. Hosenfeld also noted: *I am looking forward to a letter from* [both] *Cieciora and Hörle.*

Hosenfeld's first letter of the new year, dated January 5, 1947, was addressed to his children. He regretted not being able to teach Jorinde her school lessons. *Learn well*, he wrote. *But don't underestimate the practical skills. Those are very important. I have seen that in captivity.* Hosenfeld wished Detlev much success for his upcoming final exam. Unfortunately, there was nothing he could do to help. He asked Anemone to keep him informed about conditions in postwar Germany. At one point, Hosenfeld noted that news from home was interesting and worth knowing. In the camp, it was as if he lived on the dark side of the moon. *Do tell me more about the relatives and friends*, he wrote. He asked the children to include a flint for his lighter with each letter.

On January 16, Hosenfeld's thoughts took him back to the events at the end of the war in Warsaw. In a letter to Annemarie, he wrote:

> *Darling . . . two years ago today I was a free man for the last time. How much time has passed since then and what events have occurred! Is it lost time? No, I have grown wealthy in my impoverishment. I have found the man that you want me to be. Beloved, I know that*

you are also lonely, despite all your worries and dedication to your daily tasks. I can feel your heart wrapped around me. But you are not as alone as I am. Everything that I think of, everything that I feel, my wishes and prayers have only one goal: to prepare myself for you and my future life at your side.

During the winter months, when it was too cold to work outside, Hosenfeld helped peel potatoes in the camp kitchen. He accepted such work without complaint; he welcomed the distraction and it gave him the opportunity to talk to other prisoners. It was also very cold in Germany. Annemarie reported the thermometer had dropped to -9°F in Thalau. The postwar generation would long remember the harsh winter; the snow and ice added to the overall hardship.

***

Hosenfeld kept his distance from many of the prisoners. He did not fully isolate himself and answered when spoken to, but his private life meant more than anything else in the camp. When his wife wrote about visits from returning soldiers, he replied: *Basically, they do not know me. Even though we are together in close confinement, I keep to myself and my thoughts are directed inward. I am so rich in my loneliness that I don't need anyone. At my age one also does not find anyone to feel close to. My ring is closed; there is no room for anyone except you and the children.*

Was this the same Hosenfeld from his time in Warsaw? The man who approached people, who sought out the contact of others, who enthusiastically accepted new challenges, and who listened to the concerns and needs of persecuted Poles and found a way to help them? By this time, he had been in captivity for over two years. The camp reduced him to his mere existence. No one gave Hosenfeld fulfilling assignments to carry out. An iron discipline, a belief in God, a hope of returning home, and love for his wife and family were the pillars upon which he tried to build his survival in captivity.

The religious holidays were a special challenge for both Wilm Hosenfeld in Babruysk and his family at home. During those times, his absence was even more painfully felt. The images of happy times in days past would often resurface. Hosenfeld developed a means to overcome such phases. Almost without effort, through writing he could transport himself to his family, which provided a temporary distraction from the pain of separation.

For Easter 1947, a comrade decorated one of Hosenfeld's post-cards with idyllic scenes of home: the man drew Thalau with the church in the background, surrounded by forests and hills. In between were hopping rabbits that carried Easter eggs. On April 8, he sent his wife a portrait that had been drawn by a fellow prisoner. In the sketch, Hosenfeld has a serious face with a mustache and beard, and his hair stands off to the side. *I am not completely satisfied with it, but I more or less look like that*, he commented.

A portrait of Wilm Hosenfeld in 1947, drawn by a fellow prisoner.

On the upcoming occasion of the Hosenfelds' wedding anniversary, he included a tiny drawing with his letter dated April 14. It showed a young couple on the edge of a forest. Wilm looked back in time, almost overly dramatic. In the letter, he wrote:

> *We must stand alone and remain silent in sad forbearance. Our hands, that we interlocked so firmly on this day in May, reach into emptiness and our eyes look into the distance. My lips form a sweet name, but you do not hear it. And yet, we are standing in the splendor of our young lives. Like foolish children we stood at the new shores. We stepped onto the land of our desire, brave, joyful, and serious, made mistakes, suffered, injured and forgave, having erred and been found. Like the traveler in the dark one star after the other, so, too, did our children come to us.*

Hosenfeld remained an adviser and teacher, even in captivity, always leading the way by setting a good example. *I am continuing with my Russian,* he reported on May 31. *The children should take their language courses very seriously. Only through its language can you truly understand another nation.*

During the summer of 1947, events took their usual course. Mail from home normally arrived at the camp in batches. Sometimes, there were six or seven cards, which made Hosenfeld very happy; he would pick them up again and again. Hosenfeld wrote letters to Annemarie, which he neither wanted to—nor would have been permitted to—send because they were too long. He instead saved them so she could read them later. These letters have been lost.

Hosenfeld continued to send optimistic notes concerning his health and a speedy return in his usual letters. However, he had no specific reason to warrant such optimism. It appears Hosenfeld did not want to lose hope, and at the same time, wanted to encourage his family to patiently wait for him. On July 4, he wrote:

> *Moni [Anemone] feels that you don't have to write to me anymore since I will soon be home. That time has not arrived yet. I am doing*

well. I am sitting in the garden house, outside by the fence. The troops of the work teams are returning to the camp at their usual unperturbed pace, their heads down, with the expression of cheerless indifference. Around me [are] several comrades; one is reading, the other writes, most of them are staring at nothing in particular, thinking. In the eastern sky wonderful white mountains of clouds are towering upon the gentle white-blue of the sky. Below, the small, cowering wooden houses and six paces from me the mesh of the barbed-wire fence. I don't see it. I look over it, up to the towers of clouds.

***

After two and a half years in captivity, on July 27, Hosenfeld's life dramatically changed. He suffered a stroke that paralyzed the right side of his body and affected his ability to speak. In Warsaw, his dizzy spells, headaches, and temporary paralysis signaled a circulatory disorder in his brain, but the various examinations had not recognized it.

The conditions in the camp, especially the months of pretrial detention, severely affected Hosenfeld's health. Nonetheless, he always assured his family all was well. He tried to remain physically and mentally strong, not wanting to return home a broken man. It is a testimony to his great discipline that a few days after the stroke, on August 2, he scribbled a few lines to his family:

Dear Annemie, dear children, I am writing to you using my left hand. Since Sunday, 27.7. [July 27], I have suffered a sudden paralysis of my right side, arm and leg, and [have] difficulty speaking. I have to lie in bed, [and] am in the hospital receiving good care. It will take several weeks until I am healthy. I am confident and submit myself to God's holy will. Best wishes to Detlev for his birthday celebration tomorrow. May God protect you, your father, your Wilm. Don't worry!

The messages Hosenfeld sent from the hospital each consisted of only a few lines. He continued to write with his left hand. The awkward penmanship, as well as the contents of his letters, did not reassure his family. He did everything possible to look toward the future. He told Annemarie he wanted to drive with her next August to Witzenhausen, where they had first met 30 years prior. About a month later, he confirmed he had received eight cards from Germany. *I am doing well again, no strength in the right hand,* he wrote. *Don't you worry about me. The return draws nearer, date undetermined. Try to reach Cieciora through* [the] *Polish consulate or American authorities. Hopefully unpleasant circumstances in the house* [are] *resolved. Saddens me very much.* He referred to the renewed confrontation about the Thalau schoolteacher's residence, which his wife was to vacate. Then, Hosenfeld quoted the New Testament, from the apostle Paul's letter to the Galatians: *"Bear ye one another's burdens, and so fulfill the law of Christ. But let every man prove his own work, and then shall he have rejoicing in himself alone, and not in another."* He concluded the letter by offering his own advice: *Do not live in returnee-psychosis, you get sick from it. Your yearning tears at my heart.*

Although writing was a difficult task for him, Hosenfeld repeatedly included lengthy passages from the New Testament in his letters. Annemarie had to remain patient because the mail delivery was again held up and it took longer for her to receive Wilm's letters. Her letter dated September 10 started with a heavy sigh:

> *My heart's dearest Wilm! This unbearable waiting, one becomes ill from it. For 15 days I have not received news from you. How I am worrying. If I only knew how you were! Day and night I have only one thought of you—your condition. During the hours of strength and brightness I have courage and confidence, but when it grows dark, when I am lonesome and lie awake overtired, the worry almost kills me. My lips form the words of a prayer, but my heart does not know it.*

Since all rescue attempts and petitions were to no avail, and the news of her husband's stroke alarmed her, Annemarie again contacted Karl Hörle for help. He was now chairman of the Association of Persecutees of the Nazi Regime for the city of Hanau. Hörle sent an appeal directly to the commander of the Babruysk POW camp on October 5, asking for the immediate release of Wilm Hosenfeld.

In his letter, Hörle first addressed his own position as a functionary of the Communist Party of Germany (KPD). He then detailed how Hosenfeld reacted when Hörle told him about the serious abuse he had suffered in the concentration camp. *Now I recognized the compassion of Hosenfeld, that he was also an opponent of these Nazi criminals*, Hörle wrote. *From then on, while observing the necessary precautions, we spoke about politics and the senseless and criminal actions of the German civil*[ian] *administration in the occupied countries, especially in the East.*

Hörle expressly mentioned Hosenfeld's Warsaw journal, which by then was in his family's possession. It documented the persecution of the Jews, the gas chambers, and severe torture in very explicit terms. In October 1947, Hörle and Annemarie traveled to East Berlin. They managed to speak with Otto Nuschke, who, like Hörle, had suffered injuries in a concentration camp. (Nuschke later became Deputy Prime Minister of East Germany.) During the meeting, Hörle exercised all of his standing in order to gain Hosenfeld's release. Nuschke promised he would do everything in his power to help. Annemarie regained some hope. In her notebook, she wrote: *KPD requests release from war captivity, if possible with courier to Moscow.* In the end, however, Nuschke was not able to achieve anything.

Around mid-October, Hosenfeld was allowed to leave the camp hospital. He informed his son Helmut that he was again writing with his right hand, although it was still not as strong as it used to be. *The secret of success is practice and patience*, he wrote to Annemarie on October 18. *My return* [is] *uncertain, although they give us hope. We are too near to the catastrophe of war and are their victims. At home you believe this was all finished. That is not so.*

During November, Hosenfeld repeatedly updated his family about treatment in the camp and the state of his health. *Food sufficient, three times* [a day we receive] *three-quarters of a liter soup, 670-gram bread, 20-gram sugar, 20-gram fat daily. You probably don't have more*, he wrote. He was smoking again, but not much. The dizzy spells had decreased. *Nobody should feel sorry for us—we are taking the noble path of suffering*, Hosenfeld wrote.

In his next letter, Hosenfeld asked his wife what she had achieved in East Berlin. He told her he was skeptical and asked about Father Cieciora. [The] *connection with Cieciora* [is] *important because Cieciora should look for more Jews in Warsaw whose lives I saved*, Hosenfeld wrote. The details about his health sounded less reassuring than before: [I] . . . *often have dizziness and headaches, high blood pressure 180-130. Can walk, just as strong* [on the] *right as* [the] *left. Weight* [is] *62 kilograms* [137 pounds], *before 69* [150]. *Writing right. Homecoming uncertain. Life becoming more difficult.*

***

Hosenfeld sent Christmas greetings to his family early, on November 25, because he was to be moved to a different camp. He also announced a Christmas fairy tale he had written and dedicated to his wife. Starting in early December, he was in the Cholmy hospital in Mogilev, Belarus. The reason for the transfer is not known. Perhaps his health had again declined.

Yet another transfer took place in March 1948. Since the Cholmy hospital closed, Hosenfeld was moved to a hospital in the town of Orsha, about 45 miles away. Another interrogation took place during his time there. Among the questions Hosenfeld was supposed to answer was whether or not he had been a commander in Warsaw. He stayed at this hospital until mid-May.

After Orsha, his next stop was a labor camp in Vitebsk. At the time, Hosenfeld still expected to be relocated to Warsaw to testify against German war criminals. This was something for which he had hoped a long time. Chaplain Josef Gith had been brought to the hospital in Babruysk with symptoms similar to Hosenfeld's and transferred to Mogilev. Gith wrote to Annemarie: *Wilm himself expected that he would be handed over to the Polish by the Russians so that he could testify as a witness in a trial held against German officers in Warsaw.*

However, Gith also stated his concern that a Warsaw transfer would delay his return home because the Russians were not handing him over, but only loaning him out. *That is what we were told on the trip home in Brest-Litovsk* [Brest] *by people who had been through similar events,* Gith wrote. The chaplain, who had suffered a serious kidney infection in Mogilev, also acknowledged his camaraderie with Hosenfeld:

> *I had lost hope and temporarily refused to eat. It was comrade Wilm who spoke to me and did not let up until I ate something. He gave me small delicacies from his provisions to make the food more palatable for me. But much more important and decisive was the comfort that he provided me through his deep, sincere religiousness.*

What Hosenfeld feared had happened: his transfers to different hospitals and camps resulted in his family not hearing from him for five months. He sent a message from Vitebsk dated May 15. In it, he wrote:

> *Dearest Annemie, dear children! A few days ago, I wrote card number 49 to you. You may believe that my handwriting reveals how I am doing health-wise, but this indicator is misleading. I am really doing well despite the shaky writing. A certain weakness has remained in the right hand. I thank the dear Lord that he has healed me this much. . . . Tomorrow is Pentecost! My heart is with you! I send you my greetings, your Wilm, your father.*

Hosenfeld was not required to perform any strenuous physical work at the Vitebsk camp. He used the time to again focus on learning Russian. He regretted he was in foreign surroundings. But he was not yet too old for such a change. Moreover, the mood in the camp was better because the prisoners were younger, healthy, and content since they were required to perform physical work.

Hosenfeld was just getting acclimated to the camp when he was transferred back to the POW camp in Babruysk. At the end of May, there was just enough time before his transfer to ask fellow prisoner Rudhard Enders to inform Helmut, who worked as a doctor in the

Heilig-Geist Hospital in Fulda, of the news. In a postcard dated May 28, Enders wrote that Hosenfeld was happy about the transfer *because he hoped to receive an opportunity to exonerate himself there. He can also see old friends there again. . . .*

Upon his return to the Babruysk camp, Hosenfeld felt a certain melancholy; some of his comrades had been allowed to return home and were no longer there. Chaplain Gith was there, although only for a short time. Gith was now permitted to say mass on Sundays, which was a special comfort for Hosenfeld.

Hosenfeld fully expected to be released in July, or at least transferred to Warsaw, which would have brought him a step closer to his vision of returning home. It was his hope the Russians would keep their promise to release POWs by the end of 1948. The Soviets made this same commitment during the meetings of the Council of Foreign Ministers held in Moscow in March and April 1947.

One of Wilm Hosenfeld's numbered postcards from a Soviet POW camp.

***

Starting in August 1948, Hosenfeld's postcards to Thalau no longer contained even a hint of hope he would soon be released or transported to Warsaw. *Sometimes I have terrible headaches that depress me, but most of the time I am healthy and in a good mood. The waiting and the disappointment are the challenges we have been presented*, he wrote on August 1. One week later, Hosenfeld wrote: *Yesterday a transport left our camp for home. All of the officers who were scheduled to leave were canceled. We must continue to wait.*

Chaplain Gith told Annemarie to remain brave in another letter he sent from his German residence in Mülheim. She should not lose confidence, Gith said. When the transports were prepared, it was never certain until the last second who would go and who would stay. *These are always nerve-racking days of suspense*, Gith wrote. He also noted the health risks to which prisoners continued to be exposed. Gith also noted:

> *At the moment I view the repeated disappointments and the serious emotional distress as a danger for Wilm's state of health. I know how badly that affected me. When Wilm left us in Orša [Orsha], he was remarkably fit. Except for light dizzy spells, which affects many people who have high blood pressure, he felt very good. His day was filled with reading and studying the Russian language, occasionally a chess match; rarely did he engage in political discussions. Because he is a man who can easily occupy himself, he was not bored.*

Gith and Hosenfeld were not popular with former staff officers who, during their captivity, were only concerned with their own benefit. There were cynical comments made about the schoolteachers, but, Gith wrote, they simply viewed it as involuntary recognition. Some of the officers could not comprehend that Hosenfeld had saved the lives of Polish Jews.

The remaining months of 1948 passed without any meaningful change in Hosenfeld's condition at Babruysk. After relatively stable phases, Hosenfeld again had to be treated in the hospital several times due to acute dizziness and overly high blood pressure. Annemarie asked him to be honest about his health, and he now mostly honored that request. In any case, she learned about his condition from former prisoners who had been released.

Annemarie also had health problems. The constant pressure, the fear, the waiting, and the many disappointments—all of it affected her. Since the end of the war, she had found her surrounding environment to be hostile and peaceless. Annemarie had yearned for the end of the war, and now that it was over, faced even bigger problems than before: the struggle to remain in the house, the lack of income, the uncertain future. *A hurricane of hate and a lack of peace drown out all the tentative calls for communication and brotherhood,* she wrote in a letter on September 7.

On October 28, she depicted her daily routine with the children and the preparations for the coming winter. *As I was leaving church with Detlev today, it was snowing and the Dalherda peak* [in the Rhön Mountains] *looked toward us with a white cover of snow,* Annemarie wrote. *We fear the cold. I made a fire in the living room so that Detlev can work undisturbed.* Detlev was preparing for his medical studies.

When it became obvious in early 1949 that Stalin would not honor his promise to release all POWs, several of Hosenfeld's prison comrades contacted Annemarie. Klaus Wagner expressed his hope for a storm of protest among all concerned parties and the prisoners' wives because Russia was not fulfilling its obligations to return all German prisoners. Ignaz Fornhammer, a prisoner from Munich who had recently been released, also conveyed greetings from Wilm.

Hosenfeld had no other choice but to persevere in the camp. He no longer had any hope of an imminent release. It was too exhausting to cope with each new disappointment. The Christmas and New Years holidays greatly troubled him so much that his blood pressure again rose to dangerous levels and he complained of feeling unwell. In mid-January 1949, he again spent several weeks in the hospital. The jittery tremors in his right arm and leg concerned him. He wrote to his wife on March 1:

> *For days I have been lying in bed with a headache and nausea, without appetite, and in a poor mental state. Then a few healthy*

days follow again, during which I exercise and go walking, play
chess, and read. Blood pressure around 170. More strength in the
arm and leg. If dizzy, then shaky like an old man, jaw locking, mild
speech impediment.

He wrote to his daughter Jorinde on May 9, who was still attending
the secondary school in Fulda. *Study well*, Hosenfeld wrote. *You must*
be like a field thirsting for rain. Do not disdain people who work with their hands
and be willing to do any craft work as well. A comrade spoke of two young ladies
who had made a great and positive impact upon him when he went to secondary
school. The thought that I also [have] *such dear girls makes me happy.*

In the meantime, his youngest daughter, Uta, had also passed the
secondary school entrance exam. He wrote to her a few days later:

You have changed a lot; I almost did not recognize you in the picture
with Detlev and the other one with the dog. I am doing fairly well. I
must not applaud it too much. I think that we will soon be going home.
We already have the blue suits, but that does not mean anything. We
have already been disappointed so often. All of you have helped me
so much! You know upon which golden bridges we will meet. The
Russian railroad will one day also leave with us!

He assured Annemarie in the interim she should not think he had
become a sanctimonious old man or a pessimist. Despite everything,
he was still a man with an appetite for life who eagerly waited for
his wife. In additional letters, Hosenfeld asked his brother-in-law, Dr.
Gerhard Krummacher, to send him a new blood-pressure reduction
medication being produced in Switzerland under the name Hydergine.
Hosenfeld asked if it were at all possible for the Swiss Red Cross to
send it directly to the POW camp.

Hosenfeld was forced to watch another prisoner transport depart
the camp in June 1949; once again, he was not one of those who
were sent home. Thereupon, he wrote to his daughter Anemone, who
worked as a nurse in the St. Antonius city hospital in Fulda. She was

now engaged to Rudhard Enders, a former prisoner whom Wilm had gotten to know at the Babruysk camp, and who had been free for a long time. *Let us not talk about returning home anymore*, Hosenfeld wrote. *We will consider it to be the same as "getting to heaven." But I am hopeful that both will occur. That's something. Ask dear Rudhard what is going on with the red house. Whoever enters there loses all hope, like those who are swallowed up by Hades.*

It is unclear what this comment meant. On May 29, two weeks after his release from the hospital, Hosenfeld was again interrogated about his activities in Warsaw. Was he tortured in the "red house?" Certain information indicates this. Or, was the "red house" the office of the military prosecutor who, since April 1949, had followed new guidelines? According to these guidelines, Wehrmacht officers who, like Wilm Hosenfeld, had been assigned to headquarters and staff divisions were to be equated with members of the Gestapo and SS—in effect, to be treated as war criminals.

3

Final Years

At most, Wilm Hosenfeld could guess what was happening behind the scenes. His writings during the summer of 1949 do not paint a consistent picture, but rather indicate a state of continued uncertainty. This is not surprising in light of his situation. Where could he have found support when, more than four years after the end of the war, there was still no prospect he would return home?

In a letter to his brother Rudolf, Hosenfeld vividly described how the two of them would meet again and take in the surrounding areas where they had played as children. *Various trees*, Hosenfeld wrote, *have come to symbolize life; I look forward to seeing them, as well as good people.* His ability to transport himself into another world and to envision distant regions often helped him to at least temporarily suppress the seemingly endless existence as a prisoner of war. Hosenfeld's camp life remained a cycle of ups and downs between hope and disappointment, between phases when he suffered from dizziness and headaches and days when he felt his health was improved.

Stalin came under international pressure at the end of the 1940s when it became clear the Soviet Union was reneging on its promise to release POWs. At the time, approximately half a million Germans were still held in camps across the Soviet Union. Many of the former soldiers worked in construction, agriculture, or forestry. In the eyes of the Russians, Ukrainians, and Belarusians, the German prisoners provided reparations for the destruction caused by their people during the war. They helped with the reconstruction of public buildings and entire city blocks.

According to the Kremlin, prisoners were to be returned sometime in 1949. Instead of honoring this pledge, however, the Russians hastily made preparations to convict German war criminals in a series of trials, after which they were to remain in the Soviet Union. The trials all followed the same pattern, and the vast majority ended with an identical sentence: 25 years' camp imprisonment. Wilm Hosenfeld, savior of the pianist and other Poles, helper of the persecuted, humanitarian in a soldier's uniform, was also a victim of this judicial discretion. For him, it represented a death sentence.

***

Hosenfeld remained hopeful about a possible release until autumn 1949, although he could never be certain. On September 16, he informed Annemarie the strict rules for written correspondence would again be observed. *We are only allowed to send one card per month,* he wrote. *Don't be surprised if you do not hear from me. But I also think that more is not necessary. We were so often disappointed, but now it must be meaningful. I will come at the end of November at the latest. I do not wish to set a date, because nobody knows, even our hosts do not know.*

He was well aware his fate, as well as that of his comrades, would not be decided in Babruysk. Any decision would be made by Stalin in the Kremlin. *I hope you have copies of your cards,* Hosenfeld wrote. *I would like to read them again later. I am not allowed to take them with me.*

On September 24, he wrote another postcard, this time to his eldest daughter, Anemone. It is clear from his lines that he fully expected to be released. He wrote: *With number 45, Mother should have received my last card from Russia, but you will actually have the last one. I hope that I am not wrong. But don't start to fidget if it still takes some time before I am home.* Since he had not received any mail during the previous two weeks, he asked about the wellbeing of his wife and each of his children. It was Hosenfeld's final message from the Babruysk camp. His family had to wait a long time for the next letter from him.

At the end of October, Hosenfeld returned to the POW camp in Minsk, where he had been interred at the start of his captivity five years earlier. He was not sure what this meant. Hosenfeld may have seen the transfer from Babruysk to Minsk as a sign of his impending release. After all, he had suffered so long his health had deteriorated and there was nothing for which he could be held accountable. Hosenfeld may have thought along those lines. But things came differently. A new martyrdom began for Hosenfeld, even worse and more cruel than everything he had already endured. He was now in the hands of the Soviet military justice system, which was determined to brand him as a war criminal.

The detention order he received on December 14 was followed by solitary confinement. Hosenfeld had already been subjected to this treatment when he first entered captivity. This time, the justification used was "threat to escape." Guards searched everything he still possessed and found nothing. Hosenfeld was stunned. And yet, from that moment on he would have surely recognized he was regarded as a dangerous criminal who potentially faced the death penalty. All correspondence was prohibited. In a series of interrogations, investigators tried to force him to confess, which obviously did not occur.

***

Annemarie found out from other released prisoners that her husband's condition had gotten worse. She was aware he and around 400 other prisoners were being held in solitary confinement. Annemarie also knew Wilm refused to sign a list of indictment charges, an action that would have amounted to an admission of guilt. She started a desperate new rescue attempt. She compiled new witness testimonies for an application to the International Committee of the Red Cross in Geneva, Switzerland.

On March 29, 1950, she sent a request to Wolfgang Werner in Bomlitz, Germany. Werner had participated as a soldier and medical student in lectures as part of the vocational training courses offered by the Wehrmacht in Warsaw. In her letter, Annemarie wrote:

> *We need testimonials of former comrades for our appeal to the Red Cross that factually describe the work of my husband and emphasize that he never participated in a crime against humanity. I know this from letters and journals. You were certainly together with my husband at section IC. He only worked as an interrogation officer for a short while and only as a deputy. He stated in Russia that during his time no <u>death sentence</u> was passed.*
>
> *I know that he was happy when he could help Poles. Please answer me quickly. . . .*

A few days later, she received a response. Werner confirmed what all those who met Wilm had previously testified. The courses were professional and unrelated to military and political topics. Hosenfeld was widely respected because of his warm, humane nature. He had always emphasized that students should regard themselves as people and free academic citizens. Werner wrote: *It is to be hoped for that many of the numerous friends and acquaintances among the Polish population of Warsaw will find the courage to help an innocent man and friend, if only out of thankfulness and justice. All across the world, it should be seen as an injustice when innocents are forced to suffer for the guilty.*

On May 27, 1950, the military tribunal of the Belarusian Ministry of the Interior (now the Ministry of Internal Affairs) in Minsk met in a secret session under the chairmanship of Captain Zolotarev. Without the presence of prosecution and defense, Captain Wilm Hosenfeld was sentenced to 25 years' imprisonment. In 2000, Helmut was able to receive a copy of the court's decision. This was the court's justification for the sentence:

> *Hosenfeld has served in the German army since 1939. In September/ October 1939, he guarded a prisoner-of-war camp holding soldiers and officers of the Polish army as part of the security battalion "Francken." Thereafter, he served as an officer for the Warsaw*

> *command headquarters until 1944, where he participated in puni-*
> *tive actions against insurgent Polish citizens in August, personally*
> *interrogating and committing them to prison, thereby contributing to*
> *the reinforcement of German fascism and an enemy action against*
> *the Soviet Union.*

The sentence was in no way based upon the rule of law. Instead, it was a bureaucratic action whereby the tribunal changed the initial sentence intended for such "crimes"—death—to multi-year imprisonment.

Hosenfeld's experiences in solitary confinement, beginning in December 1949 and until the reading of the verdict in May 1950, were described to Helmut by the physician Christian Meyer-Reicheneck in a November 1950 letter from Bad Tölz, Germany. The doctor, like Hosenfeld, found himself in the isolation wing. Meyer-Reicheneck occasionally treated Hosenfeld's medical condition, and said he had been so tormented he suffered a serious nervous breakdown and one or two mild strokes. Hosenfeld was then admitted to the hospital. There is no indication from the letter about the type of interrogations to which Hosenfeld was submitted, or if torture was applied. At any rate, he was in bad shape, both mentally and physically. Meyer-Reicheneck wrote: *When I first treated Hosenfeld, he was at times completely disturbed and oftentimes had to be brought back from a state of "mental absenteeism." He often struggled unsuccessfully to pronounce words that were on the tip of his tongue; if I was able to help him, he would smile happily and thankfully.*

With the help of heart medication, vitamin C, and cod liver oil, Hosenfeld's condition improved. His balance was still impaired, and the trembling in his hands and head also affected him. Apparently, though, Hosenfeld was soon able to help others. Meyer-Reicheneck wrote: *My lungs and limbs are severely damaged; during our time together, he touchingly assisted me, brought the food for us patients, washed laundry, cleaned the rooms, heated the stoves, always offered a word of comfort. When I wanted to complain, he begged me to let him work, otherwise he would go crazy.*

Hosenfeld filed a timely appeal against the verdict with the highest military court in Belarus. It was promptly rejected. The judges did not even state a reason for their decision, simply referencing the verdict of the subordinate tribunal that had ordered a transfer to Camp 362 in Stalingrad. Hosenfeld was transported there, along with 250 other convicted POWs. The journey took them through a camp in Brest, which had already served as a midway stop on the way to Minsk at the beginning of his captivity. Meyer-Reicheneck saw Hosenfeld for the last time in Brest, after which the doctor was allowed to return to Munich.

Nothing more is known about the journey to Stalingrad. Hosenfeld arrived there in August 1950. The historian Vogel, writing about Camp 362, said normal POWs had previously been held there and were returned home. From then on, the camp—under heightened security—served exclusively as a detention site for convicted POWs. When Hosenfeld arrived, the camp held approximately 2,000 inmates who lived in primitive stone huts, and to a large extent, underground bunkers. The living conditions were accordingly spartan and difficult.

The food was also insufficient. That changed in the spring of 1951 when prisoners were finally allowed to receive packages with food as well as letters. Hosenfeld sent a card to his family on May 26, 1951; they had heard nothing from him for more than a year. He confirmed he had received 22 cards, six photographs, and two packages. He wrote: *Blue jacket still in good condition. Very happy about everything.* Hosenfeld again asked his brother-in-law, Gerhard Krummacher, to send him the blood-pressure reduction medication Hydergine. Details about his health are vague.

Annemarie received additional information from Dr. Nikolaus Daniel. The doctor, who had also been transferred to Stalingrad, treated her husband during the ensuing two years. In a letter, Daniel wrote:

> *Herr* [Mr.] *Hosenfeld had already been suffering for a longer time from very high blood pressure and advanced arterial calcification, particularly of the vessels in the brain and weakness of the heart*

muscle. Herr Hosenfeld suffered three strokes with temporary paralysis, twice on the right and once on the left side of the body, during the time I treated him in Stalingrad.

Life-threatening events were averted thanks to the application of appropriate medical measures. During follow-up treatments, the paralysis had abated to the extent that Hosenfeld was able to walk until his end.

***

Leon Warm was one of several Polish Jews whom Wilm Hosenfeld had employed. Warm had fled from a train on the way to Treblinka extermination camp, after which he contacted his sister, Maria Malina. She worked for the Schoene family in Warsaw, where Hosenfeld had been a frequent guest. When Hosenfeld heard about Warm's escape, he provided him with new papers—as he had done with Antoni Cieciora—and hired him under the name "Warczynski" to work at the Wehrmacht sports school, thereby saving his life.

After the war, Leon Warm located Hosenfeld's home address. He wanted to personally thank his savior in Thalau before emigrating to Australia. To Warm's great surprise, he found out during his visit that Hosenfeld was still being held as a prisoner of war by the Soviets. Annemarie showed him letters and postcards from her husband in Belarus. She also showed him the secret message with the names of those he had saved and told Warm that Szpilman might still be able to help.

Warm immediately wrote a long letter to Szpilman, describing the previous rescue attempts and emphasizing that Hosenfeld's family had had no sign of life from him for one year. His state of health was very poor: paralysis, heart attacks, and depression made things difficult for him. *It's a fact that villains and perpetrators were free while a man who deserved a commendation had to suffer,* Warm wrote.

As Warm finalized preparations for his move to Australia, he suggested his sister, Maria Malina, serve as a contact with Szpilman. In his letter to Szpilman, Warm listed additional people whom he believed to be living in Warsaw or somewhere else in Poland and would be willing to help Hosenfeld:

> *Chamczek Leon, Kraczyk Waclaw, Patela Waclaw, Zalegowski Wiktor, WiernikTokarska Maria,* [and] *Father Cieciora Cichocki, living in Posen. . . . Together with the family of Herr Hosenfeld, consisting of the desperate wife and five children, I refer the fate of Herr Hosenfeld to your hands, as a person who also shares a moral obligation to him. I suspect that you will immediately confirm the receipt of my letter to my sister, advising her of your opinion on this matter. I am giving this letter to a friend of mine, not knowing your address. With my expression of great respect and in the belief of your capabilities I remain your Leon Warm-Warczynski.*

The news of Hosenfeld's captivity was as much a surprise for Władysław Szpilman as it had been for Leon Warm. The pianist immediately took action. Thanks to his reputation as a composer and musician, he reached out to Jakub Berman, head of the Polish State Security Services. Szpilman later talked about the meeting with the songwriter Wolf Biermann, who pushed for a German edition of Szpilman's book, *The Pianist: The Extraordinary True Story of One Man's Survival in Warsaw, 1939-1945.* Szpilman confided in Biermann that in 1950, upon finally discovering the name of the German officer who saved him, he had been ashamed to call on Berman. "I went as a supplicant to a criminal, with whom a decent person in Poland does not speak," Szpilman told Biermann. He told Berman everything, even "that Hosenfeld had not only saved me, but also Jewish children." Many people had this German to thank for their lives.

Jakub Berman was friendly to Szpilman and promised to try his best. Several days later, Berman phoned Szpilman at the Polish Radio studios and told him that he was unfortunately unable to do anything. He said, "If this German were still in Poland, we could get him out. But the comrades in the Soviet Union will not let him go. On top of that, Hosenfeld is a citizen of West Germany. It would be easier if he were East German, especially since a senior government official of East Germany was shortly to visit Poland." With that, the last rescue attempt had also failed.

***

The messages Hosenfeld sent from Stalingrad to Thalau until the summer of 1952 reflected his physical and mental decline. He had to repeatedly ask his comrades to write to his family. At one point it is written: *Do not concern yourselves that I dictate this card; my handwriting is hard to read and I fear that it will not be sent. My condition varies,* [I] *am very forgetful.* He continued to confirm the receipt of food packages, photos, and consumer goods. However, the man speaking in these messages was no longer the same Wilm Hosenfeld whose iron discipline and strong faith in God had kept alive hope that he would again see his loved ones. Instead, this was a man whose health was destroyed by years of imprisonment and the inhumane sentence of the military justice system.

Hosenfeld's final letter to his wife, on June 25, 1952, ended with the words: *Best of wishes for all the children, especially the girls for the good grades. The headaches have lessened. Belated birthday wishes to the grandfather. Many greetings to the people of Constance! Do not worry about me, I am doing well considering the conditions. I greet all of you with all of my heart, all the best.* A fellow prisoner had written the text up to that point. In clumsy, shaky handwriting Hosenfeld himself added: *Your Wilm.*

Wilm Hosenfeld died on August 13, 1952, at 9:50 p.m. He was 57. Dr. Daniel, his comrade and attending physician, was called to see him during his evening rounds; his condition had suddenly deteriorated. *At first, I could only diagnose considerable weakness of the heart and circulatory system,* Daniel later wrote. *By chance, I had sterile syringes in the duty room and therefore immediately injected strophanthin glucose and camphor. However, while I was administering the injection, Herr Hosenfeld died, without having regained consciousness.* Within two to three minutes, he died of internal bleeding due to a tear in the sclerosis-affected chest aorta. *His death was sudden and without pain*, Daniel wrote. Hosenfeld was buried at the Stalingrad camp cemetery, which no longer exists.

Weeks passed before Annemarie found out about the death of her husband. She even sent him a letter on October 21. In it, she wrote:

> *My dearest Wilm! Today another Mass for you. Outside of me, the three youngest took part. We have not heard from you for a long time, very worried. Everything is proceeding as always with us. I am healthy again. The cause for the illness was damaged teeth. Helmut was home on Sunday; he is learning much at the Frankfurt clinic. Detlev is making himself useful at home until the semester starts. Because of his resemblance to you, he was recognized by a female patient in the Heilig-Geist hospital who had been one of your students in Rudolphshan. . . .*

A letter that ended in emptiness. When Annemarie finally held the death notice in her hands, she lost her footing. Six years of war, seven years of imprisonment—always waiting, always hoping. In the end, all in vain! It was too much. Annemarie phoned her daughter Jorinde at school. She and Uta came home immediately. "When we arrived, Mother had covered everything with black sheets," Jorinde recalled. "She was screaming and was not responsive. Only once Helmut and Detlev also arrived did she finally calm down."

Detlev, Annemarie, and Helmut Hosenfeld after World War II.

— Epilogue —

Righteous Among the Nations

Annemarie Hosenfeld was permitted to stay in the Thalau school-teacher's residency until 1954, albeit with some restrictions on the garden and farm buildings. She then rented a small single-family house in 1955 in Stöckels, east of Fulda. Annemarie received an unusual visitor on a Sunday, mid-morning, in November 1957. She wrote a lengthy note about the visit:

> *An icy wind sweeps across the frozen fields, several late churchgoers hastily return to their warm homes.*
>
> *Suddenly, an elegant French vehicle stops in front of our door, and a few moments later, two men are standing at our door, asking for Herr Hosenfeld in broken German. The older introduces himself as Władysław Szpilman from Warsaw, before introducing his friend, a Polish-American musician.*

The visitors—Władysław Szpilman and the Polish violinist Bronisław Gimpel, who had immigrated to the United States in 1937—apparently did not know Wilm Hosenfeld had died five years prior. About the visit, Annemarie wrote: *"Yes, my husband died in 1952 in Russian captivity."* Stunned, Mr. Szpilman looks at me, and after we sat in silence across from each other for a few moments, I heard the story behind the unexpected visit. Szpilman then told Annemarie the circumstances under which Wilm had enabled his survival. He said, *"It was November 17, 1944, when your husband saved my life. Although he was stationed as a German officer in Warsaw, he had a heart for the suffering of the afflicted people in the Ghetto, and he saved the lives of many people—Poles and Jews."* The connection between Szpilman and the Hosenfeld family remained intact throughout the years; the children from both families, especially, maintained the relationship.

At the end of the 1950s, Annemarie was diagnosed with colon cancer. The disease was in such an advanced stage the Würzburg University clinic did not want to perform surgery. A young physician whom Helmut knew personally, and whose lectures his sister Jorinde had attended during her medical studies in Frankfurt, was willing to operate—and did so successfully. According to Detlev, his mother lived another 10 years with almost no complaints. She died in 1971 at the age of 73. Her illness brought the five siblings even closer.

The selfless support of the older and unmarried Anemone Hosenfeld, in caring for their mother was, as Detlev said, beyond comparison. Anemone worked for several years as a nurse in a hospital and then in Helmut's pediatric clinic in Fulda. Detlev also acknowledged everything his older brother did for the family. "The actions of my older brother, concerning how he took on a representative role of the father and dealing with concerns about the two younger sisters is indescribable," Detlev said. "It is also almost unimaginable all that my brother did for me during my medical studies and afterward during my training in Munich, Bern, and Heidelberg."

***

Helmut Hosenfeld was instrumental early on in ensuring the memory of his father be upheld. He succeeded in obtaining Wilm's handwritten interrogation protocol and the documents used in the 1950 trial in Minsk. Helmut submitted a request through the German Ministry of Foreign Affairs, directed to the Republic of Belarus, that asked for the vindication of his father. This was rejected with the explanation the deadline for such a petition had expired. The attempt to convince the Jewish memorial center Yad Vashem to declare Wilm Hosenfeld as a "Righteous Among the Nations" also

A commemorative plaque on the residential building where Władysław Szpilman and Wilm Hosenfeld met.

failed on the first attempt. This title is the highest honor the Jewish people bestow upon non-Jews who risked their own lives to save Jews during the Holocaust.

In its rejection, Yad Vashem specifically referred to Hosenfeld's conviction and sentencing to 25 years of incarceration. In a letter from Yad Vashem director Mordecai Paldiel to Andrzej Szpilman, the son of Władysław, he wrote:

> *I am confident you will agree that the assessment of a German officer, who was stationed in Warsaw during a time when the German military committed the most terrible crimes to Jews, the commission and the Yad Vashem institution must act with extreme caution before bestowing the highest title of the Jewish people upon a person who held an important military position in this city and was tried for war crimes.*

At the instigation of Andrzej Szpilman, in particular, a German edition of *The Pianist: The Extraordinary True Story of One Man's Survival in Warsaw, 1939-1945* was finally published in 1998, supplemented by several entries from Wilm Hosenfeld's Warsaw journal and a lengthy essay by Wolf Biermann. Andrzej secretly read his father's memoir (then titled *Death of a City*) as a 13-year-old and understood for the first time why he had no paternal grandparents. Until then, he was unaware of his Jewish ancestry and had even made anti-Semitic jokes with his Polish classmates. The thought of discovering more about his father's ordeal and the fate of his grandparents would not leave him. But Władysław Szpilman remained silent. He did not want to talk about the most difficult and worst time of his life, and he was probably unable to discuss it. Whenever he thought about the events, it felt like the past wanted to crush him like a black wall.

The plan to republish *Death of a City* only began to take shape once Andrzej Szpilman had immigrated to Germany and worked as both a dentist and musician. During a meeting at his Hamburg home with Biermann, as well as Helmut and Detlev Hosenfeld, the project was finally launched.

The book quickly became a bestseller and was translated into many languages. Władysław Szpilman, who died at the age of 88 on July 6, 2000, lived to see its release, even though he remained opposed to it. His memories were always fraught with emotional anguish. About his father, Andrzej Szpilman said:

> Until the end of his life, my father felt guilty for having survived while his brother, sisters, and their parents died, and he had been unable to save them. He had lived with this unrelenting pain. Every time that it would become hot during summer in Warsaw, he could drink no water. At the reloading site, where they had been permanently separated, they had not given the people water to drink, and the terrible thirst made their suffering even worse. The nightmare of the last encounter was inseparable in the

conscience of my father with this suffering. He died of a stroke in just such August heat because he refused to drink.

***

The republished remembrances of Władysław Szpilman were the foundation for the 2002 film *The Pianist*. The film won many prizes, including three Oscar Awards. The central character of the movie is Szpilman, not Wilm Hosenfeld, who appears near the end of the film in a short sequence. Nonetheless, the movie represented the first time Szpilman's rescue by the German officer grabbed a broad audience's worldwide attention. The link between Szpilman and Hosenfeld provided a key for understanding a form of resistance that found its way into the history books under the term "rescue resistance."

For Andrzej Wrzesiński, the film *The Pianist* awoke memories of his father, who on his deathbed, asked him to find the German officer to whom he and his family owed their lives. The name "Wilm Hosenfeld" was like a discovery for him. Wrzesiński contacted the Hosenfeld children and had an annual mass read for their father in the field cathedral of the Polish army.

Polish television produced a film in 2005 called *Dzieki niemu Żyjemy* (*Thanks to Him, We Live*), directed by Marek Drążewski. The film features a number of those rescued by Wilm Hosenfeld, as well as his children. In light of the monstrous crimes Germans committed in Poland, the documentary featuring Hosenfeld was particularly striking.

Because of the increased spotlight on Wilm Hosenfeld, Yad Vashem took another look at him and decided to overturn its original decision. In between the 2000 rejection and the 2008 honor, notable personalities lobbied on behalf of the captain. Dirk Heinrichs, Wolfram Wette, Carl-Peter von Mansberg, Gert Weisskirchen, Witold Kulesza, Maria Malina (the sister of the now-deceased Leon Warm, who had also immigrated to Australia)—the list of supporters had grown ever larger. Andrzej Szpilman was especially unwilling to accept Yad Vashem's initial rejection. He publicized his bewilderment in

The Yad Vashem certificate and medal honoring Wilm Hosenfeld as a "Righteous Among the Nations."

Israeli and international newspapers, and in 2007, personally presented the case for Hosenfeld in Warsaw during a meeting with the director of Yad Vashem.

With the 2004 publication of Thomas Vogel's book *Wilm Hosenfeld, "Ich versuche jeden zu retten": Das Leben eines deutschen Offiziers in Briefen und Tagebüchern (Wilm Hosenfeld, "I Try to Save Everyone": The Life of a German Officer in Letters and Diaries)*, all significant documents were available in black and white so everyone could form an opinion of Wilm Hosenfeld. The impetus for this book had initially come from Wolf Biermann. The songwriter requested the German Defense Minister at the time, Volker Rühe, bring Hosenfeld back from obscurity and use him as a role model for German soldiers. Thereupon, Rühe commissioned the Military History Research Institute in Potsdam with the investigation into the life story of Hosenfeld. For four years, Helmut and Vogel sought out and organized the original documents and prepared them for publication. The nearly 1,200-page comprehensive presentation left no doubt the rescue of the pianist in Warsaw was not a random act performed by a German officer at the conclusion of his military career. Rather, it was the clear expression of a belief Hosenfeld had acted upon since the beginning of the war, repeatedly risking his own life in the process.

The clincher for Yad Vashem's reassessment of Hosenfeld may have been a pair of reviews of Vogel's book by two Israeli historians. Benjamin Z. Kedar acknowledged the book in the August 6, 2004, edition of the newspaper *Haaretz. The book succeeds*, Kedar wrote, *in following the fascinating character of Hosenfeld, who, based upon his writings, absolutely deserves a biography.* Kedar also noted the letters and journal entries attest to Hosenfeld's analytical skills.

Another review, written by Steven E. Aschheim, appeared on March 11, 2005, in the *Times Literary Supplement.* In his balanced analysis, Aschheim looked at the contradictions that characterized Hosenfeld's personal development. The man had been an enthusiastic supporter of the German youth movement and propagated its unusual mixture of progressive and nationalistic sentiment. Aschheim wrote:

> *He was injured and decorated in World War I, during which he fought with unbridled patriotism while also becoming aware of the senseless carnage. He was a dedicated teacher sympathetic to enlightened teaching methods while remaining within a general "Germanic" framework. He shared the displeasure of many others in the time after the First World War, and despite his conservative religious beliefs, succumbed at an early stage to the revolutionary temptation of Nazism.*

Hosenfeld was aware of these contradictions, particularly during World War II. He only gradually turned his back on the Hitler myth. Thomas Vogel also recommended Yad Vashem reconsider its dismissal because within *the murky mixture of complicity and conscience that is central to the story of Wilm Hosenfeld, there were a number of decisive life-saving moments in which conscience overcame complicity.*

Since 2008, Wilm Hosenfeld has been recognized as one of the "Righteous Among the Nations"—an exceptional honor that befits his exceptional life. During a commemorative ceremony at the Jewish Museum in Berlin on June 19, 2009, his children Anemone, Jorinde, and Detlev accepted a certificate and medal with its Talmud quote: "Whoever saves a life, it is considered as if he saved an entire world." Helmut was not able to take part in the event for health reasons. Uta, the youngest daughter, had died three years earlier. The historian Wolfram Wette, author of the 2001 book *Retter in Uniform* (*Rescuers in Uniform*), remarked in his speech: "The rescuers display humanity and civil courage under extremely difficult conditions. This is what makes them role models for our democratic society."

***

Wilm Hosenfeld has also been honored for his moral courage in other ways. In 2007, Polish president Lech Kaczyński posthumously honored Hosenfeld with the Commander's Cross of the Order of *Polonia Restituta*, one of Poland's highest awards, for his efforts during the war to save lives and ease suffering.

In December 2011, a commemorative bronze plaque was installed on the building where Wilm Hosenfeld and Władysław Szpilman first met. A central section of the youth exchange center in Golm, Germany, on the island of Usedom and near the Polish border, was named in honor of Hosenfeld.

The former Wehrmacht sports school in Warsaw is today a cultural and social youth center for young people from challenging social backgrounds. There, adolescents are offered a broad spectrum of opportunities for development, from sports to music, theater, and painting, and video art to handicraft skills. The director, Honorata Waszkiewicz, acts according to the guiding principle of Hosenfeld. She said, "As a teacher, it is important to me to convey certain values. Wilm Hosenfeld was an authentic human being. He had already represented his value system as a teacher before the war and he retained these values during the war, even though the conditions were much more difficult." Because of this, she feels especially obligated to him. "We have again taken up the original ideas that connected Hosenfeld with this building," she said.

The Leuphana University in Lüneburg, Germany, has awarded the Hosenfeld-Szpilman Memorial Prize since 2005. Named for the rescuer and the man he saved, the award intends to keep alive the memory of the victims of National Socialism, while also honoring outstanding examples of courage and humanity. On the occasion of the first award ceremony, Detlev said, "We children of Wilm Hosenfeld cannot visit the grave of our father because it no longer exists. However, his memory will live on in a meaningful way if his vision and humanity and reconciliation, which led him to save others, will be carried on."

The 2015 award winner was Polish professor Witold Kulesza, who teaches law at the University of Łódź. Kulesza has endeavored for years to uncover the crimes committed against the Polish people by the Nazi regime, and after 1945 while under Soviet communist rule. The criminologist and author Dieter Schenk acknowledged the honoree in his laudatory speech: "In his role as Polish Attorney General, Kulesza apologized that Poland had not done everything

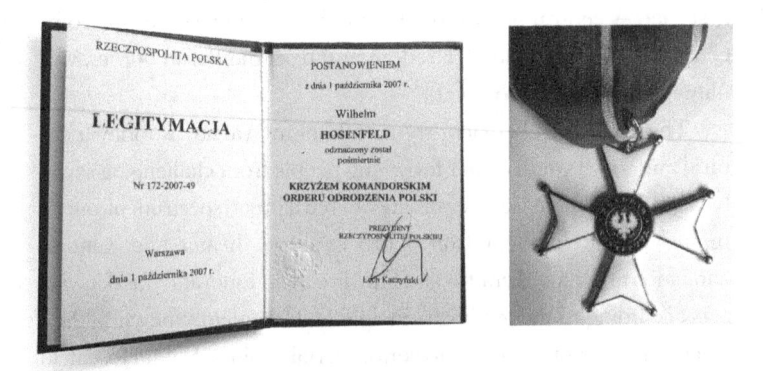

The Commander's Cross of the Order of *Polonia Restituta* and certificate awarded to Wilm Hosenfeld in 2007.

humanly possible after the war to save Wilm Hosenfeld by freeing him from Soviet captivity."

The composer Dietrich Lohff, who wrote "*Requiem für einen polnischen Jungen*" ("Requiem for a Polish Boy") in 1998, based on the texts of victims of fascism, dedicated the work to the Hosenfeld family. In a handwritten note, he said:

> *There are people who must live on after their death. Not in heaven, but here with us. We need them so that they can remind us that this life-saving mixture of courage and human kindness is possible. While others may be responsible for their resurrection, we alone can ensure their survival here on earth.*

***

Despite her advanced age, Halina Szpilman is still working to keep the memories of her husband, Władysław, and Wilm Hosenfeld alive. Together with the professor Eugeniusz Cezary Król, she travels from place to place, city to city. In February 2014, when we met for the second time, the 87-year-old complained about the snow and icy streets, which made driving difficult for her.

The film *The Pianist* has spurred the interest of Poles, so auditoriums are usually filled when Halina and Professor Król appear. Her husband's name is familiar to many, especially older, people. Władysław composed over 300 popular pieces, as well as chansons, symphonies, and film music. Sometimes, one of his popular songs is played before a discussion begins. "The body of work of my husband—his compositions, his songs that the people love—these things should remain, and this is more important to me than if, for example, another street or another place is named in his honor," Halina said. "Such requests are again coming in now."

But the name Wilm Hosenfeld also has a special resonance in Poland. He is probably more well known there as the rescuer of the pianist than in Germany, especially as Poland's historical awareness is significantly more pronounced than that of its neighboring country.

Halina Szpilman still lives in the same apartment on Gymnastic Street in Warsaw where she spent more than a half century with her husband. There are many photos on the walls—pictures of friends, relatives, and acquaintances, as well as of tours and trips in Europe, the US, and South America. The only photos of the family murdered in the concentration camp were obtained by Władysław from an aunt who immigrated to Argentina. He possessed no mementos at all. The piano on which he played and composed at home still stands in the living room. This musical instrument was the natural centerpiece around which everything else revolved.

During the visit, Halina displayed photos of her husband and Helmut Hosenfeld visiting the hiding place where the pianist concealed himself in 1944. Władysław had once more climbed into the attic space using a ladder to show his rescuer's son the hiding spot under the roof.

Halina grew up during the 1930s in the city of Radom, Poland, where her father, Józef Grzecznarowski, was the mayor. As a member of the Polish Socialist Party, he was among the first people the Gestapo arrested after the invasion of Poland in 1939. A few months later, Grzecznarowski was taken to the Sachsenhausen concentration camp, where he was held until the end of the war. During the ensuing years, his wife lived in constant fear that she and her daughter, Halina, would be sent to Germany as forced laborers.

Władysław Szpilman only met Halina Grzecznarowski after the war ended. "I visited the spa resort [town] of Krynica[-Zdrój] in the south, near the Slovakian border, with a girlfriend in 1948," she recalled. "Władysław was also there. We saw each other, and I noticed that he wanted to speak to me. However, somehow, it was not possible. The next year I saw him again. Now we were able to speak with one another. After three days, he already wanted to marry me. But I was studying medicine in Kraków at the time, so that did not work. He lived in Warsaw."

Halina is one of the few people with whom the pianist spoke about his time in the ghetto. He shared his memories with her. "Władysław had written the book *Death of a City* in 1946," she said. "In the first edition of his remembrances, Wilm Hosenfeld is identified as an Austrian officer. Good Germans were not allowed in communist Poland at that time. Newspapers printed extracts from the book. Therefore, he had not only been well known because of his musical skills, but also for having written this book. My mother was given the book as a gift for Christmas in 1947, and I subsequently read it."

The widow described her future husband's mental and physical conditions at the time when they first met as being good. Władysław apparently wanted to quickly make up for lost years. He threw himself into his work, whereby he soon had the opportunity to perform abroad. Like many other Holocaust survivors, he, too, tried to suppress the bad memories: the loss of his family, the years in the ghetto, the flight. These horrible experiences, however, did not stand in the way of Władysław's career. When his book was published, he spent several months in Scandinavia.

Halina Szpilman recalled:

He performed concerts in Denmark, Norway, Finland, and Sweden, produced albums, and appeared on the radio. When he eventually returned to Poland, he was again a very busy musician and composer. As he had done before the war, he wrote music for films and composed popular pieces that were played on the radio. When I got to know him, he was full of energy. He was funny, very sociable, and enjoyed being around other people, and, of course, more than anything, he loved his music. Did the long ordeal change his artistic expression, his way of playing? No, I don't believe so. Of course, music gave him a lot. It meant very much to him, gave him the opportunity to enter a different world. Music was a kind of medicine for his soul.

Halina Szpilman worked as a doctor at a research institute for blood disorders and circulation, focusing on the causes of rheumatism. When asked if her husband suffered any trauma during the postwar years due to his history, whether emotional stress or depression affected him, she took a moment to consider the question. She responded:

> Maybe toward the end of his life. At that time, he was not playing as often anymore and had more time to think about the time up to 1945. He once said to me, "I can do what I want, but the memories of my family being transported away in the closed wagon will not let me be." He was already older when he said that. Before he had been much too busy. We had a large circle of friends and acquaintances. Outside of music, family was important to him, [especially] our two sons Christoph and Andrzej. He practiced for three hours daily on the piano, from 8 until 11 in the morning. When my oldest son, who had lived outside of Warsaw for a while, came back one day and saw that my husband was not at the piano, he was very surprised and asked what was going on.

During the 1960s, the communist leadership in Poland initiated an anti-Semitic campaign that persuaded many Jews to leave the country and move to Israel. According to Halina, Władysław Szpilman was largely unaffected. He was held in high regard and even fellow musicians who were anti-Semitic did not let him feel it. "He was respected and never complained about insufficient approval," Halina said. However, he received fewer commissions. "It is conceivable that he may have criticized a colleague's composition and was in turn attacked for it. But such things were never made public. In 1963, he was criticized. A total of 24 composers and musicians reported him to the Central Committee of the [Polish United] Workers' Party and claimed that Szpilman was propagating Western—especially American—music. His work for the Polish Radio was thereafter limited."

Together with the violinist Bronisław Gimpel, with whom Szpilman had worked before the war, he founded the Warsaw Piano Quintet, which achieved great popularity in the ensuing years. The musicians performed over 2,000 concerts worldwide and were always enthusiastically received. Gimpel, who as a Jew had temporarily been barred from his home country, lived in the US for a long time. The two of them worked together on artistic collaborations and maintained a friendship up until Gimpel's 1979 death in Los Angeles. The Warsaw Piano Quintet was important to her husband, Halina emphasized.

As to the question of what she thought of the film *The Pianist* when she first saw it—in which her husband was portrayed by Adrien Brody—she replied:

> It is a very good and very important film. I can only say, thank God that Polański made it. Spielberg made *Schindler's List*; Roman Polański, *The Pianist*. Polański visited us in 2000 and spoke with my husband. They knew one another. Polański had read the English translation of the book *The Pianist*. A friend had, by chance, brought it to his attention and Polański was right away attracted to the story. What a coincidence! Maybe otherwise he would never have made the movie!
>
> Another coincidence was the encounter between Wilm Hosenfeld and Władysław. Somehow all of life is a coincidence. . . . Seriously, the story of Wilm Hosenfeld and Władysław Szpilman is extremely important for Germany and Poland. The story of their two lives is a symbol of the reconciliation between both countries. All those years of war, I was always afraid that the Germans would come and take us. I hid my books from them. We did not go to school, but were privately taught—not in our house because it was constantly under surveillance from the Gestapo. And today we have overcome everything. . . .

The only thing that I might critique about the film *The Pianist* is that Wilm Hosenfeld plays too small a role in it. Oh, and something else. Hosenfeld never addressed Szpilman informally as he does in the film. Instead, he always used the polite and formal personal pronoun when speaking to him.

— Photo and Document Credits —

Thanks are due to the following people and organizations for permission to use the materials as listed. We have tried to contact all owners of copyrighted material and apologize if we have missed anyone. If we have inadvertently used copyrighted material without permission, we apologize and hope the owner will contact us so we may make amends. We will make any necessary corrections in the next printing.

— Index —

Baltic Sea

Danzig

Köslin

Elbing

6

6

10

5

Stettin

1

Schneidemühl

←Oder River

Berlin

POLAND

2

2

GERMANY

1

Neisse
River →

7

2

Oder River →

Liegnitz

4

4

4

Dresden

Breslau

8

9

9

Oppeln

Gleiwitz

CZECHOSLOVAKIA

Prague

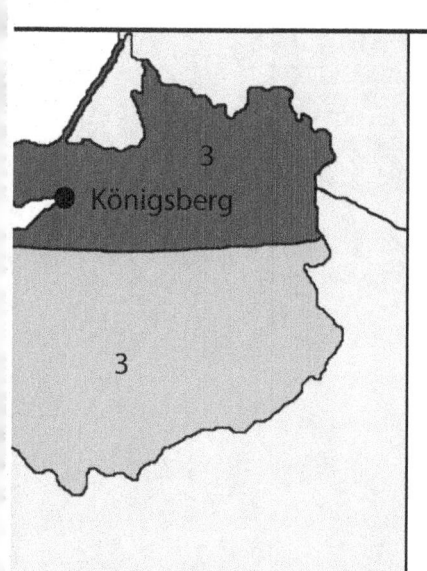

The Oder-Neisse Line and Germany's Postwar Territorial Losses

Territory lost to Poland, 1945

Territory lost to the Soviet Union, 1945

Postwar Germany

Pre-1945 German Administrative Units

1. Border Mark
2. Brandenburg
3. East Prussia
4. Lower Silesia
5. Mecklenburg
6. Pomerania
7. Prussian Saxony
8. Saxony
9. Upper Silesia
10. West Prussia

1. The Border Mark included those parts of the former Prussian districts of Posen and West Prussia that were not lost to Poland in 1918, apart from the area of West Prussia around Elbing.

2. All the areas of Germany on this map, apart from Saxony, were part of the prewar State of Prussia.

3. Danzig was a Free City administered by the League of Nations from 1919 to 1939.

4. Stettin and the surrounding area were annexed by Poland despite being west of the Oder-Neisse Line.

5. This map uses the English forms of German city and region names annexed by Poland and the Soviet Union in 1945. This does not imply any position on the "correct" form of these names.